So Few on Earth

So Few on Earth

A Labrador Métis Woman Remembers

Josie Penny

DUNDURN PRESS
TORONTO

Editor: Michael Carroll
Design: Courtney Horner
Map of Labrador by Christopher Pandolfi
Printer: Transcontinental

Library and Archives Canada Cataloguing in Publication

Penny, Josie
        So few on earth : a Labrador Métis woman remembers / by Josie Penny.

ISBN 978-1-55488-709-5

        1. Penny, Josie. 2. Métis women--Newfoundland and Labrador--Biography.
I. Title.

FC109.1.P45A3 2010   971.82004'970092   C2009-907441-9

1 2 3 4 5   14 13 12 11 10

We acknowledge the support of the **Canada Council for the Arts** and the **Ontario Arts Council** for our publishing program. We also acknowledge the financial support of the **Government of Canada** through the **Canada Book Fund** and **The Association for the Export of Canadian Books**, and the **Government of Ontario** through the **Ontario Book Publishers Tax Credit program**, and the **Ontario Media Development Corporation**.

Care has been taken to trace the ownership of copyright material used in this book. The author and the publisher welcome any information enabling them to rectify any references or credits in subsequent editions.

J. Kirk Howard, President

Printed and bound in Canada.
www.dundurn.com

Dundurn Press
3 Church Street, Suite 500
Toronto, Ontario, Canada
M5E 1M2

Gazelle Book Services Limited
White Cross Mills
High Town, Lancaster, England
LA1 4XS

Dundurn Press
2250 Military Road
Tonawanda, NY
U.S.A. 14150

First of all, I dedicate this book to my four children, Gregory, Darlene, Catherine, and Mark, who, though they were born in Happy Valley–Goose Bay, Labrador, aren't familiar with the primitive lifestyle of their mother. I also dedicate this book to my nine grandchildren, all of whom were born in Ontario and have no concept of Labrador. I wish also to dedicate this book to my parents, Thomas and Flossie Curl, especially in light of their tenacity and determination to survive in Labrador's isolated wilderness. And lastly, I dedicate this book to Violet Dyson, a dear cousin, who in the later years after my parents' deaths was the only source available to me for information about Roaches Brook and Spotted Island … place of my birth. Thank you, Sissy.

Contents

Acknowledgements   9
Introduction: The Wild Land That Is My Home   11

Part One: Early Life   17
  1 Before Memory   19
  2 Berry Picking   25
  3 Shifting in the Bay   30
  4 Roaches Brook   35
  5 Mommy's Work   47
  6 Hunting and Trapping   55
  7 Springtime and Shifting Outside   65
  8 Spotted Island   73
  9 The Making of the Fish   86
 10 Medical Care and Mail Delivery 95

Part Two: Lockwood 103
11 Heading for Lockwood 105
12 Arriving at Lockwood 110
13 School Days 118
14 Learning the Rules 126
15 Special Times at Lockwood 133
16 Longing for Home 150
17 The Children Return 159
18 Learning to Cope 169

Part Three: Return to Family 181
19 Getting Home 183
20 Muddy Bay 192
21 The Move to Cartwright 198
22 St. Peter's School 209
23 Life in Cartwright 215
24 A Joyous Winter 225
25 Spring Adventures 232

Part Four: Later Life 245
26 My First Job 247
27 Challenges 256
28 Coping with Tragedy 268
29 Early Teens 275
30 Growing Up 285
31 Love and Conflict 299
32 Leaving Childhood Behind 308

Glossary 321

Acknowledgements

A special thank-you and much gratitude to my original manuscript editor, Mary Labatt, who was extremely encouraging from the first phone call when I told her just a wee part of what my book was about.

I would also like to thank Robert Nielsen, my first teacher at McMaster University, who in our initial class told us two things: *"Write what you know"* and *"Let the chips fall ..."* He was encouraging to the point of excitement when I told him I had only a grade seven education and that maybe I didn't belong in his class.

I owe a great deal to my friends Dora (Eagles) Learning and Dr. Doris (Martin) Saunders (now deceased) and all the other family and friends from Cartwright and the Sandwich Bay area who gave me tidbits of information. I thank all who encouraged me along the 10-year journey of writing this book. You know who you are.

I want to acknowledge the help of my son, Mark Penny, who was able to scan hundreds of pages back into my computer after losing them all in a crash. Luckily, I'd printed the pages out. Thank you, Mark!

Last but certainly not least, I want to thank my husband, Keith (now married 49 years!). Over the decade it's taken to complete this book, he's been interested, supportive, not interested, and indifferent. At one point he wanted me to self-publish and he even thought about starting his own publishing and book-binding company. And when I whined about the printer or computer not working, he was patient with me.

All in all, this book has been an experience I'll never forget! It has enlightened my life beyond all understanding.

Introduction

The Wild Land That Is My Home

When I tell new acquaintances I'm from Labrador, I always get the same response. They tell me they've never met anyone from there before. I always reply with pride, "That's because there are so few of us on Earth."

In the far eastern section of the Canadian Shield, Labrador is 112,000 square miles and has a 700-mile coastline. When we think about this vast area in relation to its population of only 35,000, we can easily see that it's one of the most sparsely inhabited regions of Canada. As he approached Labrador's rugged terrain, immense mountain ranges, and stark coastal plains in 1534, Jacques Cartier is said to have remarked that it looked like "the land God gave to Cain."

Labrador is where the navy blue of the ocean is in stark contrast to the majestic icebergs that score the seabed as they make their way through the North Atlantic. Although tourists admire the icebergs, fishermen find them a problem. Icebergs are a hazard to fishing boats, destroy expensive fishing gear, and can even block passage to the open sea.

The thousands of islands off the coast are home to millions of seabirds that cling to the rocky ledges on cliffs that shoot straight up from the sea. The barren coastline is bare of trees except for sheltered crevices where bushes are dwarfed from the constant battering of ocean storms. Farther inland, tall, resilient trees stand like giant arrows piercing the clear blue sky. One can still kneel and drink the cool, fresh water from Labrador's thousands of rivers and streams as they wind through the mountains to the North Atlantic. The majestic Mealy Mountains are home to one of the largest caribou herds in the world. And sports fishermen flock to Labrador's many rivers to enjoy fishing beyond all expectations.

We are a people of mixed race. I am Métis, as are many Native Labradorians. When immigrants from the British Isles and France arrived on the shores of Labrador by ship, they married indigenous people. Living in isolation with two or three heritages in a family has given Native Labradorians a rich, unique culture and has created my branch of the Métis.

Our racial heritage comes from the Inuit people in the north, the Naskapi in the interior north, and the Montagnais who lived inland and farther south. These peoples, together with the French, English, Scottish, and Irish, produced Métis who are often short in stature, olive-skinned, and dark, usually with startling blue or hazel eyes. In my own family, Inuit features predominate, as do blue and hazel eyes. In the dialect of the Native Labradorian, we refer to ourselves as Livyers. The origin of the word is lost, but one can surmise that it has come down through time from the phrase, "living here," or perhaps "living here for years."

Strangers to our shores — Faranners — frequently speak of the kind and friendly nature of our people. When you arrive in Labrador, you can't help but notice the pride of its inhabitants. The Labrador flag is flown on many houses throughout the communities and is knit into many garments of clothing. It's also painted or displayed on garbage containers built to keep out wild animals and on coach boxes used to pull relatives behind snowmobiles. Dog teams have long since disappeared.

The survival of Native Labradorians is the story of a race's endurance. Through my memories I can share the life experiences of a people. My purpose in writing is twofold. I want to inform our children, who were raised in Happy Valley–Goose Bay, Labrador, about their roots. And I want to enlighten our grandchildren, who were born and raised in Ontario. I want them all to gain insight into the unique and authentic lifestyles of their Labrador ancestors. But as I write I realize I have a wider purpose: to give voice to the struggles of the people who lived in this harsh land, a people whose daily lives were often heroic, a people whose roots reach into the prehistory of this continent, long before European contact.

Life on the coast of Labrador has always been a day-to-day existence. Up until the 1950s we lived a semi-nomadic lifestyle. Everything we needed was shifted out of the bay each fall and moved outside again to the fishing grounds in the spring. These tough, well-adapted people lived off the land, and food had to be found. Therefore, mealtime was a constant concern, and the threat of starvation for our people always loomed as a possibility. There was very little cash in hand for anyone. Store-bought food such as flour, molasses, tea, beans, salt pork, and salt beef was bartered or traded for during square-up time. Squaring-up was done with furs in the spring and dried cod in the fall.

To some degree, coastal Labradorians still enjoy the freedom of hunting and fishing. Although fishing and hunting quotas and weapons are all stringently registered and controlled now, our people can still gather enough wildlife to help with the rising cost of living. One is sure to find wild game tucked away in freezers, unlike during my childhood when scaffolds were built high off the ground to keep game frozen and away from dogs. Snowmobiles have supplanted dog teams, and store-bought clothing has replaced the homemade garments of the past. Television and computers are now in most homes along the coast and have changed the lifestyles of our people forever.

During the past 40 years, much has changed in Labrador. Since the twin towns of Wabush and Labrador City developed in the 1950s, and Churchill Falls in the 1960s, new people have come to live and a new generation of Labradorians has sprung up. Those one-company towns constructed permanent, comfortable housing for its residents, and people enjoy all the modern amenities of a well-designed northern community. Happy Valley–Goose Bay, built during the Second World War to accommodate the hundreds of planes en route to Europe, is located at the bottom of Hamilton Inlet in central Labrador. And though it's accessible to the ocean, it isn't included in the coastal region.

My memories are of life on the coast of Labrador. My perceptions of my life as I saw it during the time period of this book are just that, personal perceptions, and aren't neccessairly how other people would see it.

Some of our people find it difficult to adapt to the new ways. Many fishermen have had to relinquish their salmon licences, and regulations dictating that cod can't even be caught for personal consumption are hard to take for a people who have known no other way. Without television and computers Labrador would still be "a world apart," as *National Geographic* described it. Although some people were concerned about the effects of the new roads connecting Labrador, for the most part the results have been positive. The new roads have brought the cost of goods and services in line with the rest of Canada and have deterred merchants from price gouging.

Many of my people wonder if the serenity and peace of Labrador can be sustained in this modern world. I would think not, but having been born and raised in this wonderful land I would hate to think that inconsiderate, uncaring people could deface such a pristine environment. Some Labradorians still try to reclaim the old lifestyle, and others are too stubborn to let it go entirely. It is the hope of our people that we keep our rich culture and maintain our integrity.

I hope, through my story, the reader will be able to form a picture of the way we lived and see how our people have survived against all odds. Records, for the most part, haven't been kept, and a family tree was something few of our ancestors either had the education to do or time to keep. However, I recently received my family tree from Dr. Doris J. Saunders, my cousin and lifelong friend, who just a few years ago received the Order of Canada and an honorary doctorate. She is a great historian, and I am very proud of her.

Because there are so few of us on Earth, I'm extremely proud to be a Labrador Livyer. Having resided in the heart of Ontario for 30 years, I look forward to going back to Labrador every summer, especially since the completion of the Trans-Labrador Highway. Labrador is now accessible to anyone who wishes to drive there. Every summer I see my homeland with new eyes. I see the proud heritage of my people in the tall pines, rocky cliffs, and navy sea. Wildly beautiful, it is the land that shaped my people. Here is one of their stories.

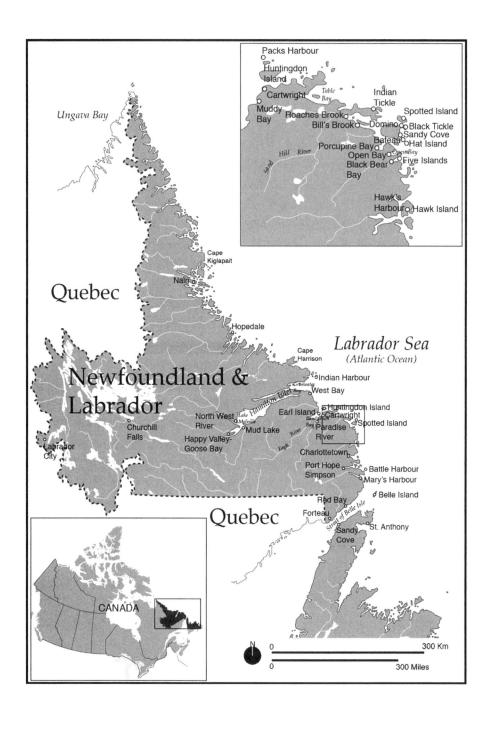

Part One

Early Life

Previous Page:

Top: My father, Tom Curl, and my mother, Flossie, along with my brother, Sammy, stand in front of their cabin in Roaches Brook, Labrador, in the fall of 1943. My mother is pregnant with me.

Bottom: Here I am, age two, holding my puppy, Blackie, in 1945. Note the sealskin slippers and hand-knitted socks.

I

Before Memory

My family lived a primitive and extremely harsh existence where only the strong survived. I was born on January 15, 1943, in our winter home of Roaches Brook, Labrador. Mom decided to call me Josephine Mildred. My eldest brother, Samuel, was born out of wedlock and was adopted by my father when Mommy and Daddy were married. After losing their first daughter, Sivella, from unknown causes, I came along, third in line behind my sister, Marcella. I was blessed with good health, strong bones, olive skin, hazel eyes, and curly blond hair.

"What was I like, Mom?" I asked many years later.

"Ya was beautiful, maid. Yer little head was covered wit yellow ringlets dat hung down round yer shoulders. An ya was a good baby, too. But yer lucky ta be alive." She rocked back and forth, her eyes gazing far into her memory.

"Why?" I asked.

"Well, maid, ya was a happy, carefree little ting, always runnin about and gettin in de way. Ya shoulda been dead long ago!" As her eyes glazed, I knew what was coming, and I never grew tired of the story.

Mom settled back to tell me the tale of how I was attacked by husky dogs. The fire crackled, throwing shafts of light on the wall. Her voice grew dreamy as she spoke of the faraway times. Her story went like this.

We were living in our summer home on Spotted Island, a rocky place in the North Atlantic. My family went there every summer to fish for cod, our livelihood and a staple in our diet. On the island, children and dogs were able to roam at will. The dogs were free of harnesses and chains. During warm summer days, they lazed underneath the houses where sea breezes kept them cool.

To shop for supplies and food, the island residents had to make a run to the mainland by boat to Dawes Store in Domino. The sea raged constantly, and there were times when some of our people starved to death because they couldn't get off the island for supplies. Often they had to wait for days or even weeks for the weather to become civil enough. That summer, when a calm day finally arrived, my mother left us in the care of Aunt Lucy, a neighbour, boarded a motorboat along with several others, and headed across the water.

I loved the new puppies that were born each spring, and being inquisitive I wanted to see them, so I meandered along the rocky path, munching on a slice of molasses bread. Unfortunately, I fell. The husky mother saw this as a threat to her litter and attacked me. The other huskies, always hungry for food, took advantage of the situation and joined in. I started screaming. Aunt Lucy heard the commotion and ran out. Her broom high in the air, she swiped at the dogs. Everyone within earshot dropped what they were doing and raced to the scene.

In just a few seconds I was mangled beyond recognition. There was panic and confusion. Seeing my grave condition, someone wrapped me in a white bedsheet, which soon was red with blood. They couldn't tell at first how badly I'd been hurt. But on closer inspection they saw that all the flesh was torn away from the back of my head, exposing my skull.

As soon as the boat landed on the stagehead, my mother dashed up the hill. Everyone tried to shield her from the horrible sight.

"No, Flossie, don't look!" they all cried.

Immediately, my mother realized that her worst nightmare had come true. Moaning and groaning like a crazed person, she grabbed her child and removed the sheet.

My mother came out of her reverie at this point. "I'll never forget what I seen dat day. It'll be in me mind ferever!" She shook her head, hesitating for a moment, then continued the story.

"As de boat got closer, I could see dat sometin awful happened wit de dogs. Lots of us had problems wit dogs before, so I was scared ta death! As I climbed de stage, I knowed t'was bad. People was screamin and cryin! As I ran up de hill, I could see someone was wrapped in a big white sheet, and it was completely red wit blood. Everyone tried ta stop me from takin ya. Dey tried ta shield me, but dey coulden. When I took de sheet off and saw yer little head, I fainted."

"What did you do then?" I asked.

"Soon's I come to, I knowed I had ta do somethin quick! I picked some juniper boughs, boiled 'em, and mixed 'em wit bread ta make a poultice. I put 'em on yer open cuts an bandaged ya up. I did dat fer t'ree or four days, till de steamer come and took ya ta Cartwright ta de hospital."

Sarah Holwell, a Spotted Island resident who was working in the Cartwright hospital at the time, had come home for a short visit. She was asked to accompany me to Cartwright, about 60 miles away. We travelled on Dr. Forsyth's schooner, the SS *Unity*. He was the resident doctor living in Cartwright then.

"What kind of shape was I in?" I asked Sarah many years later.

"Ya was some sick, my dear," she said, "but ya was alert. Ya didn't jus lie there. I changed yer dressing in Table Bay when we stopped fer the night and yer head looked terrible! We didn't have any medicines or anythin! But ya didn't cry much atall, just whimpered a little through de night. I'd seen dog bites before, but yers was de worst I'd ever seen."

"How long was I in the hospital?"

"Oh … bout a month, I tink, but ya was a tough little girl. And I remember yer beautiful blond hair. Dey took a razor an shaved it all off."

According to the story, when I arrived at the hospital in Cartwright, the doctor discovered my mother had done such a good job of dressing and treating my wounds that they couldn't sew up the badly torn flesh.

It had healed too well, so they decided to treat them as they were. Dr. Forsyth told Mom that my skull was too exposed and that a skin graft was needed to cover it.

"I'll never ferget when ya come home. Ya looked so cute in yer little red-and-white polka-dot dress," Mom told me years later. "But I was broken-hearted because all yer blond ringlets was gone. Jus gone! And now yer hair was real short an dark. Ya looked so different. Not at all like my little blond, curly-haired girl from a mont ago!"

My mother loved to reminisce about our reunion. "Even though ya was spoiled by de nurses," she used to say, "we was happy ta have ya back home." Then her tears would flow freely. Every time we had a visitor in our home, she'd gently pull up my hair to expose the terrible scars. Using her index and forefinger, she'd rub along my skull, feeling the deep grooves left by the bites.

"Dese rips on yer head was wider den two fingers," she told me. "Dere was several teet marks as well as de two big ones dat went right round de back of yer head, but dere was no udder bites on yer body. No one could understan why de dogs only tore up de back of yer head."

Later, while visiting Spotted Island on his regular trip along the coast, Dr. Forsyth told my mother the details. "The wound that came closest to killing Josie was the fang puncture behind her left ear that pinned her earlobe to her head. And there's one spot where there's a piece of skull missing. Both these areas will be susceptible to pain. However she's a very tough and extremely lucky little girl."

The community had to destroy nine dogs that had blood on them. Once a husky has tasted blood they can't be trusted, so everyone knew they had to be shot.

As with children everywhere, accidents were common. The difference in our isolated communities was the difficulty in getting medical care. Often a home remedy had to suffice.

My mother used to tell of the time I fell from Aunt Lucy's bridge, or verandah, into the slop hole. "Ya was foolin around out on de bridge, maid, an ya fell off an broke yer collarbone in two places." She shrugged at the inevitability of childhood foolishness.

"What did you do?" I asked her.

"I took an ol' sheet, tore it inta strips, an wrapped ya up till ya was healed."

In later years my older siblings painted a picture of their life as it was before my memory. Their recollections offer glimpses into the primitive life of our family.

My sister, Marcie, recalled my father's gift for song. "One of my favourite memories, when we was small, was Daddy lyin back on de settle. He'd sing ta us from suppertime till bedtime. I loved ta hear him talkin ta his dogs as he was drivin along. He'd talk an sing to 'em de whole time."

Our winter home of Roaches Brook held special memories for Marcie. "When we moved inta Roaches Brook in de fall, de grass would be all grown up real tall over our heads. We would go an pick de moss from de bogs round de ponds an let it dry. Den we would use it ta stuff de seams of de cabin ta keep out de snow an cold."

Marcie remembered one day when a hunt went very badly. "One day me an brother Sam was after a squirrel, an de squirrel bit his finger. It held on an woulden let go! He was screamin. De blood was flyin everywhere! I was toddlin long behind him scared ta death! Prob'ly screamin my head off, too!"

My mother and Marcie used to tell me often that Marcie fainted when she was hurt. Once I asked her if it was true. She laughed. "Yeh, ever time I hurt meself I'd faint. De first time I fainted, I was standin on de kitchen table. My finger was all gathered [infected and swollen]. I caught holda it, started squeezin real hard, and said, 'It don't hurt, it don't hurt.' De next ting I remember is wakin up in Daddy's arms. After dat, every scrape an bump I got, I fainted."

I asked about our brother, Sammy, who drowned tragically when he was 19. "Sammy was a good hunter even when he was small," Marcie told me.

When I asked what he hunted (besides squirrels!), Marcie said, "Mice. I member seein a pile a mouse skins on de windowsill. Dey'd be swarmin an he'd catch 'em, skin 'em, dry 'em, an sell 'em fer five cents each."

I was intrigued by Marcie's stories and wanted to know more about our home before I was big enough to remember. "Tell me about our mommy," I asked her once.

"Mom was a good hunter, too. She used ta take off in de mornin wit her short little .22 rifle, an she always come back wit tree or four partridges, or tree or four rabbits. I used ta be lookin up at de hills, an lookin up at de treetops showin up against de white snow on de hillside, and thought dey was de partridges Mom used ta get."

I asked Marcie if she was allowed to go ice fishing as a child. "Sometimes," she answered. "I member me firs trout. Minnie Rose [a neighbour] an me went down to de steady [a quiet place in the brook] where we used ta get water. I caught a trout, an was I ever glad! I brought me trout home, cleaned it, an split it meself. Den I hung it up ta dry. I musta been on'y four years ol' at de time. We had a lot a fun, us little ones growin up."

And so it is with children everywhere. Even when our parents are struggling to keep the family alive, children can still find fun.

2

Berry Picking

As a supplement to the winter's food supply, wild berries were as vital to a Labrador diet as fresh fish and wild game. With bandanas tied snugly under their chins to ward off flies, rubber boots to keep feet dry, and tin cans and buckets in hand, Labradorians roamed the marshes, traipsed through bogs, and huffed and puffed over rocky hills, picking berries.

Although there were several types of berries that ripened at different times during the summer, bakeapples, also known as cloudberries, were the favourite. The time between ripening and rotting on the stems was only a few weeks. Although berries grew in abundance on Spotted Island (our summer home), it was the day trip by boat that yielded the most bakeapples. It was important to us to get out to the little islands where we had discovered favourite berry patches.

But weather was always tricky. It had to be civil (calm) enough to go by boat, but it had to be windy enough to keep the flies away. Although the bites from crawling blackflies, also called sandflies, didn't itch too badly, they would get into every part of the anatomy and draw blood. The mosquitoes were torture, and their bites left huge welts that itched for hours. I remember Daddy scanning the skies looking for the ideal conditions to pick bakeapples, and finally it was time. I'll never forget my first berry-picking trip in the boat. I was six. The memory of every detail is clear.

"Kin I go, Mommy?" I pleaded as I watched her take fresh buns from the woodstove oven.

"No, Josie, yer too small yet ta go fer all day. Ya'll get too tired."

"But, Mommy, I can pick lotsa berries, an I won't get tired an I won't eat even one!" I cried.

"Awright den, ya can come, but I don't wanna hear ya complain," she warned as she stuffed food into the grub bag.

"I'm goin berry pickin, I'm goin berry pickin!" I yelled, running out the door.

"Yeh? And I knows yer gonna pick lotsa berries, awright," Sammy piped up, laughing.

"Yeh! And I can pick as many as ya can, cuz ya eats half yours," I retorted, taking a chance sassing my big brother.

"Where's me berry picker to, Mommy?"

"Dunno, Josie. Get yer little water can. Dat'll do."

"Awright den. It won't take me long ta fill dis up," I bragged, checking it for sharp edges so I wouldn't cut myself.

After a hurried breakfast, Mommy finished packing the grub bag with enough food to last for the day. Finally, we were on our way, and as I skipped down the hill toward the stage, I thought about how many berries I was going to pick to make Mommy proud. As the motorboat chugged through the choppy sea, I could barely contain my happiness. Daddy landed the boat on the rocky shore, and we all piled onto the rocks. In my tiny sealskin slippers I huffed and puffed up the rocks. When we reached the chosen spot, we laid our things down at a high point near a big rock. We used the rock as a marker so we wouldn't get lost. No time was wasted during berry picking.

"Get back here till I puts dis stuff on yous!" Mommy shouted.

"Pooh, Mommy, dat stinks," I squealed, trying to wriggle out of her grasp. As soon as she finished, I grabbed my tin can and ran to pick berries.

"I sees a good spot!" I hollered as I bolted for the berry patch. But I couldn't run. The ground was so soft my sealskin slippers sank into it, making me tired before I even started. When I got to the berry patch, I was huffing and puffing. I dropped to my knees to pick. One by one I picked each berry and put it into my can, fighting the urge not to pop the delicious fruit into my mouth. I kept picking and picking one at a time until my can was full.

I was so excited! But when I went back to empty my can into the big can, I fell down. All my hard work was now strewn over the mossy ground in front of me. I began to cry.

"Never min yer ballin!" Mom yelled as she kept on picking. "Jus pick 'em up an start over!"

In my mother's view, children shouldn't be coddled. There was too much at stake in such a hostile land. So I had no choice but to focus on putting the next berry into my can until it was filled up again. I emptied it into the bucket. It didn't seem to make any difference to the big one. Shortly afterward, Mommy called everyone for a boil-up. I was relieved because I was getting tired.

"Mom, Jos is eatin de berries!" Sam cried.

"No, I'm not! Yer eatin more en me."

Mommy glared at both of us. "De both of ya better stop eatin dem or ya won be comin nex time. Deed ya won't!"

The wind died down, so the fly dope didn't seem to help much. The mosquitoes were relentless, but the blackflies were worse. The tiny pests left blood running down our faces and the backs of our necks. They kept getting into our eyes, noses, and mouths. Every now and then I'd hear someone choking, and I knew that meant they'd swallowed a fly.

It was mug-up time, and Daddy found a good spot to make a fire from blasty boughs. This was the fun part. I loved the smell of burning berry bushes, and a fire helped ward off the flies.

As the black smoke billowed upward, streaking the noon sky, I felt happy and secure in my little world. We sauntered about, collecting twigs and bushes to put on the fire. Daddy gathered a couple of larger sticks and made a tripod to set the kettle on. It wasn't long before it was boiling, so Mommy poured tea into tin cans for us. After adding a little molasses to sweeten the tea, she passed around the buns she'd baked for our trip.

Afterward we were reluctant to get back to the berry patches, but it was unthinkable not to keep picking. Even though I was small I was still expected to pick my share. So we trudged on, picking some, eating a few, and brushing away the flies. I was exhausted, but I dared not complain.

Some families had favourite picking spots they returned to each year, but for the most part it was a free-for-all. Whoever got to the best patches first got most of the berries, and no one liked going to a spot that had already been picked over. Some people went too early to the berry grounds, and that made Mommy angry.

"Dey shoulden pick berries till der ready fer pickin," she grumbled.

We arrived home exhausted but content. Daddy limped around to secure the boat, then brought up the pail of berries. Sammy was always there to help. Although she must have been tired, Mommy went about getting supper.

If harvested too early, bakeapples are hard and difficult to pick, but if fully ripened, they're soft and mushy when plucked, already have the consistency of jam, and don't need cleaning. We could eat them just as they were. However, they're best when mixed with a little sugar and a few drops of canned milk. We weren't allowed to snack on bakeapples because that was considered wasteful. The berries were a precious source of food for hungry days ahead. When we came back from picking, we were thankful to be able to eat a few berries.

All the other berries had to be cleaned. It was a time-consuming job, and I just wanted to go out and play. Still, the chore had to be done. We'd collect the fruit by the handful, extract the twigs and leaves, and put the berries in a barrel. There would be pies or tarts for supper on Sunday night. Mommy would whip up fresh jam made from the various berries to spread on freshly baked bread. It was especially delicious on hot kingwaks, which were bits of bread dough roasted on the stove, then placed in the oven to finish cooking. We'd cut the kingwaks in half and slather them with butter and fresh jam.

Before we went berry picking we had nothing to put on our bread except molasses. That was why fresh berries were such a treat. Soon all the berries were stored for the winter, not to be seen until at least Christmas.

The most common berries in Labrador are blackberries, blueberries, bakeapples, and redberries. The shiny blackberry with a yellow centre blanket the ground and cascade down rocks in large clusters. They're very juicy and make a dark purple jam that turns tongues black. Blueberries grow in abundance, intermingled with blackberries. They're picked and eaten throughout the season. We canned and bottled them or made them into jams because they don't freeze as well as redberries.

Bakeapples grow on boggy hills and marshes along the coast. They're covered with a velvety shuck that's difficult to remove. However, when the berry ripens, the shuck falls away and exposes the succulent berry ripe for picking. In appearance bakeapples are the size and shape of raspberries. They're redder in colour before they ripen, then turn a peachy hue. Bakeapples grow from a single stem a few inches from the ground.

Redberries are the last to mature. Newfoundlanders call this berry the partridgeberry. But to most Labradorians they're simply known as redberries and are similar to cranberries, except smaller and tarter. They grow close to the ground, hugging rocks and spilling down cliffs. Once ripened in late summer and fall, they can still be gathered beneath the snow. Redberries are extremely hardy and freeze well.

These are the most common berries, but many others grow abundantly in Labrador such as raspberries, squashberries, red currants, and crackleberries. During my growing-up years, berries were an essential staple food for our people. They were invaluable to our health. Without an adequate supply of berries, people were prone to scurvy. It wasn't unknown for people to die of scurvy in those days.

3

Shifting in the Bay

Fishermen clad in oilskins and hip rubbers tramped about the stages, now stilled from the swishing of splitting knives and the cracking bones of cods' heads. It was time to gather fishnets and buoys, paddles and ropes, and store them for another winter. Schooners, heavily laden with the summer's catch, hoisted sails in preparation to leave the sheltered coves, harbours, and bays for faraway places.

Shifting inside was a big undertaking. We Livyers moved from the rugged, wind-whipped fishing grounds each fall to more sheltered areas in the bays and coves for the winter. Whatever the success of the catch for the season, it was now time to prepare for winter. There was no government assistance available. The skipper took the money to cover his expenses first, and the rest of the men shared what was left. Each man was a share man, so whatever he ended up with after the squaring away was used to barter for the winter food supply. The barter system worked for the most part, but because the fishermen weren't paid a fair price for fish, they were kept in the hole (in debt) from one season to the next.

I watched with pride as Daddy limped into the house, tossed his sou'wester onto the chair, washed his hands in the basin, and made his way to the table for a cup of tea. As Mommy placed the cup in front of him, he stroked her affectionately. They were tired and weary from preparing for the move inland to our winter home in Roaches Brook.

"Did we make anytin after de squarin way?" Mommy asked Daddy, looking concerned.

"Yeh. We got nough ta pay down fer de winter's grub, but nuttin extra."

"When're we shiftin in de bay?"

Daddy sipped tea from his saucer. "Oh, p'raps de firs civil day now, Mammie. We mos done cleanin up, an when we get our grub from de store, we're ready."

My ears perked up when I heard the word store. I might get a candy.

"Can I go ta de store?" I dared to ask.

"Yeh, Jimmy, we'll all go," Daddy said.

"Go on outdoors, Josie," Mommy said.

"But, Mommy, I gotta get me coppers!"

I was ecstatic as we chugged across the run, and when the boat pulled up at the wharf, I clambered ashore and ran to the store. The strong odour of rubber and rope filled the place. Hip rubbers hung from the overhead rafters, and there were fishing supplies such as jiggers and twine and cork floats. Oilskin clothing was piled on shelves around the room. As I approached the counter, I could smell something sweet — cookies, candy, or apples maybe.

Whatever money Daddy received as a share man through the summer went toward his tab from the past spring when he traded in his furs. After that was paid off, or at least paid down, he could then run it up again to get our winter food supply. Basic supplies were placed in boxes, and the cost was put on our bill. Flour, tea, sugar, molasses, margarine, onions, salt pork, salt beef, hard bread, yellow split peas, and navy beans were the extent of our store-bought food. Mommy gathered skeins of worsted to knit cuffs (mittens), caps, and scarves, and collected new flannelette to make underwear. Sadly, for us, there was no money for apples. However, we did get a few jellybeans. When I popped them into my mouth, I was in heaven.

As the day of the move approached, the men raced around in preparation. They helped one another haul out the motorboats and secure them for the winter. It was a big undertaking and involved most of the able-bodied men in our village of 25 families. The men had a method for getting the boats out. Several tree trunks were placed under the keels so they would roll easily. Finding the trunks was no small feat, since there wasn't a single tree on the island. They'd been cut during the winter, limbed out, and stored away for safekeeping, much the way one would stow valuable treasure.

Several men lined up on each side to keep the boat upright, then a long rope was attached to the bow. Together they sang, "Haul on de bowline, haul boys, haul." Slowly but surely, the heavy 30-foot boats were eased onto the shore. Once the boats were up and in place, timbers were nailed under the gunwales to keep them secure. Smaller boats and dories were turned upside down to protect them from the weather.

Most houses had a little shed called a store for stashing fishing gear. Each man sorted and put away his own gear, ready for the next year. After the boats were out of the water and the fishing gear was taken care of, everyone gathered for a celebration.

My family was known for their music and dance. At our house a dance could start up at a moment's notice, and most of the village joined in. Homebrew appeared from secret hiding places as people started assembling in our home.

Daddy was an accordion player. Once he began playing, the weary fishermen, some in rubber boots, some in sealskin boots, others in duffle vamps (soft felt slippers), and a few in store-bought shoes, danced the night away. No wonder the knots stood up in our wooden floor! Shod in sealskin slippers, all the youngsters, including me, scuffled about in the corner, happy as could be.

The day after the celebration Daddy continued getting his supplies together for the winter's work. His list consisted of different types of ropes, a new axe handle, saw blades, a sharpening stone, and ammunition. The list had to be carefully prepared because when winter set in there was nowhere to go. Since Daddy knit his trout nets during the winter, he also needed fishing twine. It was vital to make sure the dogs were fed well, so during the fishing season in the summer Daddy and Sam salted salmon, flatfish, cods' heads, sculpin, and other by-products of the fishery. They packed the salted fish in burlap bags and stored everything until moving day.

Our winter home of Roaches Brook was only 35 miles away, but the pounding sea was relentless and could keep us trapped on the island for days, sometimes weeks. Finally, the day we'd been waiting for arrived. The weather was civil enough to make the treacherous trip from Spotted Island to Roaches Brook. The distance might not seem very far, but we were at the mercy of the sea's whims.

There was much excitement and a sense of urgency as Mommy and Daddy hustled about to complete last-minute preparations. Daddy finished boarding up the windows, and Sammy, Marcie, Sally, and I had to help carry everything to the boat waiting to be loaded at the stagehead.

"Is we ready yet, Daddy?" I asked.

"Awmost, Jimmy," he said as he limped past me. "An stay outta de way."

The motorboat was crammed to capacity as all our things were put onboard. Everything we needed, including the stove, was piled into the boat. I scrambled aboard and tried to find a comfortable spot to ride out the trip. The dogs were the last to be loaded. Daddy was coming down to the landwash with the dogs practically pulling him off his feet. Sam, at age 11, was big enough to help and was very good with the dogs.

"Ouch!" I cried. "Mommy, de dogs is walkin on me!"

"Josie, yer always complainin bout sometin," she grumbled. And that was all the sympathy I got.

The dogs trampled all over us until they were tied in place. The boat was overflowing now. Everything we needed to sustain us for the winter was on that boat. All our food, the dogs, the dogs' food, our stove, clothing, bedding, pots and pans, dishes, and all seven of us — Mommy, Daddy, Sammy, Marcie, me, Sally, Rhoda, and a new one on the way.

Finally, we were away, and my excitement increased. I glanced back at the rugged beauty of Spotted Island — the rough terrain, the little houses nestled around the cove. I thought of the fun I'd had over the summer. The fishing stages seemed deserted now when only a short time ago they'd been bustling with activity. As we turned past the point and headed into Rocky Bay, the raw north wind hit me square in the face. We were in the run where even on a civil day huge waves tossed boats around like wood chips.

"Mommy, I'm sick," I said, rubbing my tummy.

"Oh, Jos, ya always gets sick, maid. Whass de matter wit ya atall?" She held me over the gunwale, and I proceeded to throw up my lassie bun.

Once we got into the shelter of the hills, I felt better and was able to enjoy the rest of the trip. The rugged, moon-like, treeless hills gave way to a gentler, sloping landscape with tall trees. It was wonderful to see that land again. As soon as I spied the trees, I knew we were getting close to Roaches Brook.

4

Roaches Brook

In the early nineteenth century, as oral history came down to us, two Curl brothers came from England and married Inuit women. My paternal grandfather, John Curl, was a descendant of one of these brothers. Born in 1867, John Curl married my grandmother, Susan (also part Inuit), raised a family of five, and built the largest cabin in Roaches Brook.

I remember that their cabin overflowed with family. In true Labrador tradition all five of John Curl's family lived at home with their own growing families. My father, Thomas, who was the eldest, had built a little cabin for us so we wouldn't have to crowd in with our grandparents. Even though Roaches Brook was completely shut off from the outside world for 10 months, the people had everything they needed to sustain them for the winter.

The cabins were crudely built. They were merely tree trunks limbed out and placed together vertically, leaving many seams to be filled with moss to keep out wind and snow. Aside from cabins, the settlement contained a sawpit for sawing logs and a scaffold built high off the ground to keep fresh game and dog food out of the reach of animals. Around each log cabin were an outhouse, a sawhorse, a chopping block, a vertical woodpile, a water barrel, a dog-feeding tub, a komatik (a wooden sleigh), and a coachbox for transporting families on dogsleds.

Our motorboat was chugging along at a good pace as we made our way through the choppy North Atlantic. It was hard to talk above the noise of the engine, and the fumes were so strong that my nose stung. I kept staring at the trees on the hillsides. They passed us by as jagged sentries against the blue of the sky.

"Is we dere yet, Mommy?" I asked, tugging at her coattail.

"Awmost, Josie. Jus round dat point dere. See?" She pointed at a group of hills.

My heart pounded as we rounded the next point. There in front of me in all its beauty was Roaches Brook. It looked peaceful but lonely, with only four log cabins nestled in the shelter of the trees and hills, unlike the rocky landscape of Spotted Island. As we got closer to our landing spot, I could see the tall grass, higher than I was, swaying in the breeze. Although it was only October, the cove had sished over (formed a thin skin of ice). The fragile ice crackled as our boat entered.

Daddy eased the craft into the landwash, trying to keep the dogs from stepping on us as they piled out and disappeared into the grass. Our cabin was the longest distance away, and all our supplies had to be transported by hand for almost a quarter-mile. I didn't want to carry anything.

"Josie, don't go empty-handed if ya knows wass good fer ya!" Mommy called out.

Pouting, I grabbed a pillow and waded through the tall grass, bumbling my way along. "Weers ever'body?" I asked, staring up at the tips of the grass. "I can't see ya, Mommy. Where is ya?"

"Careful ya don't fall in de brook!" she shouted.

Everyone old enough to walk had to help. It was an arduous job, but after many trips back and forth, we finally finished carrying all our belongings from the boat.

We stumbled, tired and exasperated, into the tiny cabin that was to be home for the next six months. Although there was barely room to move, we were glad Daddy had built us our own cabin.

Everything was done in order of importance. There was no panic or confusion as Sammy and Daddy went about taking the boards off the windows, putting the dogs' food up on the scaffold, clearing away the land from a summer's growth of weeds and tall grass.

"C'mon, Josie, let's go pick de moss!" Marcie hollered.

"Awright den. C'mon, Sally!" I yelled to my younger sister. "We gotta pick de moss."

Off we ran to collect moss that grew in abundance in the bogs and under the trees. We brought home armloads, dried it, and stuffed it into the seams of the cabin to keep out the wind. Being a free-spirited little girl, I wanted to explore. Unlike the barren hills of Spotted Island, Roaches Brook was surrounded by forest. I stood in awe among the tall spruces, absorbing the wonderful aroma and the sound of the wind whistling through treetops. As I investigated my surroundings, I was fascinated to see willows growing up through the water.

At last all the supplies were put away and we were settling in. Our tiny cabin had two small windows in the front, and a little one at the back. We entered through a tiny unheated porch that served as a freezer. Dog harnesses, bridles, and traces hung on nails on the walls. The main room contained an old "comfort" stove, a crudely constructed table, a bench, and a couple of rickety chairs. A settle (settee) that Daddy had built for himself was squeezed into one corner. Mommy had made a feather cushion for it.

The bedroom at the back where Mommy and Daddy slept held a double-size bunk similar to a bin mounted on the wall about three feet off the floor. The space under the bed was used for storage. A feather mattress comprised of bleached flour sacks stuffed with feathers filled the bin. A long pillow also crammed with feathers spanned the width of the bed.

A ladder through a small hole in the ceiling led to the tiny half-loft where my sisters and I slept. It was only a crawl space. Colourful catalogue pages covered the rafters, and 12-inch-wide planks separated our feather mattresses. Like the mattress of our parents, ours were fashioned from bleached flour sacks packed with bird feathers. They had to be dragged up onto the loft and made up with flour-sack sheets and homemade quilts.

Above the stove, skimmed tree limbs were suspended with line to hang clothes on. Nails in the wall behind the stove were used to hang caps, cuffs, and socks for drying. Mukluks were placed beside the stove to dry out overnight. Mom's iron pots were also hung on nails around the stove. They were so heavy I could barely lift them. The woodbox located behind the stove completed the room.

And so the winter days began. There was work for everyone, and no one was too young to help out. How well I remember the chores I had to do.

"C'mon, Jos, ya gotta help me wit de wood!" Sammy hollered.

"But, tis too cold!" I cried.

"Oh, Jos, yer some tissy maid," he grumbled, giving me a smack.

Freezing, I watched as Sammy's saw went *swish, swish* through the wood. The ends of the wood fell to the ground. Often I held the tips to avoid having to pick them up. But Sammy, being only 12 or 13 at the time, hadn't yet mastered his saw-cutting skills, and sometimes the saw would stick and I'd fly off into the snow.

After the wood was chopped, it had to be split. With the well-sharpened axe in hand, Sammy placed a junk (log) of wood on the chopping block, raised the axe high overhead, and slammed it onto the wood, splitting it wide open. Then he cut it in half again to make it small enough to fit into the stove, and we carried it into the house. I was cold and just wanted to go inside to play. To my mind, there was never enough time for play.

When supper was finished, there was no time for play, either. Exhausted, I was happy to climb the crudely constructed ladder and roll into my nicely made-up bed. I lay there studying the images in front of me, praying I wouldn't pee in my bed during the night. Through the flickering of the oil lamp I reached up into the blackness and touched the rafters. My imagination went wild as the pictures turned into monsters stretching out to grab me. Once the lamps went out, I had nightmares of demons and ghosts in the absolute blackness.

"Mommy, tis too dark an I'm scared!" I cried.

"Yeh? Ya better be good, too, or de boogie man'll get ya," she replied to this foolishness.

Courtesy Them Days magazine and the artist Gerald W. Mitchell.

Sawing wood in the Labrador wilderness.

We got our drinking water from the nearby brook. Daddy chopped two holes through the ice covering the water. One spot was used as a well for drinking water, and farther downstream another hole was used for soaking the salted dog food.

To fetch water, Daddy lashed the barrel onto the komatik and headed for the steady. He chopped a hole through the ice, scooped bucket after bucket from the brook, and poured them into the barrel. The water was then transferred into the barrel on the porch, which froze over during the night and had to be chopped free each morning.

For firewood Daddy had to take a daylong trip to cut wood. To do that he had to get his ninny bag ready the night before. It usually contained his ever-present knife, chewing tobacco, shells for his gun, matches, a kettle, and a small pot.

In the morning, while Daddy ate his toast and sipped tea from his saucer, Mommy hustled about, stuffing food into his grub bag — fresh buns, tea, a little salt and sugar or molasses, and a piece of fatback pork.

Courtesy *Them Days* magazine and the artist Gerald W. Mitchell.

Fetching water in Labrador.

The grub bag then went into his ninny bag. If Daddy was going to cut wood, he would use the komatik box to put his things in. It was also used as a seat. He'd lash it tightly onto the komatik, along with his rackets (snowshoes), axe, and gun.

If Daddy was going to haul the wood he'd already cut, he would tightly lash the horn junks (wooden cradles) to each end of the komatik. They were contructed from two large pieces of timber just long enough to span the width of the komatik, with a hole drilled in each end. A stick about three feet long stood up in them, providing a sturdy wooden cradle.

Eventually, the wood was cut, limbed out, and placed in a neat pile by the side of the wood path ready to be hauled out. After several days of cutting, the dogs were harnessed, the wood was piled into the komatik between the horn junks, and then it was transported home by dog team. Once the green wood arrived, it was placed in the vertical woodpile so it wouldn't be buried in a snowstorm. Dry wood was stacked separately.

Courtesy *Them Days* magazine and the artist Gerald W. Mitchell.

Hauling home firewood in horn junks in Labrador.

At dusk until well after dark each day Daddy and Sammy had to feed the dogs, top up the water barrel, saw the firewood, and chop up two armloads of splits (dry wood cut into kindling), which were brought in and neatly stacked near the stove to dry out. In our house dry wood was like gold and was always kept away from the regular wood. Some of it was used to make wood shavings, and no one was allowed to touch it. The trick was not to let the fire get so low that we would have to use the dry wood.

To cut the wood shavings, Daddy used a drawknife, a tool ideally suited for the task. It had a large steel blade about a foot long, with wooden handles bent toward the sharp edge of the blade, designed to be pulled toward you. Daddy sat on the floor, facing the stove, and squeezed the kindling between his knees for stability. He then placed the drawknife three-quarters of the way up the wood. I always watched intensely as he pulled the drawknife toward himself, afraid he would cut right into his belly. But with great precision he never failed to stop an inch from his body. I can still hear the sound of the wood curls being separated from the junk as the sharp blade forced its way through the wood. Daddy cut into it with just enough pressure and speed to make a neatly curled shaving. He then put the next one behind the first, and so on, until there were several neat curls still attached to the wood. After that he started another junk until there was enough to start a fire. Daddy made it look so easy.

"I wanna do dat, Daddy," I said. "Can I try?"

"No, Jimmy, ya can't do dis. Tis too hard fer ya."

"I can do it, Daddy," I insisted, tugging at his arm. "Lemme try."

"Awright den."

Handing me the drawknife, he showed me where to place it on the wood. With great tenderness and patience he let me pull and struggle for a while. I couldn't get the blade to move. "Tis stuck, Daddy!"

"I tol ya twas too hard fer ya," he said. "Ya can try again when yer a little bigger."

Every evening, after the dishes were cleared away, Mommy sat in her favourite chair with her sewing machine or knitting needles. Daddy, with all his outdoor work done and the shavings cut, lay back on his settle and had a little rest. If his day hunting in the woods was successful, we had roasted partridges for supper. After a short nap, he played a few songs on his accordion and Mommy danced around the room. We danced around the cabin, too, happy and secure with a belly full of food and a nice warm fire.

The husky dogs were our lifeline and had to be well cared for. Daddy made the dogs' harnesses and traces and the bridle used to pull the komatik. The dogs' harnesses were created from rope that had to be taken apart and braided back together to make it more pliable and softer around the animals' bodies. The rope was then spliced at the end with a loop where the traces were attached. The traces were made of bank line, which was the size of a pencil and had a distinct tar smell. The bank line was tightly woven and quite rigid. The traces were then attached to a bridle, which was fashioned out of a larger rope braided together from three pieces of rope with a loop at one end for the traces. The other end was forked into two separate ropes, with each side attached to the first rung of the komatik.

Feeding the dogs was a daily chore for Daddy. He took the salted fish products down from the scaffold and soaked them in the brook for a day.

Courtesy *Them Days* magazine and the artist Gerald W. Mitchell.

Feeding sled dogs in Labrador.

Then he cooked food scraps and cornmeal in a big five-gallon bucket on the stove. Outside the dogs sniffed their food cooking and began howling and yelping. Once the cornmeal was cooked and poured into the feeding tub, Daddy added the frozen food to make a nourishing meal for the dogs. I enjoyed watching them crowd around the circular tub, gobbling their food in a feeding frenzy.

By the time the dogs were fed, it was dark and suppertime. Mommy was busy cooking seal meat, rabbits, or some other game for supper. Daddy came in, washed his hands in the basin, and proceeded to his settle to wait for supper. After we ate, he cleaned his traps and guns.

"Whass ya doin now, Daddy?" I asked, leaning on his knee.

"Gettin ready ta set me traps, Jimmy," he said, his gentle voice filtering through the tiny cabin.

"Where's ya goin dis time?" I prodded, wanting to know his every move.

"Oh, jus in de woods lookin fer partridges, an I'll set a few rabbit snares an a few traps."

"Can I go?"

"No, Jimmy, yer too small yet. Maybe when ya gets a little bigger ya can go."

I knew that would have to do, so I just sat and watched him. To clean the barrel of his gun, he took a long rod with a little piece of cloth like a bow attached to it. Once the barrel was cleaned, he poured gunpowder into it. It was a charcoal-grey substance and smelled strange. He then dropped in a wad, gently padded it down, and dropped in a piece of lead, then another wad. The gun was now ready, and he carefully stood it against the wall beside him.

"Dat's not fer ya ta touch," he warned.

"Why?"

"Cuz ya could blow yer head off, dat's why." Daddy never yelled at us. However, when he used a certain tone of voice, there was no questioning his authority.

In the dead of winter the temperature could dip to minus 50 degrees Fahrenheit. The frost got so thick on the windowpanes that it formed mounds of ice, making it impossible to see outside. When our mittens got wet, they stuck fast to the icicles. If we tried to pull our mittens free, they ripped.

"Don't stick yer tongue on dem ol tings or ya'll be sorry," Mommy warned.

"Okay, Mom," I piped up as I ran out the door to play. I admired the icicles hanging from the cabin. They glistened like glass as the brilliant sunshine shone through them. Holding a broken piece of icicle in my hand, I glanced at my sister. "What'll happen I wonder?"

"Yer tongue'll stick ta it," she answered. "Dat's what'll happen, an ya'll never git off."

"Oh, yeh? Can I try?"

"No, Jos," Marcie said. "Ya'll be sorry."

Always the defiant one, I touched the icicle with the tip of my tongue. It stuck. Solid! I couldn't get it off at all. It hurt so much, and I was terrified of what my mother would do to me if she found out. I tried and tried, but my tongue wouldn't come unstuck. I started to cry and now had no choice.

"Aw, Mommy, it hurts!" I cried, racing back inside the cabin.

"Good nough fer ya, ya bloody little fool. I tol ya not ta do it."

"Aw, Mommy! Tis some sore an tis bleedin, too."

"Serves ya right," she said as she melted the huge icicle off my tongue. "Cuz ya won listen, will ya?"

Mommy didn't remember a terrible incident that happened during the winter I turned seven. She might have been somewhere having a baby at the time. I'd peed in my bed again as I did every night. With my teeth chattering from the cold, I crawled across the floor, clambered down the ladder, and pushed aside the curtain Mommy used as a door to separate the bedroom from the kitchen. Daddy was putting wood in the stove.

"I'm cold, Daddy," I murmured as I wrapped my arms around his legs.

"Awright, Jimmy, de stove's getting hot now. Ya'll be warm soon." He put me on a wooden crate in front of the curtain to warm up. At that moment Marcie came out of the room, pushed the curtain aside, and accidentally shoved me onto the stove. I screamed. Daddy pulled me off so quickly that I didn't burn too badly. I'm thankful that the stove wasn't fully hot, but it was hot enough to give me nasty burns on both of my arms. I carry the scars to this day.

The long winter dragged on, and even though we were trapped inside the tiny cabin for weeks, we found ways to entertain ourselves. There was no electricity, radio, or television, no colouring book or crayons, no storybooks or board games. And there was no space for activities. So Daddy made us little toys — a spin top out of an empty cotton spool, a crossbow made from wood. When we found a piece of string, we played cat's cradle and other simple games such as button-to-button or gossip. Cat's cradle is simply a piece of string tied together. Using our fingers, we made different designs with it. Daddy also whittled little dolls from wood. We always managed to find something to do but certainly weren't allowed to fight with one another. A crack on the head with Mommy's knuckle taught us that early on.

Life in Roaches Brook was harsh and very primitive. The daily trip into the woods to cut enough firewood for both summer and winter was daunting. All the wood for Spotted Island had to be cut and hauled out to the landing point. Then we took it by boat to Spotted Island once the ice broke up in the spring.

Monday was washday, and with temperatures at minus 30 degrees, the clothes would freeze before Mommy even got them pinned on the line. Mommy had two bedwetters, so trying to keep Sammy's and my beds clean of pee was a never-ending chore for her. She just couldn't keep up. Consequently, night after night, I went to bed in my pee-soaked feather bed on the wooden floor of the loft. It was hard, cold, and wet.

The constant struggle for food was always foremost in my parents' minds. Once food was provided and prepared, Mommy was busy sewing and re-sewing our clothing, fashioning mittens, socks, and caps, and darning everything we wore. Her tasks kept her working until she practically fell off her chair. They were such devoted parents and worked diligently to keep us alive.

We weren't without fun, however. The few families in Roaches Brook whiled away the long winter nights by playing cards, making their own music, and dancing whenever they got the opportunity. And so the long winter passed.

Eventually, spring arrived and it was warm enough to snow. And snow it did! In spring we could go outdoors and play, and play we did! We climbed onto the mounds of snow and slid down on our small komatiks. We built houses of snow and snowmen and had snowball fights. It was so much fun! We'd go into the cabin with our clothes soaking wet, and Mommy would grumble at us for staying out too long. We were a happy family then.

"Yer gonna catch yer death," Mommy would say, and we'd just grin.

Fierce spring storms buried our little cabin, plunging us into complete darkness. Daddy would have to dig us out. I didn't know we were always on the brink of starvation. I didn't know there was any other place in the world.

At night as I lay in my small bed in the half-loft, wishing I wouldn't pee that night, I heard my parents talking softly to each other. In the flicker of the oil lamp I saw the pictures on the catalogue-covered rafters. They seemed to move, dance, and clutch at me. Daddy was probably nodding off downstairs and then they would bank the stove and retreat to their feather bed. Such was the life of a hunter and trapper.

Such was our life in Roaches Brook — place of my birth.

5

Mommy's Work

"Whass fer supper, Mommy?" we'd all ask as we bounded inside after playing.

"Oh, havin a bit a fish tonight, maids," she'd say. Or sometimes she'd say, "Never ya mind whass fer supper. Ya'll fin out soon nough. An stay away from dat pot!"

The rules were very strict in our house as to what went on around the stove, and we dared not disobey Mommy. Food was all-important. The stove was dangerous, and everything had to be shared to keep the entire family alive. My mother's work was all-consuming, not only in the physical sense but mentally and emotionally, as well.

My mother, or Aunt Flossie as she was affectionately known to the community, was a short woman about five feet two inches in height. She looked quite frail at first glance but was actually very strong, both in physical strength and in character. Her strength showed in the way she ruled her household.

Mommy's pale blue eyes stood out against dark olive skin, revealing her Inuit, Innu, and European heritages. Her dark brown hair, fine as silk, was worn in a neat bun at the back. I seldom saw it worn any other way. When she let her hair down, it fell to her waist. Before she went to bed, she sat and combed it out. It was pleasing to see that softer side of her.

My mother was orphaned young and suffered a terrible childhood. Her mother died when she was only 11. Her father passed away a year later, leaving four orphans; my mother was the eldest. But even those early years weren't happy. I heard her say of her mother many times: "She was a cruel, evil woman."

The mission wanted to separate the children, but Mommy refused to go to the boarding school in Mary's Harbour down the coast. Instead she decided to take a job with a family. It was a job done solely for her keep; she was never paid a salary. The family was very harsh, and two years later they left my mother alone in a cold, unheated cabin to die. Thankfully, someone went to the pond for water, heard banging from a distant cabin, and rescued her.

Mommy's rescuer brought her to a kind and caring family where she stayed until she met Daddy when she was 17. Even though my mother had had a baby already, my father, Thomas Curl, wanted to marry her and adopt her infant son, Sammy. They married in 1938. For the first several years they lived with my grandparents, John and Susan Curl, until Daddy built his own tiny cabin in Roaches Brook. On Spotted Island he inherited his father's big house, and we lived in it until we moved to Cartwright in 1953.

Thomas Curl was a quiet, gentle man. When he married my mother, he gave her a sewing machine and a .22-calibre rifle as a wedding present. When Daddy went away to his traplines or out on a hunting trip, Mommy had to find her own way to keep us alive. She'd put on all the warm clothes she could find, strap on the snowshoes Daddy had made for her, tuck her gun under her arm or over her shoulder, and head into the woods, leaving us in the care of neighbours. Being a sure shot with her little .22, she always came back with a few partridges or a porcupine. Mommy also had her own line of rabbit snares set up around the cabin, and we had many delicious meals of rabbit. When Daddy was away on an extended hunting trip, before Sammy was big enough to help, Mommy also had to saw and chop firewood, fetch water, and nurse us when we were hurt or sick. My mother knew many home remedies for everything, from small cuts and scrapes to major cuts and life-threatening illnesses.

During the spring snows when we were outside all day and came in with our clothes soaking wet, Mommy was the one to dry them out. She hung everything, including our saturated mukluks, around the stove to dry. In the morning our mukluks would be so stiff we couldn't get them on. To make them more pliable, she got out the special softening stick Daddy had made for her. It had a wooden base attached to another piece of wood about three or four inches wide, and stood about three feet high. At the top it was shaped like an axe blade. Mommy took the boots by the toe and heel and ran them over the board, making them supple again. It wasn't an easy job as I found out one day when I tried to do it.

Mommy worked from pre-dawn until well into the night. She was busy knitting, sewing, making new clothing, mending old clothing, creating bedding from bleached flour sacks, fashioning new dickies (parkas), hooking floor mats, and producing soap. One of the most challenging jobs was crafting sealskin boots or mukluks. When I was little, I couldn't understand how she could make them waterproof just by her skill in sewing.

Spring was seal-hunting time. When Daddy was due to return from the hunt, Mommy searched the horizon for the safe return of her man. Usually, he came back with a seal or two strapped onto the komatik.

"Whass dat, Mom?" I asked, eyeing the huge bulk strapped to the komatik.

"Dat's a harp seal," she explained, not that I would know the difference.

Already exhausted from the hunt, Daddy had to skin the animals before the dogs could get to them or before they froze. If the seal froze, it would be almost impossible to skin. I watched intently as Daddy skillfully removed the skin. His sharp knife separated the fur from the carcass. Huge mounds of fat were put aside for dog food. Once the skin was off, then it was Mommy's job to clean the skin.

She got the huge galvanized tub from its nail in the porch, and a special board about a foot wide, three feet long, and rounded on one side and flat on the other. As soon as Daddy dropped the pelt into the tub, Mommy went to work. She pulled the pelt up onto the rounded side of the board and retrieved her ulu (rounded knife for cleaning pelts) from its special place. Holding the T-shaped handle between her forefinger and her index finger and stabilizing it with her thumb, she placed the blade on the fatty side of the skin. Making smooth strokes with the curve of the ulu, she slithered the razor-sharp, half-moon-shaped blade down the skin, employing the full width of it and leaving the skin clean. After removing every inch of fat, she turned the pelt over and cleaned the fur from the other side. Once she was satisfied that it was clean enough, she handed it back to Daddy. In later years when she learned to make fancier mukluks, she left the fur on.

Daddy then prepared the sealskin for drying. To do this he lashed it into a wooden frame, stretching it tightly all the way around and nailing it outside on the cabin to dry. Once the sealskin was dry, which took several days, it was ready to make into boots. One full-grown seal yielded enough hide to produce two or three pairs of mukluks.

To make mukluks, Mommy laid the large skin on the floor. She used paper cut-outs as patterns to trace around as she cut out the tongues that covered the tops of the feet. The bottoms and leggings were then trimmed to size, depending on who would be wearing the boots. Once she had cut all the mukluks out, she gave the leftover hide to Daddy. He cut it into thin strips and tossed them into a pail of water. After a few days, the strips became slimy and stretchy and were used to string snowshoes.

Mommy couldn't soak the boot parts because the hide would be too slippery to grip and she wouldn't be able to sew them. However, she had to get the edges soft enough to poke the needle through. There was only one way to do that. We had to chew it. I'll always remember the first time I had to chew sealskin! I was about nine years old.

"Jos, ya gotta chew da skins, cuz I gotta make new mukluks fer Sam," Mommy said as I stripped off my coat one day.

I didn't want to do that, but we had to do as we were told. So I took the pieces of sealskin and settled down to chew. It tasted awful and burned my tongue, but I kept chewing and grinding it with my teeth until she was satisfied.

Once the skin was soft enough, Mommy sewed the tongue to the front part of the leggings first. While she was sewing that, we had to chew all around the perimeter of the bottom section, then around the bottom of the leggings. She then sewed them together, using a very fine stitch. Pleating and pulling tightly on each stitch with immense concentration, she made the boots waterproof.

With all of us children to practise on, Mommy gradually learned to make fancier boots with different coloured fur. She cut out diamonds and sewed them onto the front of the leggings, making them both beautiful to look at and to wear. As years passed and she got better at her craft, she began sewing all manner of items for the Grenfell Mission's Industrial Store across the harbour, where authentic crafts were sold to visitors from around the world.

The main meal of the day was always dinner. And if food was available, I enjoyed watching Mommy prepare it. Sundays were our special days. For Sunday breakfast we always had fish and brewis. For dinner on Sunday, Mommy cooked a big meal of wild game, with salt beef, vegetables, pudding, and duff (dumpling). For supper we had fried fish — cod, salmon, arctic char, trout, or smelt. In later years we even had canned fruit with jelly for dessert on Sunday nights. Monday we had leftovers from Sunday. Tuesday was bean soup day. Wednesday was fish or wild meat. If we didn't have meat or fish, we had to settle for stewed potatoes or doughboys (boiled dumplings) and jam. On Thursday we had fish and brewis, and on Friday we had fish. Saturday was pea soup day.

Mommy's main concern was not to run out of flour. Homemade bread was our staple food. We could almost always rely on bread and tea, which in earlier years was our mainstay. For the most part, meals were basic: no treats, no frills, no snacks between meals, except maybe a piece of molasses bread or a clump of hard tack. And many times there was nothing at all.

Cooking wild game is an art. Ducks and geese have to be steamed to pluck the feathers out. Partridges don't have to be steamed. They can just be plucked, and my mother performed this job efficiently.

"Mommy, I wants de crop!" I cried as she was pulling the innards out of a partridge one day.

The crop was the stomach of the partridge, which always contained spruce twigs. She blew it up like a balloon and hung it near the stove to dry. Once dried, it made a hollow rattle like the sound of maracas. When we were little, we argued over who was going to get the next one. We ate everything except the guts of the bird. We consumed the heart, the gizzard, the liver, and the head, and usually fussed over who would get the wishbone for good luck.

Cooking wild meat took several hours. First, Mommy boosted the heat by adding a few pieces of dry wood to the fire. Then she fried up some fat, filling the cabin with smitch (smoke). Next she dropped the meat into the hot fat. The small room was filled with sharp smells and sizzling noises. Mommy waited for the meat to brown a bit, then added water, salt and pepper, and an onion, if we had any. Lastly, she added a sprinkle of flour. After that she gave the whole thing a gentle stir to fuse the flavours, then placed the lid on the big iron pot. Filling the stove to capacity with carefully selected wood, she proceeded to her next chore.

We were hungry and knew there was at least a two-hour wait before dinner. About three-quarters of the way through the cooking time, Mommy started to make the duff. Out came her favourite mixing bowl, flour, butter, baking powder, and a little water to bring it all together.

"Wass ya doin now, Mommy?" I asked as she flattened the dough onto the table.

"Watch me an ya'll see," she answered in her matter-of-fact way.

Once the dough was flattened, she made a big hole in the centre and placed it gently on top of the meat in the pot. It only took 10 minutes to cook. That was our cue to set the table. Sal and I lifted the table out from the wall, exposing the long bench placed there for us little ones. When the table was set, we had to make the tea. I poured a handful of loose tea into the pot and filled it with water from the huge kettle, which was always at boiling point on the back of the stove. The clang of the teapot lid and someone placing the teapot on the back of the stove to steep were sure signs that the meal was almost ready. The next thing was to cut the bread.

"Can I watch ya cut de bread, Mom?" I asked, tugging at her apron.

"Awright, but don't get too close ta de knife."

Mommy always wore an apron. Placing the bread in her lap and holding the loaf firmly in her left hand, she picked up her long, very sharp knife and positioned it ever so lightly into the corner of the bread. With one smooth stroke she pushed the knife about a third of the way through the bread. Her second and third strokes made a perfectly even slice, as if the bread had gone through a slicing machine. Every slice was uniformly cut as she piled the plate high and put it in the centre of the table.

Every Monday we had to fetch water from the well for washing. Mommy lifted the huge galvanized washtub and washboard off the nail in the porch. She stoked up the stove to heat buckets of water and then sorted out the clothes that covered the whole floor of our tiny cabin. It was back-breaking work. I felt sorry for her as she scrubbed each piece of clothing, wrung it out, shook each garment, and placed it in a pile ready for hanging. On extremely cold days the clothes froze even before they reached the line. Steam from the warm clothes billowed around Mommy in the cold air.

The washing remained on the line for a few days to dry, and if it didn't dry because of the extremely cold temperatures, Mommy had to bring it back inside and spread it over the stove to finish drying. It smelled wonderful. As the family grew, Mommy couldn't continue doing everything herself. We had to help as we got older. The blisters on my knuckles would peel and bleed, but it didn't matter. We had to keep scrubbing. I hated it!

Since my mother was never still, there was always something to be learned by watching her.

"Whass ya doin now, Mommy?" I asked as she scurried around with enthusiasm.

"I tink I got nough rags ta hook a mat, Josie." she said, pulling out a bag from under her bed.

With amazing skill, using a piece of line and a huge needle, Mommy attached the burlap bag to the wooden frame Daddy had made for her. Once the burlap was sewn into place, she drew a pattern on it. It could be flowers or a winter scene or something around our cabin. She tore the rags into long, thin strips, keeping the colours separated. When she was ready, she placed a piece at a time underneath the burlap. She pushed the hook through the top, hooked the string up through the tiny burlap hole, making a neat loop, then poked it down for the next loop, and so on, until the whole pattern was filled out. Mommy finished the mat with a colourful border.

I didn't know then that our mother was exceptionally talented in her work, and I don't think that she was aware of it, either, especially in the earlier years of her marriage when we were all babies and so very needy. I wonder how she learned everything. I don't know if anybody taught her, whether she had to learn as she went along, or if she learned out of the sheer necessity to survive. I know that she made good use of the rifle and the sewing machine Daddy had given her on their wedding day. It was all she really needed to keep us warm and fed.

My mother did the best she could under dire circumstances. Many times I watched as she rubbed her hand over her head, smoothed the straggled hair that had fallen around her face, and just kept on going. In later years she sewed every day for the mission store. Once her order was finished, she had to deliver it back over to the mission. Mrs. Keddie, who ran the store, was extremely pleased with Mommy's work, and the store continued to sell it until my mother's death in 1997. After Daddy died in 1967 at age 50, Mommy was left with seven children to raise on her own. She did this with money she earned from sewing and cleaning, and I never heard her complain. Being pregnant, giving birth to 14 children, and trying to keep them alive must at times have pushed her beyond all physical and mental endurance. She lost four babies in infancy. The pain from that alone is incomprehensible. Still, she did it. She raised 10 of us to adulthood, and we are a wonderfully warm and caring family today.

Mommy mothered us the best way she knew how, and I'm so proud of her accomplishments today. I only hope, as my story unfolds, that I can bring her the justice she so rightly deserves.

While walking down Water Street in Halifax, Nova Scotia, some 40 years later, I walked into a store and saw several exquisite pairs of duffle slippers on display. I lifted the tab of authenticity and was absolutely thrilled and overwhelmed to see written on the tag: MADE BY FLOSSIE CURL.

6

Hunting and Trapping

The Labrador fur trade started legally around the middle of October, but the actual beginning of the season was variable. It took time for the animals to grow their winter coats. Therefore trappers waited until later in the fall when thicker furs brought better prices. From year to year the success of the fur trade varied. The quantity of fur-bearing animals always ran in cycles. Some years were extremely good, while others were very poor, so there was constant concern for the survival of our people. Weather played a major part in the success of the season and the quality of the furs. The distance and frequency that the trapper was able to attend to his traps were always factors. So, too, was knowing the right place to set the traps.

The local custom was never to set foot on another trapper's territory. Many trapping grounds were kept in the family for a century or more and were passed down from generation to generation. A trapping ground was never intentionally infringed upon by another trapper. The closest trading post was many miles away. The nearest one to Roaches Brook was Cartwright, which was 60 miles distant. The forest brought everything we needed to sustain us for the winter — wood for heat, animals for food, and fur to trade for clothing and essential items.

Leg-hold traps were the only type in existence at the time. The different sizes were geared to the size of the animal. The bigger traps were used for lynx, beaver, wolf, and fox, while little ones were for mink, martin, weasel, and squirrel. Aside from trapping for the fur trade, it was crucial to go hunting each fall for edible animals. Gaming licences and permits weren't required in the 1940s and 1950s. There were no laws or law-enforcement officers to be seen. People were free to hunt at will.

Some hunting memories are very clear. I was skipping up the path toward our Spotted Island cabin one day when I heard Sammy yelling. "Der's a walrus in de boat! De men gotta walrus! Boy, oh, boy, tis some big, too!"

"Whass a walrus, Marcie?" I asked.

"Dunno, maid," she answered.

I ran as fast as my little legs could carry me down to the stage to see what the commotion was about. It was the biggest thing I'd ever seen!

"Whass dem big white tings stickin outta his mouth?" I asked, fascinated by two long curved white bones bigger than my body.

"Der tusks!" Sammy hollered.

I thought my big brother knew everything. I didn't understand tusks, so I shut up and marvelled at the scene in front of me.

It took all the men in the community to haul the gigantic carcass up onto the beach. As always, when they were needed, every able-bodied man was there to help. The carcass was carved up, and the blubber was set aside for the dogs. The remaining meat was shared with the whole village. The walrus provided a lot of meat, and it left a big mess on the beach.

My memories of Roaches Brook are equally clear. I adored my father and followed him around whenever possible.

"Whass ya doin now, Daddy?" I asked as he limped around the porch and reached for a wooden box and a tin can high on a shelf.

"I'm cleanin me guns now, Jimmy. I'm goin huntin tomarra marnin."

"Whass dat fer?" I asked, pointing at the tightly lidded can.

"Gunpowder. An tis not fer ya ta touch if ya wanna keep yer head on yer shoulders."

"Why? What'll happen ta me head?"

"Never min why, Jimmy. Jus don't ever touch it."

A hunting trip was a major undertaking, especially if the men went inland for several days to search for bear and caribou. Those trips were usually made in the winter or early spring around March and April and involved several hunters. Each hunter borrowed extra dogs from other men in the community to be sure they could transport their game back.

Hunting for small game such as partridge, porcupine, and rabbit was almost a daily event. In the fall it was mainly seabirds and seals that the hunters brought home. Daddy would return with lots of birds. Turrs (murres), geese, and ducks were the most plentiful.

The next job was to pick (pluck) and clean them. Mommy had her work cut out for her again. To pluck dozens of birds she had to get the stove hot. Once the stove was hot enough, she hauled her sleeves up, straightened her pinny, slicked back her hair, and got to work. With her left hand she held the wings and neck while her right hand kept a firm grip on the feet and tail feathers. This grip exposed the full breast area. I watched as she dipped the bird into a large pan of water and then rubbed it across the hot stove in a fast, vigorous motion. Water bubbles danced across the stove. The steam penetrated the feathers and scalded the skin of the bird, which allowed the feathers to be plucked more easily. Mommy was fast and could pick a bird in a few minutes.

The smell of scalding skin and scorching feathers was nauseating. "Pooh, dat stinks, Mommy," I grumbled.

"Yeh, Josie, it do stink. But dey'll taste good on yer supper plate, won dey?"

"Oh, yeh, Mommy. Can hardly wait."

In late October winter set in quickly. The damp frost that started in late August was thick on the ground and clung to everything. By December it became extremely cold, but the air was very still and bright with sunshine. On a calm, frosty morning the air was so still that smoke from the stovepipes floated skyward straight as an arrow. On a clear, frosty night the stars, the northern lights, and the full moon shone so brilliantly that newly fallen snow sparkled like diamonds. Glittering light blanketed my world, making it as light as day.

After Daddy secured enough wood and water for a few days, he settled down to prepare his traps. He lifted the huge bundle off the nail in the porch, which looked to me like a snarl of rusted metal. The jingling and banging stirred my curiosity.

"Whass ya doin now, Daddy?"

"Cleanin me traps, Jimmy."

"Why?"

"So dey'll work right."

He opened a huge bear trap, cocked it, then tripped it shut with a loud bang. It terrified me.

"Oh, Daddy! Better not put me fingers in der, hey?"

"Not less ya wants ta lose em," he said calmly.

When he finished cleaning all his traps, he was ready. "Everything's ready ta go," he said with a satisfied look on his face. He then retired to his settle for the evening.

"Can ya play us a song, Daddy?" I asked, tugging on his pant leg.

He picked up his accordion and began playing a tune. I danced happily around the floor.

"Time ta go ta bed now, maids," Mommy piped up after a time.

Oh, why did she have to spoil everything? I thought. But I knew there was no arguing with her. I climbed the ladder to the half-loft and crawled into my feather bed. As I snuggled under the weight of Mommy's homemade quilts, I felt sad. I didn't want Daddy to go away. I listened to him play for a while and then everything became quiet and very, very dark. It was too dark to see the printed catalogue paper that covered the rafters just above my head.

The next morning it was still dark when I awoke to the delicious smell of freshly steeped tea and homemade toast. I heard the crackling of the splits as they quickly burned away, and felt warmth filtering into my loft. Daddy had already lit the fire, boiled the kettle, and made his breakfast of tea and toast. My parents were talking softly.

I felt so scared about my daddy going away. The smell of toast made me hungry, so I crawled down the ladder and stood on the orange crate beside the stove. I watched Mommy bustle about, getting everything ready for Daddy. I wanted to see him off. Mommy had made pork buns for him, his favourite.

Daddy took his ninny bag from the nail beside the stove and laid it on the table. Into his bag he put a tiny homemade stove, a blackened kettle, a small cooking pot, some snare wire, a small ball of line, ammunition, fish hooks, and a skinning knife. Into an old shaving kit bag he placed his chewing tobacco and matches. Before he left he used a whetstone to sharpen his axe and all his knives.

"Whass ya doin now, Daddy?" I asked as he spit on the stone to wet it.

"I'm sharpnin me knife, Jimmy," he said, swirling the blade around and around in a circular motion and making a soft, grinding sound.

"Wha fer?"

"So it'll cut better."

My father worked efficiently and effortlessly, almost as if in slow motion, very focused and methodical. He picked up his axe and braced it between his knees to check the sharpness of the blade. Then he pinned the handle on his thigh with his elbow, held the heel of the axe in his left hand for stability, took his sharpening stone, and pushed it across the blade. He started from the inside corner and pushed outward, making that soft, grinding noise. Spit and grind, spit and grind. I could see the tip of the steel blade start to gleam.

"Looks sharp now, Daddy," I said, my face close to the blade, studying it.

"Yeh, Jimmy, tis," he said, wiping it clean and leaning it against the wall. "Don't touch it," he added, looking at me with a warning grin.

Daddy then double-checked his supplies. He was ready. With quiet anticipation he hung his ninny bag and his traps on his gun barrel, slung the gun over his shoulder, and set out. *Swoosh, swoosh* went his rackets, rubbing together as he limped through the snow. I could hear the traps jingling, and a tear trickled down my cheek as I watched him disappear into the woods.

Everything became silent as we wondered if he would be safe. He might travel several miles in a day, setting his traps as he went. It was a time-consuming job, and finding the right place to set each trap was critical.

Courtesy *Them Days* magazine and the artist Gerald W. Mitchell.

Loading up a komatik for a trapping trip in Labrador.

For fox and mink a trapper would usually set traps along the shoreline under a large tree or in the mouth of a burrow. Mink traps could be set in a river in air pockets where the animals travelled in and out for food. A trapper had to know the habits of the animal. The better he was at predicting the animal's behaviour the better chance he had of trapping it. Lynx preferred heavily wooded areas. Mink and weasels were the easiest to trap. Weasels were plentiful, and since they weren't suspicious, the trapper didn't have to conceal the traps, which was a difficult process. However, traps for fox and lynx had to be hidden because they were such crafty animals. For fox and lynx a trapper had to be sure to leave as few clues as possible. After the traps were set on the initial run of the line, the trapper had to wait overnight and hope he would get something. Exhausted and weary, he would put up his little canvas tent, cover the floor with boughs, and set up his tiny stove. All these items he carried with him. There were no sleeping bags then and none of the warm synthetic clothing we have today. In order not to freeze to death the trapper had to keep the stove going all night.

First thing in the morning the trapper made the rounds, checking each trap, emptying and resetting them as he went. The animals were frozen solid and remained that way until he got them home.

Daddy hung the frozen animals near the stove to thaw out before they were skinned. The few animals not yet frozen were skinned right away. The skin was turned inside out and pulled and stretched over special boards carved in the shape of the animal. Little nails tacked the skins to the end of the board to keep them from shrinking while drying. They were then placed high on the cabin beams to dry. Once thoroughly dried, they were turned right side out and kneaded until they were soft and supple. The pelts had to be cleaned thoroughly. Not doing so would leave an odour and reduce the quality of the fur. Traders wanted only clean, odourless, well-cured pelts.

Getting to the trading post was another feat because the closest one was a two-day trip to Cartwright, 60 miles away. Winter storms were brutal and could come without warning. During a major storm or a cold spell, we were trapped for days inside the cabin. With the temperatures at minus 50 degrees and winds up to 100 miles per hour, nothing moved. A mound of snow was all we could see of the dogs as they were completely buried.

The silence was deafening after a storm. It was dark, but not like the darkness of night. This was different, like a grey hue everywhere. Many times I heard Daddy get up from his quilts, limp to the window, blow a peephole through the frost to check the weather, and see nothing but a wall of snow.

"Der'll be no wood cuttin or huntin taday, Mammy," he'd say with a sigh.

"Is we buried again, Tom?" she'd ask Daddy from her bed in the darkness.

"Yeh, Mammy, and tis too starmy ta go anywhere."

"My, oh, my, whass we gonna do I wonder? We got nuttin fer de youngsters ta eat."

"We needs ta get sometin soon or we'll starve," Daddy would answer, concern evident in his voice. The possibility of starvation was very real.

To go hunting for big game involved several men in the settlement as a group, and they could be gone for a week or more. Daddy used all his dogs to hunt big game, and any spare dogs he could borrow, especially if they went inland for caribou.

The hourglass was the only way to monitor the weather. So if it looked favourable for several days, the men geared up. To prepare for such a trip, Daddy cleaned his guns and loaded them and checked his harnesses and any other supplies he might need. Mommy packed his grub bag with flour, molasses, salt, fatback pork, and tea. She made sure he had a change of clothes in case he got wet.

Daddy was up well before dawn to harness his dogs in the darkness. They ran around in a frenzy, anxious to get going. Daddy had to place a heavy chain under the runners as a brake to hold them back. Hunters loaded the komatik boxes and lashed them down. They took snowshoes, axes, guns, ammunition, food, extra clothing, and stoves. They had to be well prepared. Survival depended on it.

The dogs were pulling, trying to get going, as Daddy loaded the komatik. When everything was lashed down, Daddy lifted the chain and off they went, racing at full gallop into the forest on the well-beaten path.

"Bye, Daddy!" I hollered as the komatik raced effortlessly over the newly fallen snow.

"Be careful!" Mommy yelled.

With a wave of his hand he was gone.

We were left alone again. I have often wondered how we survived, how Mommy kept us alive in the total isolation of the wilderness. I have often wondered how she felt. Was she terrified that Daddy would get hurt and never return? There were so many things that could have happened to him all alone in the forest. A trap could accidentally snap shut, he could cut himself with the axe, he could fall through the ice, and he could get knocked of his komatik and freeze to death.

When Daddy was gone for several days, it was essential that Mommy go hunting, as well. She was very capable of keeping us alive under extremely adverse conditions.

"Weers ya goin, Mommy?" I asked as she hauled on her pants, dickey, and sealskin boots.

"Jus goin in de woods ta try ta fin sometin ta eat," she answered as she slung her rackets and .22 over her shoulder. She was accurate with that gun and seldom missed. We all knew we would have partridge, rabbit, or porcupine stew for supper that night.

By this time Sammy was 11 years old (five years older than I), and old enough to set a few rabbit snares close to the cabin. He checked them each morning and often brought a few rabbits home.

When Daddy returned from a hunting trip, we watched anxiously as the team approached the cabin to see if he brought fresh game. We were hungry! The dogs started yelping as they approached the settlement as if to say, "We're back! Get the food ready!" They were always happy to get going but just as delighted to return home. When Daddy came to a stop, they rolled gleefully in the snow, grooming and licking their fur, content that they'd gotten their master home safely.

The caribou carcass was unloaded and placed on a scaffold out of reach of wild animals and dogs. The small game was stored in the porch where it stayed frozen. This time the hunters had had a successful trip, and it was a joyous occasion for all of us. The meat was shared among everyone in the settlement.

On stormy days when my father couldn't go into the woods to cut wood or check his trapline, he worked on his furs or made a pair of rackets, new harnesses for his dogs, a new bridle, or a whip. Sometimes he knitted a fishnet for the summer fishing season or even built a new komatik. One day he brought two long pieces of wood into the cabin.

"Whass dey fer, Daddy?" I asked as he laid them along benches he'd placed at each end of our tiny cabin.

"Gonna make a komatik now, Jimmy, an ya better stay outta de way," he warned. With his hand drill he punched out a line of holes down the edges of each plank. He was very careful not to break his drill bit.

"Whass all de holes fer?" I asked.

"Jus watch an ya'll see."

I sat and watched my father work for hours on end. It was a big undertaking to build a komatik. For the sides he used two straight pieces of timber about eight to 10 feet long. Several days earlier some neighbours had helped him rip (cut) the planks on the huge pit saw set up in the centre of the settlement. The first thing he did was plane the wood. Once the planks were planed out and smooth, he attached a curved nose piece to them. Then he had to saw and cut all the wooden bars, the end of each piece carved similar to the cap on a bottle. He drilled two holes in the ends of each board. He didn't use nails. Nails were hard to come by and they cost money, which we didn't have.

To assemble the komatik he lined the boards up along the sides and threaded babbish (sealskin strips) through the two holes in the board and down through the holes in the sides of the komatik until all the bars were snugly in place. As the babbish dried, it shrank a little, making the construction quite sturdy. Once all the bars were strapped firmly to the sides, Daddy turned the komatik over to attach the steel runners along the edge of the wooden sides.

"Whass dat?" I asked as he placed a runner along the side and drilled the holes to attach it.

"Runners. Makes her slide better in de snow." Daddy glanced at my big brother. "'Tis awmost done now. Can ya help me turn it over, Sammy?"

When they turned it right side up, it looked huge.

"'Tis some big, hey, Daddy? Looks beautiful, too. Will ya take me randying [sledding] now?"

"No, Jimmy, not now," he answered a little sharply. He was tired, so I sat quietly, thinking in my little six-year-old mind of the wondrous thing he had just accomplished.

In the darkness each day when Daddy arrived home, he unharnessed the dogs and fed them. Then he unsnarled the harnesses and gear, hung everything on the nails on the porch, cleaned out his komatik box, sawed the wood, brought it inside, and fetched water from the brook. When all that was done, Daddy was finally able to come inside, wash up at the basin, and sit down at the table for supper.

After supper he skinned the animals he'd trapped that day and cleaned the fur. Mommy placed his clothing around the stove to dry, turning his sealskin boots inside out. All the work was done systematically and in order of importance. Nothing could be left undone.

Hunting and trapping were very hard jobs. And even though Daddy was partially handicapped from polio, he still had his work to do. He had only shrivelled flesh on one leg. When he walked, his foot flung outward as if there was a spring in his knee joint. In spite of his condition there was no such thing as being too tired or too cold or too hungry.

To stay alive every task was important and had to be done.

7

Springtime and Shifting Outside

By the end of March, we were getting spring fever, the feeling of wanting to be outside. Our faces were turning brown from the sunlight, wind, and snow. The springtime sounds of warm breezes whistling through the forest and birds chirping happily in the trees were captivating. Spring had its own smells, too. One of the most compelling aromas was when the snow melted into the ground, leaving it exposed to the hot spring sunshine and releasing the distinct fragrance of mud, sawdust, and wood chips. That unique scent filled our nostrils as we played joyfully around the cabin. We had such fun randying down the hills. Sometimes we had our own komatiks. Other times we used a piece of sealskin or anything else we could find.

"Can ya make me a komatik, Daddy?" I asked as my tiny hands wrapped around his legs.

"Awright, Jimmy, I'll makes ya one tomarra," he said, tousling my ringlets.

The next morning Daddy took my hand and we went into the woods. He selected two little trees with natural bends in them to make the runners, and two small straight trees to make the crossbars. As soon as we got home, he cleaned the bark off with his pocket knife and tied the pieces of wood together.

"Oh, Daddy, tis some nice, hey?" I said, bounding for the hillside.

We also had fun wind-sailing on the ice, which thawed during the day and froze again as smooth as glass overnight. All we had to do was stand on the ice, raise our coattails over our heads, and fly across the steady. Another joyful activity was going scittering (sliding on the ice). I don't know where that name came from, but that was what we called it. The trick was to run fast until you reached the patch of ice, then glide across it, getting as much distance as possible.

"Whee!" I squealed with glee as my sealskin boots slid effortlessly across the pond.

In the dead of winter it was usually too cold to snow. However, once March came the temperature warmed up enough to snow, and snow it did! Mounds of dense windblown snow created ideal conditions for digging snow houses and huge tunnels big enough to crawl through. We made playhouses with little shelves for our pieces of broken dishes.

Heavy snow was good for snowball fights, but they weren't always fun because Sammy made the snowballs so hard it was like getting hit with a rock. Fluffy snow was good for making snow angels and especially fun for jumping into. We leaped from trees, from the cabin, from the scaffold — anywhere we could get some height.

We loved to go out in a snowstorm. And there were many times when we couldn't see our hands in front of our faces. I'd get so involved in playing that I didn't notice my fingers were freezing. After playing outdoors for hours, I'd run into the house with my skin tingling from the cold. As soon as I got inside, my fingers started thawing out and the pain was excruciating.

One of my favourite activities was ice fishing, not only for the lovely fresh smelts we would catch for supper but for the sheer joy of it. And we didn't have to go far — just down to the steady.

"Pass me fish hook, Daddy," I said. "Will ya bait it fer me?"

"Sammy'll put it on fer ya."

"Will ya, Sammy?"

"Oh, Jos, yer a bother," he said, grabbing my hook and sticking a piece of salt pork on it.

"I wonder who'll catch de firs one," Marcie said.

"Betchya I will," Sally piped up, still struggling to bait her hook.

"No siree!" I cried, never wanting to be left out. "I'm gonna catch de firs one."

"I hope we catch some trout or a salmon or two," Sammy interjected.

"Yeh," I agreed. "I love salmon."

The dead silence of the forest was interrupted by the tiny sounds of birds. I stood there, a little awed, absorbing the majesty of limitless forest. Suddenly, my dreamlike trance was broken. *Chop, chop, chop* went the axes. Snow and ice flew from the blades as Daddy and Sammy cut each of us a hole. I watched as the hole got bigger and deeper. Finally, gurgling water surged through and spilled onto the ice.

"Oh, goodie!" I shouted. "Can I have dat one, Daddy?"

"Awright, Jimmy. Ya can have dis one."

I skimmed the slob (ice chips) away and dropped my hook into the hole. "I'm gonna catch de firs one I bet."

In the late afternoon it got colder, and we gathered up our smelts. They glistened in the sunlight. We sauntered home, tired but happy. Mommy cleaned the smelts and started cooking some for supper. There were so many and they smelled so good fried in my mother's special way. We could hardly wait for suppertime.

"Mmm, dey's some good, hey, Sally?" I said, stuffing the fish into my mouth, bones and all.

Another source of food in the spring was snowbirds. They were so cute that it seemed a crime to kill them. But at that time they were food for us. To catch them, Daddy got an old window frame or made one from sticks tied together and filled it with window screen or mesh. Sometimes he strung it with line as he did his rackets. Then we got a stick and fastened a long piece of string to it, propped up the screen with a stick, and placed breadcrumbs under the screen. Holding on to the string, we hid and waited for the little birds to come for the food. As soon as we had a lot of birds underneath pecking at the crumbs, we pulled the stick and *wham!* They were trapped. I don't ever remember killing them, but I do recall trying to pick the feathers off. It wasn't easy because they were so small. But they were delicious.

I turned seven in January 1950. One warm March day I got the surprise of my life.

"Do ya want ta come wit me tomarra marnin, Jimmy?" Daddy asked suddenly. "I'm jus goin in de neck path ta haul out a load a wood."

I couldn't believe what I'd just heard. "Yeh, yeh, Daddy," I babbled. "Can we have a mug-up?"

"Sure, Jimmy. I'll bring us a mug-up."

I was so happy that I could hardly sleep. The next morning I woke up early to find Daddy already lashing the horn junks onto the komatik. Dressing quickly, I hauled on the dickie Mommy had made for me. She was busy getting the grub bag ready, and I was tempted to look inside, but I knew better than to get in her way. I ran outdoors, back inside, then back outside again, beside myself with excitement.

"Stop runnin in an out, Jos!" Mommy yelled. "The bloody youngsters is always runnin in and out."

"But, Mommy, I'm so happy."

Daddy was harnessing the dogs, attaching the traces to the bridle and taking the box off the komatik. He didn't use it when he was hauling wood; it would be in the way. Finally, we were ready to go.

"Jump on, Jimmy, an hold on tight, cuz de dogs is gonna go fast," he said.

I leaped onto the komatik and gripped the bars as tightly as I could.

"Is ya all sought?" Daddy asked.

"Yeh!" I cried over the yelping dogs.

He lifted the chain from the runner, and we were off. The dogs galloped at full speed over the path, and the komatik slid effortlessly through the newly fallen snow.

"Auch! Auch! Auch!" Daddy yelled in quick succession, and the dogs turned right.

When we came to a fork in the path, Daddy shouted, "Edder! Edder! Edder!" And the dogs turned left.

The huskies raced at a full run for a few minutes, then slowed to a comfortable trot. The path was familiar to them, so they knew where they were going. It was only when they reached a fork that Daddy had to shout directions. The leader, usually a female, knew where to go with very little guidance.

I looked to see if all the traces were taut, which meant that every dog was doing its share of the work. Pulling the komatik was serious business, and if one trace was consistently slack, it meant that a dog might be lazy, which wasn't acceptable. All the dogs were all pulling with great enthusiasm, tails curled over their backs. That meant this was an easy run. On the way back they would be pulling a full load of wood and working harder, so their tails would be down.

When we reached the woodpile that Daddy had cut and stacked beside the path, I jumped off and tried to help him put the wood into the wood horse.

"Tis too hard fer ya, Jimmy. Go collect some boughs fer de fire."

"Awright, Daddy, I'll do dat."

My father took his axe and chopped small pieces for the fire. I watched in admiration as he put dry boughs and freshly cut sticks of wood into place. He took out his matches and lit the fire. It was such a beautiful spring day. Filtering through the trees, the brilliant sunshine splashed on the fresh snow like millions of diamonds. The scent of spruces, junipers, and birches filled the clean air, and the smell of woodsmoke filling my nostrils told me it was mug-up time.

Daddy took the grub bag from the komatik and started pulling out the food. He scooped some snow up with his little kettle and hooked it onto a twig over the fire. When it was boiling, he added loose tea leaves. Then he poured our tea into tin cups and passed me a big slice of bread and a lassie bun. There was something about eating in the woods that made it very special.

"Tis some good, hey, Daddy?" I said. "Is ya tired?"

"No, Jimmy, I'm not tired yet. I'm goin ta look round fer some partridge an check a few snares. Den I'll finish loadin de wood." He paused. "An ya gotta be quiet when I go huntin, cuz ya'll scare em away."

"I'll be quiet. Won make a sound," I said chewing on my bun. He put on his rackets, threw his gun over his shoulder and ventured a little way into the woods. I didn't have any rackets, so I couldn't follow him because the snow was too deep. He hadn't gone far when I heard a loud bang. I jumped. It sounded very loud as it echoed through the dead silence of the forest.

"Whass ya got, Daddy?" I squealed.

"Got two partridges wit one shot!" he yelled back, sounding as excited as I was.

"Two wit one shot! Dat's good, hey, Daddy?"

It was always a joyous occasion to get food. He laid the birds on the snow and proceeded to finish loading the wood. I watched as the snow turned red from the blood of the birds but all I thought of was how good they would taste for dinner tomorrow. I sat on one of the logs he had placed beside the fire and watched him. The dogs lay down, patiently waiting for us to finish. Some were napping, some were rolling in the snow and others were grooming their fur, but they were happy. I was beginning to feel tired and sleepy. Daddy finished loading the wood, piling it higher than my head. He'd turned the komatik around before he'd started loading, so we were already headed in the right direction. He then lashed the wood onto the komatik, hooking the line onto the bars and over the wood to the other side. He was making sure the wood was secure.

"Jump on, Jimmy!" he yelled.

"Awright, Daddy."

I sprawled on top of the wood and hung on tightly. Daddy grunted something to the dogs, and we headed for home. The dogs were working extremely hard. Their tails and heads were down as they strained to pull the heavy load uphill.

Spring was the time for the seal hunt. At that time of year the sun was quite bright and strong, and there were either no sunglasses available or no money to purchase them. Consequently, Daddy became snow-blind many times. This was a painful condition and sometimes laid him up for several days. The sunlight and wind in his face while travelling caused his skin to burn and peel.

As the sun melted the snow, it became heavy and wet, making the komatik harder to manoeuvre. Another problem occurred each spring when the snow thawed during the day, then froze overnight. Ice shards like broken glass cut through our sealskin mukluks. It was painful for the feet with only duffle vamps and socks as protection. But for the dogs it must have been excruciating. Their feet bled from cuts, leaving red footprints in the snow.

The seal hunt was the event that heralded spring. Seeing seals piled on Daddy's komatik was a happy sight. My parents shared the work of preparing the seal pelts. Mommy meticulously removed fat and fur, while Daddy stretched the pelts on frames and hung them on the cabin to dry. I remember watching him nail up the enormous pelts.

"My, oh, my, tis big, hey, Daddy?"

"Yeh, Jimmy, tis big nough ta make ya lotsa nice slippers an new mukluks."

Melting ice came as a surprise to us after such a long winter. One day while we were sliding down the hill onto the brook my tiny komatik slid right into the steady. I started to cry as I leaned over the hole, trying to spot it.

"I lost me kumlik down de brook, Mommy!" I cried, running into the cabin. "Tis gone ferever!" I kept wailing until Sammy began to make me another one. Then my loss was forgotten.

Spring breakup was a difficult time for all the families in the community. By the end of April, the ice became too dangerous to travel on as the snow melted rapidly. Daddy couldn't get to his traps. Finally, he had to pull them up and prepare for the trip back to Spotted Island. The move occurred in April every year. By this time food was running low because Daddy couldn't tend his traplines. We were poised to make the move, but the waiting could go on for days, sometimes weeks.

Daddy and Mommy constantly watched the sky and read the weatherglass, waiting for the right time to shift outside. When conditions finally became civil enough to take the risk, everyone had to move quickly. It was a race against time because the Labrador climate, always relentless and unforgiving, could change quickly. There were so many last-minute jobs to be done, such as collecting the furs, packing our things, storing all of Daddy's winter belongings, and securing the cabin. The other three families in the settlement moved about the same time.

We had to carry all of our things down to the landwash. It was such a long walk! But every family member had to do his or her part to move from one place to another. As the komatik was piled high with our belongings, I got more and more excited. I watched with pride as Daddy rounded up the dogs and harnessed them. The dogs took us from Roaches Brook down to the shore. If the run was frozen, we would continue on to Spotted Island by dog team. If there was open water, we would have to wait until a neighbour with a boat showed up to collect us. Every year the weather was different.

I was thrilled when we were finally off. It was time to prepare for the fishing season. I wasn't afraid of the choppy sea. I was anxious to get to my favourite place in the whole wide world — Spotted Island!

8

Spotted Island

One year I remember being picked up by a boat. As the vessel pulled out from our inlet, my mother eyed the icebergs in the distance.

"Don't go too close to dem ol tings, Tom! Dey might founder down on top a us!" Mommy was yelling over the *putt, putt, putt* of the Acadia engine that powered the motorboat. We were chugging through the choppy ocean, and she was terrified of the gigantic icebergs floating majestically southward on the open sea.

"Awright, Mammy," Daddy assured her.

As we made our way to Spotted Island, I gazed in awe at the craggy cliffs looming straight up from the deep blue of the North Atlantic.

All along the Labrador coast tiny fishing outports were tucked away in sheltered coves, bays, and tickles (tiny inlets). As the boat rounded another point of land, our summer home came into full view. The hillsides of this rugged and treeless place looked as though millions of boulders had been dropped from the sky. Standing out in sharp contrast were the berry bushes and low-lying foliage sprouting from cracks and crevices in the rocks. With its rugged peaks and valleys, Spotted Island appeared moonlike.

As we drew closer, I spied the tiny beach at the mouth of the brook that ran through the centre of the village. The beach was walled with jagged rocks. Perched precariously on the shore around the cove were the fishing stages. Just beyond the stages, past the high-water level, were the pebbly bawns (rocks) used for drying fish. Beyond the bawns were the mission buildings.

From far off, bunches of white long-haired pussy willows sprouting from the rocks looked like patches of snow. Houses were scattered around the cove and up onto the stony hillside. There were no roads or groomed properties, no fences or flower gardens, just footpaths connected by huge rocks, boggy pathways, and small streams with a large flat rock or wooden planks to cross them. Most of the houses were covered with clapboard and painted in various colours, while a few were grey, the original hue long since weathered away. Scattered storehouses and outhouses completed the community.

After living for six months in Roaches Brook with just a few log cabins, this settlement of 25 families seemed huge. Spotted Island bustled with people during the height of the cod fishery in the 1940s. The entire village turned into a beehive of activity. After arriving from secluded winter homes, the fishermen lost no time preparing for the new season. There were boats to launch, nets to repair, firewood to cut, water to haul from the brook, and stages to get ready. There was no wood on the island, so timber had been cut on the mainland during the winter and transported by dog team over the ice. Other residents made numerous trips across the run in their small boats to bring wood, which was piled near the harbour, ready to be cut into lengths for fires.

Already exhausted from the move, the women heated up gallons of water to do the washing, and clotheslines hung heavy with homemade garments. Dusty mats were banged out on rocks in the landwash. Some women collected wood chips to start fires, chopped wood, or swept out porches and bridges (verandahs). Some screamed at their youngsters or chatted with neighbours about the winter's trapping. There was sure to be talk of the weather, and there were always complaints about the flies. Conversations about the arrival of new babies during the winter and a whole lot of laughter were constant. Everyone was happy to be back doing what needed to be done to prepare for the busy summer ahead.

Daddy inherited the Curl residence when my grandfather, John Curl, passed away. Facing the shoreline from the boat, our house was situated on a small plateau to the right of the cove. Compared to the tiny log cabin in Roaches Brook, it was a mansion — a two-storey house, roomy, and comfortable. We entered through a small porch that led into a large kitchen with a wooden floor. At the back there was a bedroom. Instead of a ladder through a hole in the ceiling, this house had stairs. Upstairs there was one large room, divided by a curtain.

Directly behind our house, tall pink flowers swaying in the breeze stood out against a white picket fence that enclosed the graveyard. To the left of the cemetery was the focal point of the community — the nursing station. It was a large white building once used by itinerant doctors and nurses who travelled the coast and cared for the sick. By the time I was six years old, though, it had ceased to operate. A community building called the club was beside the nursing station.

Some of the boats that had been hauled out in the fall sat stately and tall in their winter cradles, revealing their full bulk, undisturbed by fierce winter winds. Others were upside down. Looming mounds of wood dotted the shoreline. Soon the boats would be right side up and filled to the gunwales with fish.

When we reached Spotted Island that summer, Daddy eased the boat into the stage and tied it to a post. People who had arrived before us ran to help. As I clambered onto the stagehead, I was so delighted to be home. All I wanted to do was run and play. But I knew better.

"Now, maids," warned my mother, "don't go empty-handed."

"I'm too small," I protested. "What'll I carry?"

"Ya better carry sometin!" Sammy hollered.

Reluctantly, I grabbed what I could lift and headed for the house. Staggering up the road and grunting under the weight of a pile of blankets, I wished I was bigger. Everybody was lugging, hauling, and carrying. It went on for what seemed like hours.

The dogs were let loose from the boat and allowed to roam freely among the houses. They ran here and there, and when they were tired, they crawled under the houses to keep cool. I loved the puppies that were born each spring.

"Weers me puppy to?" I cried, running around in circles. "Weers Blackie?"

"Dunno, Jos," Mommy answered. "Havn't got time ta be bothered wit yer puppy."

"I'm not goin anywhere till I finds him den," I said.

Daddy was busy taking the boards off the windows. Then he had to set up the stove, while Sammy lit the fire for Mommy.

"Sam, ya gotta go get some water from de brook," Mom ordered just as he started running off to see his buddies. "Yer not gonna get away wit dat."

"Awright, Ma." He flung the carrying hoop over his shoulder, dug out the water buckets from the pile on the floor, and headed for the brook.

"I wanna go, too, Sammy," I said.

My brother was happy to have company. "Awright den."

Daddy had made us little water carriers out of tin cans with a string threaded through holes at the top. Searching through our stuff, I found two, and Sammy and I bounded for the brook, just up the hill past the graveyard. I placed my little can under a galvanized pipe protruding from the rocks. It was anchored in the brook with stones. My little bucket filled quickly with cold, clear water.

"Who put de pipe der, Sammy?" I asked.

"Dunno, maid. Tis been here a long time is all I know."

Sammy filled his buckets and placed them in the carrying hoop. The hoop made the arduous job of water carrying much easier and kept the buckets away from his legs. I grunted and groaned as I struggled back to the house and emptied what was left in my containers into the water barrel on the porch. Then we returned to the brook for another turn — not that my tiny cans made much of a difference in the huge 45-gallon drum. But I was helping. Getting water was a daily task we couldn't escape. Once the water barrel was filled, we had to bring in wood for the fire. We all had to do our share.

After a few days, we were settled in, and I was happy to be released from the seemingly endless chores Mommy had laid out for us.

"Okay, Mommy," I said, grinning, "gonna make me playhouse now."

"Awright, Josie, go on outdoors outta me way." She sounded exasperated.

I liked Aunt Lucy next door and sauntered in and out of her house at will. In those days we didn't knock before entering a home. Aunt Lucy was a jolly, little old lady who always wore a dress with her pinny tied neatly around her well-padded body. I was sure to get a slice of lassie bread from her.

Many of our neighbours were related. As was the custom then, several relatives lived in the same house. At Aunt Lucy's place lived her sister and her sister's little girl, Mary Jane. A pretty girl with fair hair and blue eyes, Mary Jane was a few years younger than I was. I thought she was rich because she had a swing on her porch. It was just a long piece of rope tied to a high beam, but it seemed wonderful to me because I had never seen a swing before. One day I gathered the courage to ask her for a turn. I was enthralled at the sensation of moving freely through the air.

On the other side of our house lived Sis (Violet) and Esau Dyson and their four children. Sis was my father's niece. Esau had a large bell that hung on their house, which could be heard throughout the community. It rang at mug-up time, dinnertime, and suppertime to call the fishermen up from the stages. Many years later Sis told me that Esau had acquired the bell from a fishing schooner he'd worked on. She let me ring the big bell sometimes. When the bell tolled, all the dogs in the community howled in unison. It was the strangest thing.

Our neighbours were a mixture of friends, adopted family, and blood relatives. Uncle Ken and Aunt Winnie Webber were our true aunt and uncle. Aunt Winnie was Daddy's sister. They lived close by with their five children. One neighbour I hated was Hayward Holwell. He would pop in almost every day just to tease Mommy. And he teased us constantly, as well, which made me angry and fearful. But I was much too little to do anything about it.

One day Hayward barged into our house and yelled at Mommy, "Flossie, how can such an ugly blood-of-a-bitch like ya have such good-lookin youngsters?"

Mommy wasn't fazed. "Dunno, boy," she snapped. "I know one thing's fer sure. You never had nuttin ta do wit em."

Aunt Tamer Rose, a kindly lady, short in stature, with grey wispy hair and soft brown eyes, lived just across the brook in the big house. One of the rooms contained a small store. She had a little white dog. Almost every day my sister and I meandered over to the shop, drooling at the sight and smell of candy and chocolate. Of course, there was never money to buy any, but I loved their fragrance. I enjoyed petting the dog and hoped I'd get a penny candy or two.

"Can I have some candy?" I asked as I stepped inside.

"Have ya got money?"

"Gotta copper. What can I buy fer a copper?"

"I can give ya a few candies fer a copper," she said, scooping a few jellybeans into a tiny brown bag. Elated, I skipped along the rocky path, popping the delicious sweets into my mouth. But most of the time I just gawked and drooled at peppermint knobs, candy kisses, and gumdrops lined up behind the counter.

Sunday was a sacred day. No matter how plentiful the fish, how busy the men, or how pressing any situation might be, everything came to a dead stop on Sundays. Every Sunday of the year Daddy got up, put on a white Sunday shirt, and pulled on armbands to keep his sleeves up. Then he snapped braces over his shoulders to keep his pants up and put on his sealskin slippers. Finally, with a sigh of relief, he leaned back on his settle to wait for dinner.

Mommy moved quietly around the house, her pinny snugly tied, hair combed and tucked neatly in a bun at the back. She was now ready to cook Sunday dinner — boiled seal meat topped with a duff, a couple of ducks, or some type of fish or seafood, depending on the time of year. Sunday dinner was always at noon, while supper was at 5:00 p.m.

Aside from all the work, there was still time for play. One day Sammy and a friend from down the hill rigged up two tin cans with a long string that went from our upstairs bedroom window to Sammy's bedroom window. Then they started talking to each other! Of course, I had no idea what they were doing. I'd never heard of a telephone. They had gotten the idea from somewhere, and I was all eyes and ears as I followed my brother's every move.

"Can I try, Sammy?" I asked, unable to contain my curiosity any longer.

"Oh, awright, Jos. Here, put dis on an listen real good." He knew I'd kick up a fuss if he didn't comply.

I placed the tin can to my ear, but all I heard was a roar. "Don't work. Can't hear nuttin."

"Dat's cuz yer stun," he said sarcastically.

The summer was passing quickly, and I was happy roaming the hills and enjoying myself. I loved to skip, and one day while skipping down the road, I fell and skinned my knee. I ran home crying to Mommy.

"Ya bloody little fool, what now?" she grumbled, wrapping a piece of rag around my leg.

"I was skippin an fell down, Mommy. Ouch … tis some sore, too!"

My mother knew only one way to prepare us for the hardships of life. She felt she had to toughen us up. She didn't like us to show emotion. If we were caught crying, she'd swear at us, call us terrible names, or smack us around a bit.

"Whass de matter wit ya now?" she'd demand. "I'll give ya sometin ta cry fer in a minute!"

Suppertime was an example of how my mother viewed life. How well I recall her attitude when the big bell rang to call the fishermen up to eat.

"Whass fer supper, Mommy?" I asked as I barrelled through the door and sat in my place at the table.

"Never mine whass fer supper. Whatever it is, ya'll eat it or do witout."

She said that because there were many days in the winter when there was nothing to eat. We were lucky to get a pork bun or a piece of molasses bread in the winter months. During summer, it was fried fish, stewed fish, baked fish, fish cakes, fish heads, or fish and brewis. Maybe Daddy or Sammy would catch a salmon, arctic char, or saltwater trout that day. When the berries ripened in late summer, we were in for a real treat. Along with tarts, Mommy made jam that we spread on her freshly baked buns and bread.

I'll always remember the unique scents on a hot summer day. The sea air was rich with aromas as I walked, skipped, or bounded about:

seaweed as it warmed up at low tide, salt cod drying on the bawns, cod livers rendering out under the hot sun. But none of those smells were as strong as the stench of fish parts rotting on the beach. And nothing could beat the sweet fragrances of Mommy's cooking.

I was an inquisitive and observant child. In the summer of 1948, Mommy's belly was getting big again.

"Whass happened ta ya belly dis time, Mommy?" I asked.

"Oh, Josie, ya're too small ta understan, but ya will when ya gets bigger," she said in a soft voice I didn't hear often.

Wee Edward was found (born) soon afterward, and I enjoyed my baby brother. Mommy would let me hold him if I was careful.

"Don't drop him," she warned. "Feel dat soft spot on his head? Don't touch it."

"Why, Mommy?"

"Cuz ya might kill him."

That terrified me. I couldn't figure out what she meant because she didn't explain why touching that spot might kill him. The year before wee Wilfred had died at seven months old and had gone to heaven. I'd cried and cried and wondered and worried that I might have killed him.

"Oh, Mommy, Mommy, I dint touch Wilfred's soft spot," I wailed.

"I know, Josie. God jus took him ta heaven, dat's all," she crooned in a soothing voice.

"Where's heaven, Mommy?"

"Heaven's a good place. He's safe an warm der," she assured me sadly.

"God must really love yer babies, hey, Mommy?"

Sister Rhoda was now three years old, sickly, with terrible nosebleeds. It seemed there was always a bucket to catch the stream of blood from her nose. I didn't understand what was wrong with her, and that frightened me.

Mom had let my hair grow long since my return from the hospital with my shaved head. She would tell me over and over about my beautiful blond ringlets and how proud she'd been of them and how heartbroken she was when I returned with my head shaved and my gruesome scars exposed. The deep gouges left by the dog bites were constantly itchy, and I was always scratching. Soon the scars became sore and I had a head lice problem. It seemed impossible for Mommy to keep our heads clean, though she tried to desperately. Where we lived there was no salve or ointments or solutions to kill lice, so she guarded her fine-tooth comb as if it were made of gold. It was the only tool she had to combat the problem.

"Come here, Josie," she said to me one night.

"Why?"

"Cuz yer mangy, dat's why."

I sat on the floor, and she went to work. With her thumb and forefinger she picked the lice out one at a time. Then I heard *crack, crack, crack* as she killed them with her thumbnail against the wooden bench.

"Nobody's ever gonna cut yer hair again, Josie," she kept saying as she worked. As horrific as the lice were, they still left fond memories. It was during those gruesome occasions that I became closer to my mother. It was the only time I had real intimate contact with her. I can't recall ever being hugged or cuddled by my mother. And even though she was wonderful with her babies, it seemed once we got bigger we were just "them old good-fer-nothin maids," and that hurt.

I loved my little sisters and brothers, but they were a continual blur of being found somewhere and then dying. Sammy and Mommy were very close. He could do no wrong. I became a tomboy and tried to imitate my brother, thinking maybe I'd receive some of that attention, too. Despite his closeness to Mommy, which I craved, I did love my brother very much.

After the fishing season slowed down, there was time to jig for cod. That was when we got our winter supply of fish for our dogs and for our own personal consumption.

"Wass ya doin, Sammy?" I asked my brother one day as he raced around.

"I'm helpin Dad so we can go jiggin tomarra," he said proudly.

Sammy was big enough to help Daddy, and eager to learn. He had never stepped inside a schoolhouse or a classroom, but he could handle a boat like a professional. Sammy was meticulous in his work and was overjoyed when Daddy took him hunting. I could tell he was excited to go fishing with Daddy tomorrow.

"Josie!" Mommy yelled. "Stay outta de way!" She gave me a bat on the shoulder.

"I wanna go, too," I said. "I won't get in de way. I'll be real good. Can I go, Daddy?"

"No, Jimmy, pr'aps some udder time when yer bigger."

"But, Daddy, I'm awmost six, an I'm strong, too."

"No, Josie, ya can scream all ya like, but ya can't go, and dat's all der is to it," Mommy said with finality.

I had to give in, so I stomped outside, screaming and crying. After settling down, I went looking for something else to do. There were lots of things to do, but what? I shuffled next door to Aunt Lucy's house, seeking comfort, hoping for a turn on Mary Jane's swing, but it was being used. That made me wail all the more. Aunt Lucy came out onto the porch, wanting to know what the ruckus was about.

"Mary Jane won let me take a swing!" I cried.

I had no choice but to return home to Mommy, but she didn't care a bit about the swing. "Go on outdoors, Jos," she ordered.

I meandered around, trying to find my sister. "Wanna play tag, Sally?" I asked mournfully when I located her.

"No, I'm gonna make a playhouse."

"Oh, goodie. Can I come, too?"

"Awright. But ya got ta get yer own dishes!"

Happy once again, I set out to look for bits of broken dishes and glass to put on the rock shelf of the playhouse.

In the long evenings of summer it didn't get really dark until almost eleven o'clock. The bigger kids played cricket on the only flat surface between our house and the graveyard. I didn't know what cricket was other than batting a ball and running from end to end, but it seemed like fun.

"Can I play?"

"No, yer too small," Sammy said. "Ya might get hurt."

So I sat and watched them play, making sure I was out of harm's way. Not understanding the game, I soon got bored and went looking for something else to do. *I'll be glad when I gets bigger,* I thought to myself.

Another favourite game in the long evenings of summer was Alley Over.

"Wanna play Alley Over?" someone shouted.

Children came running from all directions, yelling, "I wanna! Me, too!"

We split into two groups, the first team on one side of the building and the second on the other. Someone with a good arm threw the ball over the roof and cried, "Alley over, alley over!" The team on the opposite side lined up along the building to catch the ball as it came over the top. The person holding the ball raced to the other side and tried to tag someone from the opposing team with it. It was then their turn to throw the ball over. This continued until we were all too tired to play anymore, or Mommy called us in. It was such fun. There was always something to do during the long summer twilight.

The next day I was feeling happy as I skipped down the road in my sealskin moccasins, heading for the stage. Everyone was busy curing the morning's catch. I dared not get in their way. So I sauntered back up the hill to the house. Mommy was cooking fish for dinner, and it smelled wonderful.

"I'm hungry, Mommy," I declared as I entered the door. "Can I have a piece of lassie bread?"

"No, ya can't. 'Tis too close ta dinnertime."

"But I'm starving, Mommy! An Eddy gotta piece!"

My baby brother, Edward, was born one year after wee Wilfred died. One day Eddie was crawling around the floor, sucking on a crust of bread, and I picked him up and began playing with him. He was heavy, so I put him back down. Eddie started crawling out to the porch, the piece of bread between his teeth. Everything happened so fast. Before I could do anything, the dogs were attacking my baby brother and biting his head!

"De dogs got Eddy!" someone shouted. "De dogs got little Eddy!"

I screamed.

"Oh, my, Jesus!" Mommy cried.

As quick as a lightning bolt, she grabbed a broom and lashed out at the dogs, driving them off! It was another heart-stopping, terrifying moment for my mother. Another one of her children attacked by dogs! Eddy was screaming, and blood gushed from a large gash in his head. A closer examination revealed a few other cuts and scratches around his head and face, but my baby brother was safe. Thank God!

Mommy dressed his wounds in the loving, caring way she had with babies, and they healed quickly. It could have been so much worse. The dogs were hungry. They smelled the food on my brother and simply wanted it.

Daddy, and sometimes Sammy, made us little wooden boats, and we'd play in the landwash for hours. I enjoyed watching the beachie birds, as we called them, as they scampered around and fed on sea lice left high and dry as the tide fell. I'd lean over a big rock and watch them swimming on their sides through the seaweed and kelp.

Mommy was terrified of us going into the water. However, one day when she came back from Dawe's Store she handed me a brand-new pair of store-bought rubber boots. I was so proud.

"Ya better not get 'em wet, Josie," she cautioned.

"I won't, Mommy. I'll be right careful." I bolted for the landwash.

"Ya better be careful, cuz ya knows what yer in fer if ya gets 'em wet."

"I won't, Mommy."

I was careful and kept looking at the tops of my boots. The trick was to see how far I could go. The water got deeper and deeper, and suddenly I stepped into a hole. Water trickled into my boots. I panicked. There was no way to get out of this one.

"Jos, ya little blood-of-a-one!" Mommy yelled when I returned home. She struck me with a belt across my back.

"I dint mean ta get 'em wet, Mommy."

"Ya jus won listen, will ya?"

The belt smacked down again. *Whack, whack* came the blows, almost knocking me off my feet. I escaped and ran outdoors, stumbling my way into the graveyard behind some bushes. Tears came fast, not so much because of the beating but because I knew I was going to lose my new rubber boots. Why did she have to be so cruel? I didn't mean to get them wet.

I loved Spotted Island. Carefree, happy, and content, I was gaining a sense of who I was as a little girl. My spirit soared as I roamed the rocky hillsides, competing with my friends as we skimmed rocks across the water, played for hours in my playhouse, and raced tiny wooden boats in the landwash.

On any given day I could stretch out in the soft berry bushes and listen to the sounds of our little village. I'd lie on my back and watch the cotton-ball clouds roll across the clear blue sky and hear the roar of the sea crashing onto the rocks. At night during a full moon I'd sit and marvel at its reflected light on the ocean, broken only by gigantic icebergs that cast huge shadows. At dusk on a calm night I was in awe of the beauty of the fishing stages protruding into the water at high tide. The natural splendour of Labrador never ceased to astonish me even as a child.

9

The Making of the Fish

Once the families were settled, it was time to prepare the boats and nets for the busy fishing season ahead. There was so much to do and very little time. Because the summers were short, and the making of the fish so vital to our survival, everyone went into high gear. The men, clad in oil clothes and rubber boots, prepared their boats for launching. They stuffed vile-smelling oakum into dried-out cracks and scraped and painted weather-worn hulls, though for some, paint was scarce. When each boat was ready to launch, all the men gathered to help. The poles that had secured the boats throughout the winter were now removed from under the gunwales and placed on the ground to roll the vessels into the sea.

Every year the nets had to be repaired. With fishing twine threaded through large wooden needles, fishermen skillfully filled the holes in the nets. Then they were ready for barking. To do this the fishermen filled large puncheons (tubs) with a black tarry dye that smelled awful. They submerged the nets, soaking them completely for a while, then hung them to dry. After that they strung the nets out all over the place, and the odour permeated the air. They worked from before dawn's first light until late into the night, through sunshine, rain, and blinding storms, mending boats and nets, preparing the stages, and ordering salt and supplies for the busy fishing season.

Fishermen were up well before dawn. They donned oilskins, sou'westers, and hip rubbers as they got ready for a day of making the fish. In earlier times most fishermen had only punts, skiffs, or dories rigged with makeshift sails to get them to the traps (a four-sided box to catch fish) and nets. By the 1950s, each crew had motorboats equipped with a five-horsepower or an Acadia engine to get them to their cod traps. Many fishermen were lost at sea when they got caught in raging storms that could wipe out a fleet of dories in one fell swoop.

Both Stationers and Livyers fished together — Livyers, the permanent residents, and Stationers, the visitors who came to fish. Stationers travelled every year from Newfoundland to Labrador to reap the benefits of the rich fishing grounds. During the peak of the cod fishery, from the early twentieth century until the 1950s and 1960s, Stationers arrived on the first trip of the coastal steamer SS *Kyle* or in their schooners. Often they brought their entire families, but sometimes just a cook, usually a young girl, would travel with the fishermen. The Stationers came by the hundreds, carrying all of the provisions needed to sustain them through the summer. They lived in makeshift cabins they had built on the shore. Some of them had bunkhouses for the fishermen. Most of the skippers had a fishing crew. In their boats they brought along a wooden Labrador box that contained provisions and valuables. It was sturdily built, about the size of a large trunk, with a lock, wider at the bottom and narrower at the top, to keep it from tipping in rough water.

Also involved in the making of the fish were Floaters. These were the transient fishermen who came each year from Newfoundland. Usually, they carried a crew of four or five men and worked onboard. They travelled along the coast, following the fish northward, and were equipped with small dories and punts that were launched from the schooners. The cod was then pronged into the schooners and processed for European markets. Dozens of Floaters sailed into port at night and mixed with the locals for entertainment and dances. Their vessels were crammed into the tiny coves and bays so tightly during storms that you could walk across the harbours, hopping from one boat to the next.

Methods of catching cod varied. One technique was the trawl, a long line with many hooks attached and baited by hand. Some fishermen used squid from Newfoundland for bait. It was back-breaking and time-consuming work to bait hundreds of hooks by hand. But as one old fisherman once said, looking forlornly out to sea, "It didn't take that long once you got used to it."

The cod trap was the most popular method and the most efficient way of catching cod. It was huge. One side was weighted and sunk into the water, while the other side was pulled to the surface with floating corks, making an inescapable trap for the fish. The traps were hauled in two or three times a day, scooping up thousands of cod at a time. Although it was efficient for catching cod, there were other species captured in the traps, as well. The traps and the trawls belonged to the owners of the big boats. We Livyers were most often sharemen who worked for the big fishing boats. Consequently, when the season's fishing was done, though the sharemen were paid, they still had to think of their provisions for the coming winter. That was when the small boats, punts, and dories were used to jig for cod.

During the two-week period between the salting and drying of the cod, the Livyers got out the jiggers. This was a totally different way of fishing. The fishermen had to jig enough for the dogs and for their own consumption for the entire winter. The equipment was simple — a solid piece of lead six inches long shaped like a fish with barbed twin hooks on either side. A long piece of twine was attached to the tail of the fish-shaped jigger and wrapped around a square wooden spool, similar to a picture frame. The jigger was dropped over the side and allowed to sink to the bottom, then pulled up a little way. It sank quickly because of its weight. The sound of the line as the jigger plunged and then was yanked upward against the side of the boat was like a saw ripping through wood. Once a fish was hooked, it was hauled up and shaken off the hook. Then the line was tossed back into the water, sinking so fast that it often burned the men's fingers. Galled hands were common during the jigging season.

A fisherman could easily catch five or six barrels of cod a day, but it was gruelling work.

Fishing boats were usually hand-built by a local builder and were about 30 to 35 feet long. There was usually one boat builder in each village or just a few miles down the coast. A good boat builder was a well-respected member of the community. Engines varied in design and efficiency. The six-cylinder Acadia was a popular engine during the 1950s. Prior to engines, the fishermen had to row or construct a makeshift sail to take them to the fishing grounds.

When the boats arrived back at the stagehead after a day's fishing, everyone got busy. There was no time to waste as the fishermen pronged the fish up onto the stage. Men and women, ready with knife blades thin thanks to sharpening stones and gloves soon to be soaked with gore and blood, stood waiting for the first fish. It was now time to make the fish.

Everyone had a job to perform. The cutthroat was the first to take the fish. Some of the cod weighed 15 or 20 pounds, causing the cutthroat's arms to ache very quickly. The cutthroat stuck his or her finger into the gills and lifted the cod onto the table. *Swoosh* went the razor-sharp blade across the throat and down the belly of the fish, blood and guts spilling onto the table. The cutthroat had to be fast, passing the gutted fish on to the header and grabbing the next one.

The header, with one clean, swift swoop of the knife, cleared the head from the body. The liver was pulled out and tossed into a puncheon for cod liver oil. Then the entrails were plucked out and dropped through a hole in the cutting table.

Next in line came the splitter. He made two cuts down each side of the sound bone (backbone), freeing the flesh from the bone cleanly and swiftly. Then he grabbed the sound bone and pulled it clear, transforming the fish. Now a splayed cod, it was dropped into a waiting puncheon filled with water. Then, with fluid movements, he went on to the next fish, making two cuts down each side, grabbing the sound bone, pulling it clear, and dropping the splayed cod into a puncheon. A good splitter could clear away five or six quintals (pronounced *kintal* — a measure of cod equivalent to 112 pounds) an hour if he was skilled and the fish was an average size of about 10 to 15 pounds.

The salter reeved (stuck) his hand into the elbow-deep tub, grabbing the now-flat, triangular-shaped fish, and placed it onto the wheelbarrow next to a puncheon. The dead weight of the wheelbarrow pulled heavily on a salter's shoulders. Salters often felt as if their arms were being pulled from their sockets. Limbs numb with the cold, they kept going, taking fish after fish after fish from the tub, grabbing a handful of salt, sprinkling it over the fish in generous quantities, turning around and heading back to the waiting puncheon of fish. Each stack was about three or four feet high, the water squeezed out from the weight of the fish. After they were salted and neatly stacked on the stage, the cod were left to sit until they were cured, then they were hand-barrowed to the bawns for drying.

The drying bawns, a wide area of smooth pebbles, were stretched along the beach. All the available space around the cove was used up at drying time, and every man, woman, and child was needed to get the fish spread, turned, dried, and stacked before the fish merchants arrived in late August or early September.

Drying flakes (racks) were used in other communities, though not often on Spotted Island. They were constructed well off the ground with spruce logs neatly placed side by side on sturdy spruce foundations. The fish were spread head to tail, like carefully placed shingles on a roof, though they didn't overlap. They were turned once or twice to ensure even drying on each side. It would take several sunny, breezy days to dry the cod. However, everyone kept a close eye on the weather. If there were even a possibility of rain, the cod would have to be stacked and wrapped in tarpaulins to keep them dry. It only took a week and half to two weeks to dry the entire season's catch of 150 quintals.

The Labrador coast was alive with many types of sailing ships, especially schooners. Hundreds of sails moved about into Domino Run. The ships were there to fish for cod or to supply the fishermen's needs and those of their families. Most of the Labrador coastline was, as was said many times, "a proper home for fish." And the men coming from Newfoundland for the season were wished a good voyage or "a fine time along."

Bankers were schooners that arrived late in the fall. They were generally much bigger than fishing schooners and carried a crew of up to 14 men. There were no females onboard. There was talk around the village of contraband liquor, and the fishermen would come ashore at night and mix with our people. They would drink, play cards, and sometimes get rowdy. It scared me if an argument or a fight broke out among the men. Nobody liked liquor in their homes, especially our mother.

Planters were the merchants who came each year to set up shop. They supplied fishermen and locals with basic needs. The one closest to Spotted Island was Dawes Store across the run in Domino. The inventory was very basic: rubber boots, oilskins, sou'westers, splitting knives, and fish-processing supplies. Food included meagre supplies of flour, beef, sugar, salt pork, molasses, and very little else. There were materials such as cotton, duffle (a coarse heavy woollen material like soft, thick felt), flannelette, skeins of knitting wool, and bolts of dress material. The store also sold oil lamps, kerosene, glass chimneys, candles, matches, tobacco, chewing tobacco, cigarette papers, and cigarettes.

We were always excited when a schooner sailed into the cove. Trading ships stocked with dry goods travelled the coast each summer. They carried many of the supplies found in the merchant's store. The ships moved from harbour to harbour until all of their cargo was sold.

Hospital ships belonged to the International Grenfell Association or IGA, as it was known. We simply referred to the ship as the mission boat. The mission boat sailed into port with all flags flying to let us know the importance of its arrival. When the ship anchored, the doctor and nurse started giving shots and X-rays to our people, caring for the sick and transporting them to the nearest hospital when necessary. The mission boat that I remember was the SS *Maravel*. There was always a strong odour of medicine as I went onboard. To this day I think of those ships when I walk into a hospital.

During good weather, the clergyman's schooner came around the point to Spotted Island. It was always a welcome sight to our tiny shut-away villages. It didn't matter what day of the week it was, once the minister arrived, there was always a Sunday service. We wore our Sunday best, which included bandanas or anything else we possessed to cover our heads.

Couples who had been waiting months to get married rushed to get dressed. Babies were scrubbed and clothed for baptism. The service was held in the nursing station, and greetings abounded. There were prayers to be said for the fishery, for the sick, for the deceased long since buried in the rocky ground, and for the many sins committed since the minister's previous visit. Religion played an extremely important part in our upbringing, and my parents had great faith. If we were caught doing anything that went against their beliefs, there was serious punishment.

Rangers' schooners weren't quite as welcome on Spotted Island. Even though there was very little illegal activity or law-breaking, there just might be contraband liquor or petty theft somewhere. Like people everywhere, the sight of law-enforcement officers made people nervous, even though we lived a reasonably peaceful and serene existence.

Whaling ships were large and didn't anchor at Spotted Island very often. We only saw a whaling ship if it got caught in a storm and couldn't make it back to the whaling factory in Hawk's Harbour, a few miles down the coast.

A lot of Newfoundlanders hired Livyers for the season. As mentioned earlier, a hired Livyer was known as a shareman. The skipper was responsible for supplying the boat, equipment, board, and lodgings for his crew. The sharemen supplied the labour for a share of the profits when all was squared away at the end of the season.

Each fisherman had a fishing berth, a special place that belonged to him. It was understood that you didn't interfere with anyone else's fishing berth. Some fishermen didn't return for meals. Instead they brought their provisions with them in Labrador boxes. A small fire could boil a kettle in a few minutes, and a quick mug-up could sustain a crew for a few more hours.

As a little girl, I saw lots of schooners off Spotted Island whose sails could be seen for miles. One of my favourite pictures to draw was that of rocky hillsides sloping steeply into the ocean, with little schooners scattered everywhere. I drew puffy white clouds and a big sun in the sky, but no trees, since there weren't any on Spotted Island.

Caplin (a small fish the size of a smelt) was the mainstay of our diet in the summer. They landed by the millions in the coves. It was so exciting to see everyone grab buckets, nets, or anything that would hold the caplin. We had to catch as many as we could. Then we had to salt and dry them. They were delicious with homemade bread. The cod we jigged for our own consumption was salted and dried, too. Fish and fish heads for dogs were salted and placed into burlap bags, which kept them from spoiling and being contaminated by maggots. The sight of maggots always made me sick.

During the fishing season, there was little time for sleep. Even the wood for fires had to be hauled from the mainland. Maybe it was a good thing that the summers were short, because the pace was so fast and furious. I don't know how long the fishermen could endure that tempo. I cringe to think of the suffering our fishermen endured — hands cut and bleeding from line blisters, skin turned white with open sores, the salt in them causing excruciating pain. They ignored their discomfort. The work had to continue.

In the fall during a brief period between the end of the fishing season and shifting in the bay, there was time for a little relaxation. Our neighbours on Spotted Island included a surprising number of musicians, my father being one of them. He was often asked to play at a dance, which could start up at a moment's notice.

"Der's a dance over ta Uncle Tommy's tonight," someone would say.

In a community of 25 families, word would spread quickly.

"Oh, goodie, I loves dances!" I would say, grinning.

Even though I had to go to bed, I could listen to the music playing late into the night from my lofty bed. Daddy played his accordion until he got tired. Then someone else would take over, or Uncle Johnny would play his fiddle. There was no store-bought liquor to be found anywhere, but occasionally there was homebrew.

The Labrador reel is unique to Labrador. To start the dance, eight people gather in pairs in a circle on the floor. As the music starts, they join hands, and the reel gets underway. It lasts for 20 to 30 minutes, and unless there is a change in accordion players, the participants dance the whole set without taking a break.

At dances the sweat ran down Daddy's face as he struggled for the stamina to keep playing. And it certainly rolled down the faces and bodies of the dancers. In addition to dancing, there were card games and tall tales to be shared around oilcloth-covered tables. Our neighbours knew how to make their own fun.

There were phenomenal dancers on Spotted Island. Dancing skills were handed down from generation to generation. When I got older, I knew I had a talent for music and dance. I can't recall ever learning how to play the accordion; I just did. And even today when I hear the right type of jig or reel, I get itchy feet and automatically respond to the music.

In my childhood, summer's end always seemed to approach rapidly. Once the salt fish was dried and shipped to faraway places, the jigging for cod for personal consumption and for dog food was the next job of the fishermen.

Work never stopped, and each season brought its own challenges. As the summer waned, we all wondered what winter would bring. Would there be enough to buy new flannelette and yarn, enough to buy candy for the youngsters at Christmas? Would there be enough food?

Only time would tell.

10

Medical Care and Mail Delivery

Life in Labrador can't be understood without knowing about The Doctor. The International Grenfell Association was founded in 1912. It all began with one man, Wilfred Grenfell, who was knighted in 1927 for his work. He was a man destined for greatness, though he would never admit until his dying day that he had achieved special status or recognition, let alone becoming a world-renowned leader whose friends included Alexander Graham Bell and Henry Ford.

Sir Wilfred Grenfell was born on February 28, 1865, near Chester, England, the second son of a schoolmaster and clergyman. Young Wilfred was lucky enough to have parents who allowed him the freedom to take incredible risks. He became extremely fond of the River Dee, which wound through hills and valleys close to his home. The future doctor was soon an expert at stuffing and mounting the birds he hunted in the marshes. Grenfell tagged along with local fishermen in their daily route to the fishing grounds and became fascinated with their work.

In 1883, Grenfell went to London Hospital Medical College to study medicine. His father was the chaplain there. During his studies, he met many North Sea fishermen who told him of their medical and spiritual deprivation during long sea voyages. In 1888, two years after he qualified as a doctor, he began service with the Royal National Mission to Deep Sea Fishermen.

During his time with the mission, Grenfell heard about the appalling conditions of Labrador fishermen and discovered there was no medical care available for either the local Labradorians or the 20,000 fishermen who thronged the Labrador coast each summer. In 1892 he was selected to head an expedition to investigate the needs of fishermen who fished off the Grand Banks of Newfoundland. Grenfell outfitted a sailing ship as a mission ship and crossed the Atlantic to begin his life's work. When the vessel arrived at St. John's, the city was in flames. But despite the fire, Grenfell never forgot the warm reception he received from Newfoundlanders.

The doctor left on his first trip to Labrador in August 1892. He came upon the fishing fleet in Domino Run where all the schooners were anchored in the well-sheltered harbour. There he started doctoring the sick and disabled. He found the people's medical needs and lack of spiritual comfort very grim. And he discovered a unique people. Innu, Inuit, and descendants of early settlers from Great Britain mingled with one thing in common — their fight to survive.

After that first summer, Grenfell returned to England to raise funds to fulfill his mission. As soon as he acquired a steam-propelled vessel, he loaded it with enough supplies to last the summer and set sail again, determined to help the unfortunate people living in appalling conditions on the Labrador coast.

Grenfell built his first hospital in Battle Harbour in southern Labrador in 1895. Once that one was up and running, he established a second in Indian Harbour farther north. The next year he built a large facility in St. Anthony on the northern tip of Newfoundland, which was to become the administrative centre for the mission. It operated efficiently, caring for the fishermen and the Livyers of Labrador for decades to come.

There were schools, nursing stations, orphanages, and hospitals to be built. In the winter months Grenfell travelled abroad to raise funds for hospitals and boarding schools to carry out his work. Every summer he cruised thousands of miles of coastline to deliver aid to isolated people. Local people developed a system of setting out distress flags to be certain he would stop.

Grenfell was in his seventies in 1939 when he made his last visit to Labrador. The people gave him a rousing welcome. The modern new hospital at St. Anthony was now headed by the highly qualified and capable Dr. Charles Curtis. Grenfell was extremely proud of Curtis and knew he was leaving his mission in capable hands.

Sailing north for the last time on the steamer SS *Kyle*, Grenfell visited Cartwright and all points north. Everywhere he went he was greeted with celebration and joy. His dreams and aspirations for his beloved Labrador had for the most part been achieved, and he was satisfied to retire. Grenfell died quietly in Vermont in October 1940. The local people he helped and healed in numerous ways were changed forever, both medically and spiritually. His lifetime achievement included the establishment of hospitals, nursing stations, schools, agricultural and trade co-operatives, and churches.

My memories of his legacy, though, are from a different perspective.

"Get dis shack cleaned up!" Mommy yelled "De mission boat's comin."

I was six and didn't know how to clean up yet. Clean up what? I glanced out the window and saw a large schooner coming around the point. The fancy hospital ship was carrying Dr. Charles Curtis. Suddenly, Spotted Island was alive with activity. People milled about in a frenzy, tidying up for the doctor. Mommy shouted at us to wash our faces.

Racing to the porch washstand, I scooped cold water from the barrel into the basin, then took the corner of the already filthy towel from its nail and rubbed it over my face. It was cold and there was no soap, but I did the best I could and placed the towel back on the nail.

"Whass de doctor comin fer, Mommy?" Marcie asked.

"Dunno, maid, he jus comes."

The schooner looked majestic coming into our tiny sun-splashed harbour under full sail, with hundreds of coloured flags strung across the top of its spars flapping in the wind. The men went out to the ship in punts and dories to bring the doctor and his party ashore. He was a very important man. We weren't accustomed to having people of such stature in our little world, so this was a major event. I ran around not knowing whether to be happy or scared. After all, he might just have a piece of candy! We ran down to the stagehead and stood in awe.

Is he a god? I wondered. *Is dis what God looks like?*

We all gathered around Dr. Curtis as he made his way up the road to the nursing station. Since it was the middle of summer, the doctor found most of us in good health. He went around the whole community, administering medicine to patients who needed it. The doctor talked to children about germs and told us how important it was to keep ourselves clean.

"What'd de doctor do ta ya, Sally?" I asked my little sister.

"He was pokin at me eyes an me ears an he puts dis cold ting on me chest," she said excitedly. "Seems like he was tryin ta hear sometin in me belly. Den he puts it all round me back. Twas cold but it dint hurt."

Then it was my turn. The doctor smiled. "And what's your name, little one?"

"Josie, sir."

"Josie, huh? Is that short for Josephine?"

"Dunno, sir."

"Well, Josephine, you're healthy as a horse as well." He placed his ear-poking thing back in his pocket.

"Whass a horse, sir?" I asked.

The mailman brought the mail by dog team in the winter, and in the summer it was delivered by coastal steamer. The first trip of the SS *Kyle* was loaded to capacity with supplies and the first mail of the summer. The ship brought hundreds of Newfoundland fishermen who came to fish off the Labrador coast each summer. They lived and slept in appalling conditions and endured filth, hunger, and hardship in the holds of the vessel.

Starting in St. John's, Newfoundland, the *Kyle* made its way northward, steamed up the east coast and across the Strait of Belle Isle, then sailed to all points in Labrador until it reached its final destination at Nain, the farthest northern settlement at the time. Someone with a radio spread the news to each community as the ship drew close.

"The *Kyle* left Battle Harbour at midnight last night," Mommy said as she charged through the door with an armload of wood. "She'll be here by the end of the week."

And so we waited. The *Kyle* was our only connection to the outside world. Eventually, after many days, we heard its horn blow! Everyone tried to get a ride out to the *Kyle* as it rode anchor in our harbour. As our little motorboat chugged along, I looked up in awe at the huge craft of iron and steel. "Look, Sal, de people is wearin funny clothes," I said, pointing at the top deck.

"Yeh, an look at de way they's pointing at us," Marcie said.

"Why is dey lookin at us like dat, Marcie?" I asked. She was two years older than I was and had already spent a year away at school, so I thought she might know about such things.

"Dunno, maid," she answered. "Der outside people, dat's all I know."

We reached the side of the ship and tied up to one of several boats beside the steps. I clambered onto the gangplank, making my way to the deck. My plan was to find the galley. Maybe the cook would give us an apple or an orange. And I was right. We each got an orange! It was delicious. For the first time in my life I had an orange to myself.

"Don't eat de peel," Marcie said. "Jus bite it an tear it off like dis." Using her thumbnail, she pulled off the peel and tossed it into the water.

Sally and I followed suit. That orange was so good. Its taste remains in my memory still. The oranges satisfied our hunger for a little while, so with the fruit's smell sweet in my nostrils we explored the ship.

We came upon a room and saw men with crisp white jackets setting the table. Later I found out they were stewards wearing uniforms. I'd never seen anything like that in my entire life. The tables were draped in white linen, though I didn't know then what linen was. We had oilcloth on our table at home. There were fancy glasses with skinny stems, and cloth things sticking out from the tops of the glasses.

"Whass dem tings, Marcie?" I asked.

"Der napkins," she told me importantly.

"Whass dey fer?"

"Fer wipin yer face when yer eatin, maid."

Even at that young age I couldn't help but compare the dishes to the little tin cup Daddy had made me from a Carnation can. The shiny forks and knives, two or three to each setting, were placed perfectly straight on the tables. Why did they need so many? It was so fancy. Were these people all gods? Where did they come from? My mind couldn't comprehend it all. And I didn't dare ask any more questions. I just followed my sister around like a lost, frightened puppy.

The *Kyle* was built by the Reid Newfoundland Company at Newcastle upon Tyne, England, and was designed specifically for service to the Labrador people. Launched on April 9, 1913, the ship was 220 feet long and had five watertight bulkheads and 1,580 horsepower. The vessel was built with particular attention to the ice conditions it would encounter on the Labrador coast. The formal dining room, music room, main salon, and smoking room were elaborately furnished with beautiful plate-glass windows and rich mahogany walls. The settees and chairs were magnificently upholstered in the finest of fabrics. The staterooms were outfitted with their own washbasins, while ladders gave access to top bunks. The 40 cabins to accommodate the ladies had mirrors and fine furniture. The men's quarters accommodated 120 men. The ship was well ventilated and lit with electricity. The *Kyle* began the Labrador run in early June and finished the round trip every two weeks.

The last mail trip ended when the shipping season was over in November. There was no more mail delivered until after freeze-up, sometimes not until the end of January. However, connections were made all along the coast to try to get one run in before Christmas and one in late winter or early spring. The southern mailman connected with the northern mailman in a kind of relay system up the coast.

During the winter, local people were hired to carry the mail overland, much like stagecoaches long ago. But there were no stagecoaches or roads in Labrador. Using komatiks and dog teams, mailmen braved the intense cold and hardship to get letters and parcels delivered. Labradorians were phenomenal in their kindness to the weary travellers transporting the mail.

Stewart Holwell recalled his experience delivering the mail in the quarterly magazine *Them Days*: "I used ta carry de mail from Buckle's Point ta Battle Harbour fer $200 a winter. That was five trips, and cuz I was with another feller, I only got $100." He went on to say, "Now, de people along de coast were good ta us an dey took turns feedin us. We never paid fer our meals or board or even meals fer our dogs."

But mail was infrequent. As one woman bluntly put it, "When de mail was run by dog team, de whole world could go ta blazes outside an we'd never know." In my early years I don't recall ever receiving any mail at our house.

In the Labrador of my childhood there were no radios, electricity, or railways. It was an existence that bore no resemblance to the lives of city people in the twentieth century. Cut off from all modern forms of communication, we were extremely isolated. Medical care and mail delivery, though primitive, were never taken for granted when I was little. We owe a great debt to the doctors and all the other brave souls who endured extreme cold and hardship. Native Labradorians and Stationers appreciated the people who risked their lives to make sure we got the mail and the medical care we so desperately needed.

This picture was taken when I was eight years old in 1951 at Lockwood School in Cartwright, Labrador.

Part Two

Lockwood

11

Heading for Lockwood

In the late summer of 1950, at age seven and a half, I heard my oldest sister, Marcie, talking about going back to Lockwood School. So I wanted to go with her.

"Can I go, Mommy?" I begged. "Please, please can I go?" I'd learned to say please from Marcie, who was educated.

"Awright, awright, I'll write an ask if ya can go," my mother grumbled. With a grade three education, she sat down and wrote a letter to the house mother at Lockwood School:

> Dear Mrs. Forsyth,
>
> Josie wants de go de school terrible bad, an she pees in her overalls when she got a peer on, and she wets de bed also. But she's a cheerful happy little girl, and not much trouble. She wants to go to school wid Marcie terrible bad, and could you let me know on de next

boat up, and I will send her wid her sister.

Flossie Curl

I was beside myself with excitement, and I pestered my mother with questions. "When'll ya know, Mommy?"

"When de *Kyle* comes wit de letter."

It was torture for two weeks until the *Kyle* arrived with the mail. And sure enough, there was a letter from Mrs. Forsyth!

"Yippee!" I squealed. "Whass she say, Mommy?"

"She says ya can go ta de school wit Marcie. Tank God!"

"Oh, goodie, goodie!" I yelled, running around in circles. "I can go ta school! I'm goin ta de mission wit Marcie!"

"Ya better be good den," Marcie said, a warning look on her face.

"I'll be good, Marcie. I'm always good."

"Yer not always good. Yer spoiled and ya cries ta get yer own way."

"But I be good, Marcie. I promise. Will ya tell me wha tis like again?"

"No. Not goin ta tell ya now. Ya'll see when we gets der."

She seemed mad, and I didn't like my big sister being angry with me, so I shut up. But my mind was racing. I couldn't wait to get to school, even though I had no idea what it would be like.

I tried to comprehend what Marcie had already told me about the playground, the swings, a see-saw, and a merry-go-round. The only swing I knew of was Mary Jane's next door. However, Marcie tried to explain how big the dorm was, how large the school was, and how the bathroom had hot and cold running water.

"Whass a batroom?" I asked. "And where do de water run from — a brook?"

"Comes from a tap an it runs inta a ting called a sink," she said, a little exasperated. "Ya jus turn de handle an out it comes. Oh, Josie, yer some stun. Ya don't know nuttin." She threw her arms up in frustration. I asked so many questions she gave up trying to tell me what it was like.

I never knew what transpired beyond the letter to Dr. and Mrs. Forsyth asking permission, but I think there was a fee or a cost of $10 per child for the year. Maybe Mommy paid the fees using the barter system, or perhaps she took care of the charges in cash, though I'd never seen money at that point. Maybe the fee was waived for a large family. In any case, I was soon on my way to Lockwood School.

It was a six-hour run from Spotted Island to Cartwright on the *Kyle*. Children living in the Sandwich Bay area were sometimes delivered to Lockwood School by their parents or the mission boats *Loon* or *Maravel*. Sometimes Dr. Forsyth's schooner, the *Unity*, travelled to the closer communities to collect children. But children living farther south around Bateau, Black Tickle, Domino, and Spotted Island were transported by the *Kyle*.

"She's come! She's here!" I ran for the house in my sealskin slippers as fast as my little legs could carry me. We were told not to bring clothing, so I hugged Sally, Rhoda, and wee Eddy. Then I took Mommy's hand, and we headed for the stagehead.

A tear trickled down Mommy's cheek, even though she was very self-controlled. She held me for a little while, then said shakily, "Ya be a good little girl now, Josie, an listen ta de teacher."

"I will, Mommy. I be good, an don't cry, or ya'll make me cry, too."

Climbing into the boat, I was too excited to care what my mother was thinking. I had no idea that it would be two years before I would set eyes on my family again — and no notion that the school experience would change my life forever.

I hung tightly to my sister's hand as the little motorboat putted toward the *Kyle*. The ship seemed monstrous to me. My neck got tired as I gazed up at the top deck. A lot of people were clutching small black boxes in their hands and pointing them straight at us.

"Whass dey pointin at us fer, Marcie?" I asked.

"Cameras," she said.

"Whass a camera?"

"Dey take snaps. Dey're takin a picture of us, see?" Marcie was trying to be patient. "Ya know? Like de one Mom got of ya when ya was little … remember?"

I didn't remember and I didn't understand, but I kept quiet and tried not to get seasick. The sea tossed the motorboat around like kindling as we tied up to the ship's side. I clung to Marcie as she led me up the rickety ladder. It was very difficult.

"How long do it take ta get dere?" I asked Marcie as we stepped off the ladder and onto the deck.

"Dunno, maid. We should be dere tanight an ya'll have yer very own bed, too."

"My very own bed? Hope I don't pee in it."

Suddenly, I was scared, because I knew I would pee in it. I always did, and I was deathly afraid of what was going to happen to me. I'd been too excited to think of that before.

Soon it was noon, and the captivating smells made my mouth water. I put the disturbing thoughts of bedwetting out of my head. Then the bell rang, and we made our way to the dining room. I'd looked in through the glass doors when we were on the *Kyle* before and had seen the white tablecloths, the napkins, the shiny silverware, and the pretty glasses. But I had never seen them up close before. Would I actually be sitting and eating in there?

"What do ya use dis fer?" I asked, poking the stemmed glass in Marcie's face.

"Dunno, maid." She grabbed the glass from me and placed it back on the table.

"Sometin smells some good, hey, Marcie?"

"Yeh, an I'm starved, too. De men in de white coats'll bring de food to us."

I was in awe of everything.

We had a tasty meal of fish and potatoes with scrunchions. When we were done, we explored the boat. It was too cold on deck, so we went to the lounge, which boasted fancy draperies and stained-glass windows. Some people were playing cards, while others were enjoying checkers. A man blew on a harmonica. I wanted to hear him, so we sat and listened to the music. Men told stories, and ladies talked about their voyage and the interesting sights they'd seen along the way. The way they all spoke seemed funny to me. They made me feel small and insignificant. These people looked so grand in their elegant clothes, and I was pretty sure they were whispering about us. I hid behind my sister and hung on to her hand. I was frightened and shy at first, but after a few hours I realized these people weren't going to hurt me, so I came out of my shell a little and started being more like myself.

I watched the coastline, marvelling at the huge cliffs rising from the sea. The ship rolled violently with the ocean's swell, and when Marcie and I went below, my stomach lurched. Many of the children were seasick. They were heaving and groaning, and the smell was terrible. My sister knew better than to stay below deck very long, so we headed back up on deck and managed to keep our dinner down.

"Let's see if we can get an apple or an orange, Marcie," I suggested.

"Awright den, we'll go back an ask 'em. Tis no harm to try."

We went to the galley and peeked in the doorway. The cooks were busy preparing the evening meal, which smelled delightful. One of them spotted us and grinned. "What're ya looking for?" he demanded.

"Nuttin, sir, jus lookin," Marcie said.

"Oh, yeh? Are ya sure yer not lookin ta get an apple or something?"

"Oh, no, sir," Marcie said with all the courage she could muster.

We didn't know whether to run or stay. Then he reached into a bin and handed us each an apple.

"Tank ya, sir, tank ya," Marcie said.

I was speechless. We ran to a quiet place to eat our apples, enjoying every bite. It was such a treat.

"We'll be dere real soon," Marcie said as she chewed around the apple core and tossed it over the side.

"Oh, goodie, I'm some glad, too. I can hardly wait ta see de mission." I tossed my apple core into the sea, too.

I was lost in wonderment and fear, but I tried to remain calm and not upset my sister with a barrage of questions. I didn't know it, but our destination was just around the next point, and it would take about an hour to get there. Soon the *Kyle* was entering the sheltered harbour of Cartwright and Lockwood School.

We were there!

12

Arriving at Lockwood

Before I was born there were several attempts to get a school started in the Sandwich Bay area. The Reverend Henry Gordon of the Anglican church in Cartwright built a residential school in Muddy Bay just five miles from Cartwright in 1922. It ran successfully for several years, housing a lot of the children who had lost their parents in the Spanish Influenza epidemic of 1918–19. Tragically, that building burned down in 1928.

Mrs. C.S. Lockwood, a friend of Dr. Grenfell, donated a large sum of money to establish a new school and dormitory in Cartwright, so the doctor named the institution Lockwood School after her. It opened in the fall of 1930 and was staffed primarily with volunteers from Canada, the United States, and Great Britain, who worked without pay.

Unfortunately, a fire destroyed the first dormitory after only four years of operation, but that didn't deter Dr. Grenfell. He raised funds immediately to construct another boarding school, which was ready for occupancy in 1935–36. Fifty children attended that first year. Dr. Garth Forsyth was the resident doctor at the hospital, and Mrs. Claire Forsyth was the resident nurse. She was a volunteer and worked without pay for many years. The Forsythes met at the school, married, and became the house parents for the children from 1940 to 1950. They resided in the dormitory and lived comfortably there.

Dr. Forsyth composed the first Lockwood song, which was sung regularly in the school for many years. The rules and regulations, reminiscent of English public schools a century earlier, were very strict, even cruel. Students soon learned that disobedience brought harsh punishment.

As the *Kyle* rounded the point and entered Cartwright's harbour, I noticed the community was divided into two distinct parts. On the left stood Cartwright itself and on the right was Lockwood School. Cartwright had about 400 people then and was dominated by the buildings of the Hudson's Bay Company, which were located in the centre of town. The Hudson's Bay store and warehouses with stark white siding and red roofs were in sharp contrast to the modest homes staggered along the shoreline. From the Hudson's Bay buildings the village branched out in both directions.

Dozens of small boats bobbed on the waves near the shore. Several small wharves dotted the bank and protruded into the harbour. Just beyond the landwash at the edge of the water, in various sizes and colours, were sheds for storage and several outhouses. Beyond the sheds the low road, not much wider than a footpath, circled the harbour around a rocky beach. Houses, most of them with white clapboard siding, lined the road. Behind the houses was a gradual incline to the top of Flag Staff Hill where a flagpole had been erected. From there the hill sloped toward the point, jutting into the sea and half encircling the town. Birches, mixed with spruces, balsams, junipers, and firs, were already clad in colourful fall foliage.

Lockwood School consisted of three magnificent buildings and several smaller ones nestled on a small plateau. The white siding of the hospital, school, and dormitory stood out against the dark green forest covering the hillside behind.

When I saw the buildings, I knew without having to ask that this was my destination. Suddenly, I was terrified. Roaches Brook had five tiny log cabins. Spotted Island was blessed with 25 families. To me this was the biggest place I'd ever seen.

"Weers de school at, Marcie?" I asked while we were waiting for the ship to anchor.

"Over der! Look!" She pointed at the enormous building in the middle of three or four large buildings.

We were herded into a smaller vessel, the *Loon*, the mission boat that made the short run to the wharf. When we disembarked, I gripped my sister's hand and walked with her up the gravel road toward the dormitory. The road forked at a plateau. To the left was the hospital; to the right was the schoolhouse. At the end of the road loomed the three-storey dormitory. The playground was strategically placed between the dormitory and the school. I recognized the swings, but they were very different from Mary Jane's swing on Spotted Island. I had no idea what the other contraptions were.

"Off de road!" someone yelled. "De truck's comin!"

All the youngsters who had been here before knew exactly what to do. I, of course, had never seen a road before, let alone a truck.

"Dat's de mission truck," Marcie explained when I asked. "It carries supplies from de boat."

The truck zoomed past, and the dust almost choked me. I was astonished by this new, strange world and was mesmerized by all the commotion. Clinging tightly to my sister's hand, I followed the crowd up the concrete steps to the front door. That was to be one of the only times we ever used the front door. Oh, but it was so beautiful to my eyes! Shiny brown linoleum glistened all around us, and the smell of fresh paint tickled my nostrils.

We were conducted up the wide stairs. Immediately to the right was the little girls' dormitory. Twenty beds were strung along both sides of the room, with a wide corridor between them. At the end of the room long windows overlooked the harbour. Next to the dormitory was the main bathroom. A huge white free-standing bathtub with claw feet took up the far corner. The toilet was close to the door, and several sinks were situated against the wall. Just beyond the bathroom were teachers' bedrooms and stairs down to the main-floor living quarters of Dr. and Mrs. Forsyth.

Beyond the stairs at the end of the hallway was the linen room. Across from the stairs were the boys' dormitories and the sewing room. Toward the front of the building was the big girls' room, and directly across the hallway from that room were stairs to the attic, which contained Christmas things and general storage that we weren't supposed to know about.

Downstairs, to the right of the entrance, was the well-equipped kitchen. On the far side of the kitchen, windows looked out on the harbour and counters stretched along the entire wall. Against the opposite wall were two big stoves. Beside the kitchen was the large dining room with four or five huge tables with benches. At the end of the dining room facing the back of the building was a door to Dr. and Mrs. Forsyth's living quarters. Downstairs, on the other side of the entrance, were two study rooms with couches and soft chairs.

Immediately upon entering the basement to the left was the maintenance room or small carpenter shop. Directly across the hallway at the bottom of the stairs was the cold storage room where dried fruit and other non-perishable food were kept. And on the same side were the stairs to the main floor. Just past the stairs and down the hall on the left was the boys' washroom. Across the hall was the furnace room. Farther down the hall on the left was the large laundry room, and at the end of the hall was the girls' washroom. All along the hallway walls were clothing hooks and lockers for storing our outdoor clothing and rubber boots.

The school stood in front of a small marsh. The playground was well situated, with swings to the right of the gravel pathway and a see-saw and a merry-go-round to the left. Closest to the dormitory and to the right were the hens' and pigs' pens. Beyond them the sprawling vegetable garden, with its white picket fence, stretched to the edge of the trees. Along the side of the dormitory were clotheslines strung in several rows. Beyond that was the root cellar.

To the right of the school, nestled under the hill, stood the magnificent hospital; the same one that had cared for me when I was mauled by dogs. A small powerhouse containing a generator supplied the mission's electricity. It was located on the far left at the top of the hill. We were fully self-contained and lived there completely isolated for 10 months.

My experiences at Lockwood transformed me from a happy, carefree child into a rebellious, angry girl. The process started immediately. First, Mrs. Forsyth and her aides separated me from my sister. I held on to Marcie's hand as long as I could, but my screams fell on deaf ears as I was dragged in the opposite direction. Marcie had to go to the big girls' room, and I had to go to the little girls' room. Although I was herded into the little girls' room with 10 or 15 other girls, in my mind I was completely alone.

I can't recall all the details of what transpired next, but I vividly remember being terrified, lonely, and lost. I was frantic for my family already and wanted to go home. The house mother, Mrs. Forsyth, lectured and advised us what to do and what not to do. She was very clear about what we needed to fear.

"You will address us as Miss, Mrs., or Mr. You will learn and use your manners at all times. You will obey the aides and do as you're told at all times. There will be no fighting, running, or roughhousing in the school or in the dormitory."

Boy, oh, boy, I thought. *I'm in trouble now fer sure.* I tried to stay very small. Then, all of a sudden, I was singled out.

"Which one of you is Josie Curl?" an aide asked.

"Here, miss," I replied timidly, trying to hold back the tears.

"Little Josie. My, we're a tiny, wee thing, aren't we? This is your bed here by the door."

I felt ashamed and degraded from that first moment. Then another girl came forward and laid her few things on the bed next to me. She also looked terrified, sad, and uncomfortable.

"All right then," the aide said. "I'll get some rubber sheets for your beds. Strip everything off and get ready for your bath." The aide threw our little bundles of clothing onto each bed. "Your lockers are at the end of the room there. We'll label, bundle, and store your personal clothing in there for now."

When my turn came, I was issued a face cloth and toothbrush with my name on them. I was instructed to hang the face cloth on the nail provided.

I can't remember what came first, the haircuts or the delousing, but there was no escaping, either. My head was forced under a tap just like Marcie had tried to explain to me, and a foul-smelling solution was applied. My head was then wrapped in a white triangular cloth that had to stay on for a while to kill the lice. It didn't matter whether you had them or not. Everyone was herded like cattle to the sinks.

Snip, snip, snip went the scissors, straight across my forehead and straight from the bottom of my ear, around the back of my neck to my other ear. The aide was rough, and I thought she was going to cut my head off.

Once we were deloused, we were thrust two at a time into the huge bathtub. I thought I was going to drown. The water was shivering cold, and I was scrubbed until my skin was sore. It hurt.

"De soap floats," I managed to mumble.

"You've never seen floating soap before, Josie?" the aide said.

"No, miss. Wha kind is it? Smells some nice, too."

"It's Ivory soap. It floats so you won't have to dig at the bottom of the tub for it."

"Oh, yeh," I marvelled.

"Inquisitive little one, aren't you?" she said as her fingernails dug into my skull.

"Wha, miss?"

"What happened to your head? It's all bumpy."

I shivered. "De dogs bite me."

Finally, the torture was over. I put on the little cotton shirt with the Peter Pan collar trimmed with rickrack and pulled on my bibbed overalls. My new rubber boots were three sizes too big. When I finished dressing, I sat on the edge of my bed and waited. I looked like everyone else.

"Can I go see Marcie, miss?" I pleaded with the aide with all the courage I could muster. I tried desperately to stop the tears and be brave when my request wasn't granted. "Whass dey gonna do wit me clothes?" I asked one of the other girls next to me.

"Dey're gonna be packed way an we won't see em till we go home next spring."

"Next spring! Why?"

"Dunno, maid," she said sadly. "Dat's what dey do here." Then she added, "We gotta wear de mission clothes till we goes home in June an dat's dat!"

We retrieved our clothes from the lockers at the end of the room, and the aides tied them in bundles that were then labelled and placed in baskets. I watched my aide's every move. I wanted to see what she was doing with my clothes. Tattered as they were, they were mine. She took the basket across the hallway to the sewing room and put it in a cupboard.

New children were still arriving from points closer to the school — Muddy Bay, Paradise River, Separation Point, Cape North. Wherever they came from, they had to go through the same things we did.

At the bottom of the stairs there was a small office. As soon as we were all deloused and dressed in our mission clothing, we were herded downstairs to register. They asked us our names, our ages, our parents' names, and where we were from. Then we shuffled into the dining room where there were several large tables. I saw my sister and ran to her, grabbed her hand, and wiggled in beside her on the bench.

As soon as we were seated, we were given a lecture on table manners. With a crystal-clear voice, loud enough for all to hear, Mrs. Forsyth said, "Sit up straight. Wait for grace to be said before you start eating. Place only one hand on the table, the other in your lap. Never put your elbows on the table. Always say please and thank you. Don't chew with your mouth open. There will be no carrying on at the table, and when your plate is empty and all is done, you will be given permission to leave."

Once the dishes were done and put away in the cupboard at the end of the dining room, we went outside to play until bedtime, which was around 7:30. When we came back in, we were treated with hot chocolate. It was delicious. Then we lined up for the bathroom to brush our teeth and clean up. We were ordered to fold our clothes neatly, then donned long flannel nightdresses, knelt to say our prayers, and climbed into bed.

Lights were out at eight. We had to remain quiet, which was almost impossible for us that first night. I heard other girls crying into their pillows, and I wept, too. I was so homesick. Besides I was worried about peeing in my bed. The rubber sheet felt hard and cold under me, and I cried myself to sleep. *If only I could go and be with my sister,* I thought.

In the middle of the night I woke up in a pool of urine. The rubber sheet contained it so well that it soaked my whole body. At first it was warm and then it got cold. I lay there shivering the entire night. I thought of being at home in my little feather bed on the loft floor. It was so much better than this place. "Oh, Mommy, Mommy, Mommy … wat ya done ta me?" I sobbed.

That was only the beginning.

13

School Days

"When're we startin school, Marcie?" I asked my sister.

"Soon as ever'body gets here."

"I wanna go home. Can I go?" I could feel the tears welling in my eyes.

"No, Josie, ya can't go home now." Marcie sounded sad, too. "Try ta be brave. Sides, ya'll like school once ya get started."

We were finally all settled in the dormitory, and school was going to start on Monday morning. I was scared and excited at the same time. I didn't even know what a person did in school. And I didn't remember why I had wanted to come here so badly.

On Monday morning at seven o'clock sharp we were all woken up. *Ding-a-ling-a-ling* went the bell. *Cock-a-doodle-doo* cried the roosters.

"Rise and shine!" shouted the aides. "Rise and shine!"

We had to move quickly and follow instructions. After we made our beds, we folded our nightgowns and placed them under our pillows. Then we were herded into the bathroom to wash our faces, dig out our ears, brush our teeth, comb our hair, and clean our nails. Once we were dressed and ready for school, we went down for breakfast, which was porridge, and I hated it. It was full of lumps big enough to choke me, and it had a revolting, slimy consistency.

"You will sit until it's all gone or do without until dinnertime," one of the aides said.

"Can't eat it, miss. Tis too lumpy." I gagged and gagged and couldn't get it down. So all I had to eat for the first day of school was a slice of toast.

After the dishes and chores were done, we went outside to wait for the school bell. I shuffled along the gravel path toward the school, interested in the sound the stones made under my oversize rubber boots. I felt sad as I sat back and watched the other kids. Then Marcie took my hand and showed me how to play on the see-saw.

I was just beginning to have fun when suddenly the bell jangled. *Ding-a-ling-a-ling.* I glanced up to see a lady standing on the school steps, shaking a big bell. It was so loud. Youngsters ran from all directions, heading for the classrooms. Some of the bigger students had ventured into the marsh behind the school to pick berries, but they made it to school on time.

The most remarkable memory I carry with me from the moment I entered the big white school is the smell. It was a combination of fresh paint, a musty odour from the dust that had settled into the wooden floors, and the fragrance of new books. Those aromas were so distinct that to this day when I sniff new books it takes me back to my first day at Lockwood.

I started out in the primer. The teacher handed out pencils, and scribblers with brown paper that smelled oily. The first lesson was arithmetic, which lasted until recess. I was learning how to count. When arithmetic was finished, the bell rang for recess, and I meandered out to the playground.

After recess we had a writing lesson. I practised my printing: *AAA, aaa, BBB, bbb* ... I wanted a gold star. I wanted to see lots of gold stars beside my name on the big chart that hung on the wall beside the blackboard. But after sitting in my seat and being a good girl for a while, my mind wandered and I gazed longingly out the window at the garden and the woods beyond. I wondered what it would be like in those woods. That was where I really wanted to be.

Whack! The teacher smacked a ruler across her desk so hard that it made the whole class jump.

"Josie, what are you looking at?"

I recoiled in my seat, startled as my name was yelled so earsplittingly loud. "Nuttin, miss, jus lookin."

"Get back to work or you'll be staying after school!"

I was good for a while, but I wanted to talk to somebody, so I turned around in my seat.

Whack! "Josie, turn around! I'm getting sick and tired of shouting at you. Now go and stand in the corner."

I was horrified. "Wha corner, miss?"

"This one here beside me!" she bellowed, pointing at it.

I got up from my seat, feeling ashamed and humiliated. I tried to shrink inside my overalls.

Then it got worse! When I reached the corner, she said, "Now turn around, face the corner, and put this on."

She handed me a tall pointed hat. I didn't want to put it on.

"Put it *on*! *Now!*" The teacher was so angry that I thought she was going to hit me.

I had no choice but to put the dunce hat on and stand there. I heard stifled giggles and felt the taunting from the class go straight through me. Crying silently, I was humiliated beyond description. For the rest of that morning I had to stay in the corner and was thankful when the bell rang. Removing the hat, I tottered outside, feeling belittled, angry, and alone. I was seven years old.

For a while after that I tried harder to be good in school. I didn't want to go through that embarrassment again. I was smart and learned to read and write with very little effort. With pleasure I discovered that I thoroughly enjoyed the process of learning to read.

Halloween was soon upon us. My spirit soared as we sat around the big tables in the dining room making jack-o'-lanterns, witches, ghosts, and black cats with arched backs. To my delight we pasted them on the walls and windows of the dormitory. *Snip, snip* went my tiny scissors as I cut strips of orange and black construction paper and glued them into garlands.

I didn't know that Halloween was going to be a terrifying experience for me. Even while I was enjoying the decorations, my apprehension grew. I heard tales of witches eating little children, stories of cats scratching out eyes, ghosts and goblins flying about, and bats sucking the blood from your body until you died.

"Whass a goblin?" I asked Marcie.

"Dunno. Kinda like a ghost, I s'pose."

"Whass a bat den?"

"All I know is dey only comes out after dark. Kinda like a big black bird wit sucker lips."

"Is dey real?"

"Yeh," chimed in Peggy from across the table. "Bats is real and dey sucks de blood right outta ya!"

I was too frightened to ask any more questions, and that night I was afraid to go to sleep. I kept looking out the windows, trying to see all these creatures I'd heard about.

Finally, Halloween arrived, and I was scared out of my wits all day. All around the school I spied people in scary costumes making squealing, squeaky sounds. After supper the big dining-room tables were stacked, Mrs. Forsyth and the aides dished out Halloween treats, and ghost stories were recited. We were then taken to the basement and told to look into the laundry room. Years later I realized a sheet had been set up with a light behind it. At the time, though, all I saw was the profile of a witch in a tall pointed hat stirring a huge pot of brew!

"Hee, hee, hee," she squeaked. Beside her was a big black cat with its tail sticking straight up and its back arched in rage. The witch continued to stir her brew. "Hee, hee, hee, watch out for the cat. She'll scratch your eyes out. Come here, little girls and boys. It's almost hot enough for you now!"

"I'm scared, Marcie!" I cried, clinging tightly to my sister.

"'Tis not real, Josie."

The bigger pupils knew what was happening, but they didn't tell the little ones. Looking back, I imagine they meant no harm, but I was petrified.

"Look, miss, a giant bat jus flew by de window!" someone yelled.

I screamed and gripped Marcie's hand even harder. Terror overtook me.

After the ghosts and goblins were gone, we settled down for hot chocolate and cookies. But I was too upset to enjoy them. I couldn't get the bloodsucking bats, eye-scratching cats, and the witch's brew out of my head. For days I couldn't sleep.

A few days after Halloween I heard some older students talking about a bonfire. Guy Fawkes Night it was called.

"Whass a bonfire night?" I asked Marcie. "An who's Guy Fawkes?"

"Tis where we gets a big pile a wood an lights a huge fire an we're allowed to toast marshmallas an sing songs an tis lotsa fun."

I was looking forward to having some fun. It seemed I wasn't fitting in very well, and I was sick with longing for home. I found I couldn't adjust to all the rules. I couldn't stand being so confined. And I couldn't cope with the anger from Mrs. Forsyth and her aides.

Despite my heavy heart, as Guy Fawkes Night drew closer, I began taking part in building the bonfire. We piled everything we could find onto the pile of wood in the middle of the marsh behind the school.

"Boy, oh, boy," a boy said as he threw a huge tree onto the pile. "Tis gonna be a big one dis year."

"When we gonna light it, Marcie?" I nagged my sister every day.

"Sunday night, Josie. Ya jus gotta wait."

Sure enough, on Sunday night everyone was in an uproar. As dusk approached, we all became more and more excited. It was getting darker and darker until finally someone hollered, "Miss! Hey, miss! Tis time ta light de bonfire! Tis time ta light it, miss!"

"All right then, let's do it!" the aide said, approaching the pile. She struck a match on the paper and kindling at the bottom of the pile. Flames licked through the wood, quickly rising to the top. I was totally absorbed in the experience, and my heart soared as I watched the flames leap into the night sky. The sound of the crackling spruce boughs and the scent of the smoke calmed me. My mind went back to the mug-up in the woods with Daddy. A tear trickled down my cheek at the thought. I quickly brushed it aside.

We had a lot of fun that night toasting marshmallows and singing songs. The older boys dragged pieces of wood and whatever else they could find and added them to the fire. However, all too soon it came to an end, and as the flames died, so did my spirits. Just the thought of having to go to sleep in that hard bed with the rubber sheet so thick that it felt as if I were lying on concrete twisted a knot in the pit of my stomach.

Mommy had told Mrs. Forsyth in her letter that I was a cheerful little girl, and for the most part I think I was. I loved to compete and always wanted to do my best at everything. I worked hard in school, and even though I didn't like the angry treatment I received, I enjoyed my lessons and continued to learn quickly.

Every day I studied the big chart. My name was at the centre of the ladder for a long time. Then ever so gradually it moved up the ladder. I began to understand and accept what I had to do to get a star. As my name moved up the chart, I gained more confidence. Then one day, after working hard at my printing and feeling good about what I'd achieved, I got a gold star for excellence. I was so excited!

"I done it!" I cried in delight "I done it!"

"Done what?" one of the girls said archly. "Pissed yer pants again?"

I was getting tougher despite myself, so I promptly slapped her. I wasn't going to sit back and let her ridicule me after I worked so long and hard for this. I had learned to fight back.

"Marcie, Marcie!" I shouted as I ran to my sister during recess. "I gotta gold star!"

"Good fer ya, Josie. I told ya, ya was smart."

I needed reassurance, and those charts gave me the incentive to do well. The bell rang for dinner, and I bolted for the dining room.

"Josie, don't run!" one of the aides cried. "How many times have I told you not to run?"

"Sorry, miss!" I hollered, but I kept running, anyway. I just couldn't stop.

As I became less afraid and gained more confidence, I wanted to explore this strange new world. I asked Uncle Mickey, the mission worker, if I could help him feed the chickens and pigs. He was the maintenance man, the carpenter, the gardener, and the general handyman. I collected eggs for Mrs. Forsyth and always wanted to help.

Snowdrifts accumulated quickly around the dormitory. I loved playing in the snow, randying down the hillside on a piece of cardboard, a barrel stave, or a piece of plastic. I enjoyed building snow houses and making snow angels. Snowball fights weren't always fun because the boys made the snowballs so hard they hit like rocks. I'd race to the see-saw, wrap my hands around the frame, and whirl myself through my arms. And everywhere I went I climbed something or other.

One day, as I was climbing the woodpile, my heel got caught between two large logs and I fell backward. I ended up hanging upside down by one heel and was stuck fast. "Help, somebody!" I screamed, dangling my free leg, whirling both arms in the air for what seemed like forever. I was terrified that I was going to fall, land on my head, and die. Finally, one of the bigger boys came along.

"Whass ya doin up der, Jos?"

"Nuttin. Ony climbin de woodpile. Can ya lift me down, please?"

"What if I don't?"

"Please lift me down," I begged. "Me foot's hurtin. An I think tis broke," I added, trying to gain sympathy.

Once he finished tormenting me, he pulled the two logs apart and gently lifted me to the ground, just as the bell rang for the afternoon class. That woodpile was at least 12 to 15 feet high, and I was halfway up when I fell. The other students teased me when I went into the classroom, but I ignored them. I sauntered over to my seat and sat down as if I didn't care. I gazed out the window at the enormous woodpile and thought how lucky it was that I didn't get hurt.

A sharp voice broke into my thoughts. "Josie, what are you looking at out there?"

"Nuttin, miss. Jus lookin." I opened my book, picked up my pencil, and started printing from my reader.

I have many memories of the authority that I tried so hard to comprehend. I found some rules incomprehensible, and my experiences began to fuel a deep anger inside me. A few examples will suffice.

After school we weren't allowed to go inside until wash-up time for supper. Once, when I needed to use the bathroom, I banged on the door and there was no one there to let me in. I was frantic! There was nothing

I could do except sit on the windowsill and wiggle back and forth, desperately trying not to wet my pants. I cried silently to myself and watched the other children playing. Why did I have to be so different?

When the bell finally rang, I rushed inside and sneaked into the furnace room to dry my overalls with the heat of the furnace. I recall the strong urine smell as steam billowed around me. I didn't want to get in trouble again, and I hadn't thought of how to hide the odour.

As I entered the classroom, one of the boys held his nose. "Phew! Watta stink! Did ya piss yer pants again, Jos?"

I was ashamed and just wanted to crawl away somewhere and die. "No, I dint. Tis jus from de snow."

"Gonna tell Miss on ya," one of the girls said.

"Oh, please don't tell," I whispered.

"Yeh, gonna tell Miss on ya," she snarled as she walked away.

It was suppertime, and they didn't want to give me clean clothes, so they simply put me to bed. I lay there crying for hours, aching for my mother, longing for home.

One day I was tossing bits of paper to my friend Florence and got caught again. The angry voice rang out. "Josie, will you please come here and stand in the corner!"

"Yeh, miss." This time I didn't care what she thought. I stood there until finally the bell sounded and I was free again.

Another day I was deeply involved drawing pictures with my fingernail on the frosty windowpanes when suddenly I heard a crack.

"Josie, what do you think you're doing?"

"Nuttin, miss, jus drawin." I was trying desperately to curtail her anger.

"You're supposed to be working, not drawing pictures on the windowpane!"

I scrunched in my seat, feeling indignant and belittled once again. *I must be a bad girl,* I thought as I tried to work on my sums. But I wanted to be good. I wanted to learn my lessons and get gold stars, but it was such hard work and I didn't like that. Having to sit all day in a classroom was torture.

I decided then that I didn't like school, and I certainly didn't like this teacher.

14

Learning the Rules

I became more and more rebellious and feisty, but strangely, Mrs. Forsyth liked me. Maybe it was because I was so tiny. She singled me out and invited me into the Forsythes' living quarters. I was flabbergasted at how fancy it was and felt very privileged.

Soon I discovered that this wasn't a good thing. In fact, it turned out to be disastrous. As soon as those visits became common knowledge, I was mercilessly teased for being the house mother's pet. I experienced a new wave of despair as I cried myself to sleep night after night.

How well I remember dinnertime and the *ding-a-ling-a-ling* of the bell to announce that food was ready. Starving, I bolted for the basement door. Inside I hung up my coat and removed my rubber boots and placed them under my small wooden locker. We all crowded into the washroom to wash our hands before dinner and lined up for inspection before going upstairs to the dining room. I sat at the big table and wondered what food would be served this time. Dinner was usually sandwiches or soup with brown bread. I didn't like brown bread, but I had to eat it and everything else on my plate whether I liked it or not. This rule caused a lot of unnecessary suffering at the dinner table.

We were fed well, though not necessarily with food we liked. But we were given meals that were good for us. Some of the food was very strange to me. I'll never forget the first time I was forced to eat tapioca pudding. I remember how suspicious it looked to me.

"Ya're not gonna eat dat ol stuff, is ya?" the girl next to me whose name was Peggy asked.

I glanced at it again. It looked like snot. I was afraid to taste it, so I left it in my dish.

My name rang out over the dining room. "Josie, eat your dessert!" one of the aides ordered.

"Whass dessert, miss?"

"Your pudding. Eat your pudding."

"Can't, miss," I mumbled. "Don't like it."

"Eat it, anyway, or you'll go straight to bed."

"Can't, miss. I'll get sick."

But my pleas fell on deaf ears. At last I knew I had no choice. I picked up my spoon and tried to eat the pudding, but it felt slimy, and the little lumps made me gag. After choking down a few mouthfuls, I threw it up all over the table.

"Okay, Josie, go to bed right now!" the aide shouted.

"But, miss, I tol ya I coulden eat it!"

I left the table along with a few other youngsters, went upstairs to the bedroom, and sat on my bed. I hated being sent to bed. I hated that place. As I lay there, quietly crying into my pillow, I thought of home. How I wanted to see my family! I needed my daddy to hold me and comfort me. How was I going to live like this?

After dinner certain pupils were assigned to clean up. I hadn't been given any tasks yet, so I had to go outside and wait for the bell. We were never allowed to loiter around the dormitory or the school. When we weren't eating, studying, or doing chores, we were outside, no matter how cold it was. Rainy days were special. Then we were permitted to play inside and sometimes linger in the sitting rooms. It was so nice in the sitting rooms with the fireplace on. We played games or worked on puzzles. I enjoyed tinkering with the wooden blocks with the animals on them. When properly assembled, each side made one animal. There were also tiddlywinks, pick-up sticks, Snakes and Ladders, checkers, and Chinese checkers to help while away the time.

The weather turned cold quickly in November and then even colder as fall became winter. We were issued winter coats. I can't recall what they looked like. I just know I was freezing most of the time. The Forsythes had a dog named Uncle Remus. He was big, with black wavy hair, and I liked playing with him, as did all the other students. Life at Lockwood wasn't all gloom and doom.

At the end of the day, when the dishes were cleared away, we had to sit at the dining-room tables and do our homework. There was very little time to play before we had to go upstairs to bed. I loved the hot chocolate we got on weekends. Little by little, life at Lockwood became more bearable. I started to feel a bit more comfortable, and though I didn't make a best friend, I began to get along with some of my classmates. I was learning coping skills despite myself.

I remember feeling sorry for Hazel Williams. She had a tubercular hip and was wrapped in a full body cast. I was also drawn to Florence, the other bedwetter, and we supported each other as much as we could. I found out that fighting wasn't the answer and was able to control my temper better. It was better to obey than to resist, and I also realized that I enjoyed learning and did so quickly. Drawing was fun, too. We had an art class every Friday afternoon, which I looked forward to all week.

During school hours, when it was too wet or cold to go outside, we were allowed to go upstairs to the gym during recess. I'll never forget seeing the rings and swing being lowered from the ceiling. Of course, I couldn't reach them, but I managed to get one of the bigger children to lift me up.

"Whee, whee!" I'd squeal as I went back and forth high into the air.

Early on I discovered that I liked competition. Stretching my athletic abilities made me feel powerful because I was able to take advantage of my upper-body strength and it didn't matter that I was tiny. Once I was on the swinging bar or the rings, I felt free. There were also tumbling mats on the floor for us. We had fun playing on them — doing the monkey dance, grappling with one another in Indian wrestling, and performing somersaults and headstands.

When the bell rang, we had to put everything away. Then we raced for the door to get ready for dinner.

"Don't run!" yelled the teacher as we bolted for the door.

"Awright, miss," I replied but kept running.

"Josie, come back here!"

"Okay, miss."

"Do you know what the word *don't* means?"

"Yeh, miss."

"What does it mean?"

"Dunno, miss. I shoulden run when ya says don't run."

"That's right, Josie. You can be pretty smart when you want to be. Why do you choose to put yourself through punishment simply because you don't want to listen?"

"Dunno know, miss."

"You'd better start listening, or you'll keep getting into trouble."

"Yeh, miss, I will," I mumbled as I sauntered toward the door, feeling alone, sad, and humiliated that I'd been scolded yet again.

When I entered the dining room a few minutes late, everyone stared at me because they all knew the teacher had chewed me out. The grins on their faces made me want to wipe them away with one clean sweep of my hand. But I knew better. That wouldn't do any good, so I sat silently at the big table and picked at my food.

My defiance and rebelliousness grew. I hated being teased for being Mrs. Forsyth's pet, for being so small, for peeing in my bed and in my overalls. I was so angry. It wasn't the schoolwork that I hated; it was the strict rules. I wanted to learn, but at my own pace. I didn't want to fit into the system — the rules of the classroom, the rules of the dormitory, and the rules of the playground were driving me crazy. I felt constricted and longed for the freedom of the woods, being able to putter about on the landwash, the joy of following big brothers and sisters around, climbing trees, and watching my father shoot food for supper. Instead I was in prison.

Many times during recess I had to play outside in clothes that weren't adequate to keep me warm. Frequently, I needed to use the bathroom, but when I tried to get inside, the door would be locked. Countless times I sat on the windowsill wiggling back and forth, trying not to pee. I'd bang on the door in desperation, hoping that Uncle Mickey would be in his workshop, which was just inside the door. Sometimes he'd hear me and let me in. On other occasions I just had to wet my clothes.

"Der goes pissy-ass Jos," one of the students would say as I walked by.

"Yeh, an she stinks, too," another would chime in.

And then I'd hear the other youngsters giggle.

This tormenting occurred during my entire stay at Lockwood. No wonder I became so rebellious and mean. Occasionally, my sister and her friends tried to protect me.

"Ya gotta be brave an stand up fer yerself," Marcie would say, trying to soothe me.

"I tries, but dey're all bigger'n me," I'd reply.

"Ya can't let em beat ya, Josie, cuz dey'll jus keep doin it."

"Awright, Marcie, I'll try," I'd whimper.

She was right. It eased up somewhat once I became brave and strong enough to fight back. I didn't always win, and the taunting never ceased completely, but when I began to fight back, life became a little better. I had been plunged into a strange world and had to learn to adapt or be crushed.

One night, after crying myself to sleep, I recalled that the next day was Saturday and there was no school. That meant I could play outdoors. The thought of being free to play cheered me up. I woke up that morning, feeling stronger within myself than I had in a long time. But it didn't last. It never did.

The bedwetting was constant, and the punishments got worse. It didn't matter what they'd do to me to try to make me stop. It didn't matter whether they made me sleep on the stairs, under the stairs, in the bathtub, or on the floor in the hallway. Nothing worked. I couldn't control it, and I truly think the punishments made my situation worse.

The first night the aides put me in the bathtub to sleep was a nightmare. Shifting from side to side, trying to find some form of comfort, only made me hurt all over. "Why're dey doin dis ta me?" I cried, my tears flowing into the drainpipe.

I had been an inquisitive, free-spirited, happy little girl when I arrived at Lockwood. I'd had such high hopes and dreams of going to school, even though I hadn't known what to expect. I certainly didn't think children would be so cruel. I didn't even know what being mean or cruel meant.

By March of my first year, I had become a tough child, but I had absorbed enough rules to get by. Although I can't recall when it started, I became a thief. I didn't know what a thief was then or what stealing was really. I just took things because I wanted them. I'd never even heard the word *thief* before. At home Mommy's laws were rules about safety and survival. We had no rules about belongings. All belongings were shared.

After being sent to bed one day without supper for taking a comic book from one of the lockers, I lay on my bed crying and wondering what all the fuss was about. Soon afterward I received a visit from Mrs. Forsyth.

"My little Josie, Josie, Josie … what are we going to do with you? You're such a sweet little thing and we love you very much, but you have to learn that you mustn't steal. It's very wrong to take other people's property."

"Whass propaty, miss?" I sobbed, confused.

"All of the things you have with your name on them are your property. They belong only to you. All the things that are given to you are yours alone. No one else has the right to touch them without your permission. These things are your property. It's the same with your father's tools and your mother's dishes. Your mother's dishes belong to her alone. What would happen if you stole your mother's dishes?"

"Oh, miss, I'd never do dat!"

"And why not?"

"Cuz, miss, she'd gimme a big lacin!"

"Well, then, what makes you think the same thing won't happen here? Do you understand?"

"Yes, miss, I understan," I quavered, feeling grateful that I'd learned this lesson about other people's property. I was especially thankful that I wasn't going to get a beating this time.

Slowly and painfully, I adjusted to Lockwood. I learned the rules and tried to abide by them as well as I could. At first I didn't know the rules, then I defied them deliberately. Eventually, I obeyed and found some form of comfort in receiving praise for being a good little girl.

I heard horror stories of beatings with belts, slippers, willow switches, and sticks. Cracks on the knuckles with a ruler were painful enough. I tried so hard not to cry, but if you didn't, the teacher thought it didn't hurt enough. Being kept in after school and being sent to bed without supper were the most common punishments I endured. Going to bed early, especially during the warm, sunny evenings in May and June, was brutal. Compliance was difficult for me to learn, but I found that when I obeyed the rules, when I listened to the teachers, when I avoided punishment, things weren't so very bad at Lockwood.

15

Special Times at Lockwood

Halloween, Guy Fawkes Day, Christmas, Valentine's Day, and Easter were all celebrated at Lockwood School. Shortly after Guy Fawkes Night, I started hearing talk about a Christmas concert. It sounded like an important event. A lot of the pupils were whispering about who would get the lead part, who would be the baby Jesus, who would play Mary, and so on. I'd never seen or heard a school play and had to ask lots of questions. I knew about the big stage in the gym upstairs, but I didn't know why it was there.

"Whass a concert, Marcie?"

"Tis like actin, when we pretends to be somebody else, like a mommy or a daddy," she explained.

"Is it like when we plays house?"

"Yeh, sorta like that cept we goes up to de stage an we gotta remember our lines an we gotta remember de words to de songs, too."

I was mystified. This was something new, and I loved adventure.

Marcie was a good singer and sang louder than anyone. Her voice rang out clear and beautiful over everyone else's, but what about me? Being a competitive spirit, I wanted to be in the concert badly. And my dream came true! A group of little girls got to sing a Christmas song. "Jolly old St. Nicholas lean your ear this way" was the first line. We practised every day after school, which I loved.

I heard all sorts of stories about Santa Claus, St. Nicholas, and Father Christmas, which confused me. Whoever he was, he was going to come down the chimney. I was afraid he might get stuck, and for sure he was going to get all black with soot.

One day after school I bounded into the basement and smelled something awful. The whole place was steamed up. As I bolted for the bathroom at the far end of the hallway, I glanced into the furnace room. Mickey was pouring scalding hot water over the carcass of a pig hanging upside down from a beam in the ceiling. Its belly was wide open and completely cleaned out. Later I found out that Mickey had slaughtered the first pig of the year. At Lockwood, Christmas dinner was always celebrated with fresh roast pork.

"Whass ya doin, Mickey?" I asked, a little shocked at the sight in front of me.

"I'm gettin yer Christmas dinner ready."

"Dat looks real bad." I watched as he scalded the skin and started shaving the hair off. It was one of those scenes I'll never forget. Because of Daddy's hunting and trapping, the sight of a dead animal wasn't new to me. After all, we were brought up around dead animals. I think it was the size of a whole pig that fascinated me.

Soon everywhere I looked I saw evidence of Christmas coming. Garlands fashioned from red and green construction paper, bells, and Santa faces trimmed the windows and walls. The dormitory looked pretty decorated with tinsel, bells, and streamers. And the big Christmas tree was so beautiful when it was strung with sparkling lights that it took my breath away. I worried constantly about being bad in case Santa decided not to bring me anything.

Then, early one morning, a girl shouted upon awakening, "Tis de day! Tis Christmas Eve!"

The day dragged on and on. I wanted to hang my stocking, and every moment seemed like an eternity. "Wass de time, Marcie?" I nagged my sister. "Is it time yet?"

"No, Josie, ya gotta be patient. We gotta wait till after supper."

I was so excited I could barely eat my supper.

At last it was time to hang our stockings. I sat in the corner and carefully printed my name on mine: JOSIE CURL. Once the stockings were neatly hung, we were given a treat of hot chocolate along with Christmas cookies decorated with red and green icing. Then we sang Christmas carols, which made me very happy.

"If you're a good girl for the rest of the night and go to sleep early, Santa might bring you something special," Mrs. Forsyth whispered to me as she tucked me in.

"What, miss?"

"Never mind right now. Keep your sheets dry and we'll see."

"Please, God, don't let me pee in me bed tonight," I prayed.

As I drifted off to sleep, I thought about my family at home and wondered if Santa would bring my brothers and sisters anything. I'd never received a toy before. All we ever had was something Daddy made for us. I'd always looked forward to Mommy's sweet bread, tarts, and fresh berry pies. Sometimes at Christmas, Mommy even made molasses candy. She'd boil down the molasses until it became stringy, add a little butter or lard or seal oil for flavour, then stretch it out and cut it into chunks to set. Once set, it was brittle and delicious. I tried to put thoughts of home out of my mind, though. Finally, I drifted off to sleep from sheer emotional exhaustion.

"Tis Christmas!" everyone shouted as we jumped out of bed the next morning. "Yahoo! Whoopee!"

I can still see that scene with 60 or 70 youngsters gleefully bouncing around with smiles and laughter. Many of them, like myself, were receiving their very first toy.

"Santa's comin!" someone cried as we cavorted.

I knew what Santa would look like, because we'd been drawing pictures of him all week. I couldn't take my eyes off the door. Then, suddenly, there he was in front of me! I was scared at first. He had a big sack stuffed with toys on his back. I was so excited! He started calling out names and handing out gifts wrapped in pretty paper.

"Ho, ho, ho! Merry Christmas, boys and girls. Were you all good boys and girls this year?"

Fear gripped me. That was it! I wasn't going to get anything.

"Ho, ho, ho, Hazel Williams!" he rumbled as he reached into his bag and pulled out a handsomely wrapped parcel. "Ho, ho, ho, Peggy Dyson! Ho, ho, ho, Winston Hopkins! Ho, ho, ho, Florence Turnbull!"

Name after name was called, and I was shaking with fear. However, after hearing Florence's name, I became more hopeful. After all, she was a bedwetter like me and she was getting a gift.

Finally, after what seemed like forever, Santa shouted, "Ho, ho, ho, Josie Curl!"

"Dat's me!" I squealed in delight. "T-tank ya, sir," I managed to sputter when Santa gave me the present. I walked back to my place and ripped off the paper. "A dolly! Look, miss! I gotta dolly! She's some pretty, hey?"

"Yes, Josie, she's beautiful," Mrs. Forsyth said. "Now you take good care of her, all right?"

"Oh, yeh, miss, I will," I promised.

I entered my own little world then, totally wrapped up in the doll. She had a porcelain face with sparkling blue eyes that closed when you put her down. Her dark curly hair was crowned with a lacy bonnet. She wore a gorgeous sky-blue dress with a white lace collar and a blue-and-white-striped apron trimmed with lace to match her bonnet. Over her shoulders was draped a splendid navy blue velvet cape. I couldn't stop gazing at her. She was prettiest thing I'd ever seen.

We had so much fun on Christmas Day as we played with our new toys. I also received a plastic Cupid doll and a tiny set of porcelain dishes, which I tucked carefully away in my locker upstairs. The roast pork dinner was unbelievably delicious. I have yet to experience roast pork like that first Christmas dinner at Lockwood. During Christmas week, I had a wonderful time playing with my dolly. But all too soon everything returned to normal.

Suffering from a cold one day, I was sent home from school. Feeling lonely in that big dormitory by myself, I decided to do some exploring. I sneaked into the sewing room across the hall and found my own clothes tied neatly in a bundle. I couldn't believe they were mine. They smelled exactly like home. As I cried out my heartbreak into that bundle, I tried desperately to remember what Mommy and Daddy looked like.

When I couldn't cry anymore, I went into the big girls' room. In their lockers I found perfume. It smelled wonderful. I'd never seen perfume before. The big girls had interesting things I'd never seen before — nylons, lacy underwear, sparkling jewellery, and boxes of Kotex. Back then the last thing really mystified me. What were they used for? I felt a tinge of guilt, but I was fascinated by this new environment. Amazingly, I didn't get caught.

Time passed slowly. On the night of my eighth birthday, January 15, 1951, Mrs. Forsyth decided to put me to bed on the hallway floor close to the head of the stairs, which led to the Forsythes' suite. I was scared to sleep on the floor, but this barbaric treatment was toughening me up. At last I fell asleep. When I awakened in the middle of the night, I saw in the darkness a terrifying creature leaning against the wall beside my head. I screamed, waking up the whole dormitory.

Mrs. Forsyth came racing upstairs. "Josie, Josie, what's the matter? What's wrong?"

"Dere, miss!" I pointed at the shape. "Dere's a monster over dere! See?"

"Oh, Josie, my little Josie! That's not a monster. It's a stuffed kitty for your birthday."

"Tis, miss? Fer me birtday?" I sobbed, shaking uncontrollably.

"Yes, I put it there so you'd see it first thing in the morning."

"Oh, miss! Tank ya, miss." I grabbed the kitten, not knowing whether to hug it or throw it away.

Mrs. Forsyth held me for a little while until I stopped shaking. It felt so good to be held. Then she brought me to my own bed in the little girls' room and settled the other girls back down. I'd caused quite a stir on my birthday night of terror!

The next celebration was Valentine's Day, which I'd never heard of.

"Whass a valentine?" I asked Marcie at recess. I didn't dare ask anyone else for fear of being called stupid.

"Tis a card we makes in school."

"How'd we make 'em?"

"Oh, Josie, ya'll see soon nough."

After recess in the common room, Mrs. Forsyth told us what we would be doing for Valentine's Day. "At Friday's art class we're going to make valentines for your favourite people, and we'll place them in here." She pointed at a large box covered in red tissue paper. "Then, on Valentine's Day, we'll have a wee party and they'll be given out to each of you."

"Who's I gonna make one fer, Marcie?" I asked my sister.

"Make one fer ya teacher or a friend. Don't ya have any friends?"

I didn't know what to say. I couldn't think of anyone to make a valentine for. I was worried, and I didn't know what to do, so I asked someone nearby. "How do ya make 'em, Gladys?"

"We jus draws big hearts an colours 'em red. Den we draws an arrow trough it. An lacy trim all round. Den ya draws flowers on em. See?"

On Friday we were given sheets of red construction paper and bits of ribbon and string to make our valentines in our classroom. I was thrilled, because I could use my own creativity. To my surprise, I discovered I was quite inventive. I made a valentine for my teacher and one for Mrs. Forsyth, who by this time was like a mother to me. I loved her very much. The teacher brought in the heart-shaped box with a big slot at the top to drop our valentines in.

"There," she said. "We'll have the draw on Valentine's Day in the common room."

On February 14 we were called to the common room, and Mrs. Forsyth started picking the valentines from the box. She read out the names in a clear voice. "Hazel Williams, Minnie Rose, Becky Dyson, Winston Hopkins, George Morris, Marcella Curl."

"Marcie, Marcie! Who's it from? Lemme see." This was the exciting part — finding out who had sent it.

"No, Jos, I'm not gonna show ya now," she said indignantly.

Finally, I heard my name. "Josie Curl."

"Da's me!" I shouted as I jumped from my seat. I was so happy to get a valentine, though now I don't recall who gave it to me.

There were times when we celebrated for no reason at all. I loved to hear someone play the piano. We'd sing our hearts out whenever we got the opportunity. I'll never forget the first movie I saw. It was a home movie of Mrs. Forsyth and her pet seal. They were on a smooth, sandy beach that stretched for miles. A baby seal followed along beside her, and Uncle Remus, her dog, frolicked about. She picked up the seal and carried it in her arms. The only seal I'd ever seen was a dead one — to be skinned, cut up, cooked, and eaten.

We also played games such as Musical Chairs, London Bridge, Farmer in the Dell, and many more. I was never bored, and we were kept busy all year. One of the most memorable events was when Mrs. Forsyth asked me to sing in the spring concert.

"All by myself, miss?"

"Yes, Josie, you can do it. Isn't that what you wanted?"

"Dunno, miss."

On the night of the concert I was extremely nervous. I was shaking so badly I could barely breathe, but I had to follow instructions.

"Now, Josie, go stand in the centre of the stage," Mrs. Forsyth said. "Ann will be right behind you playing the guitar, and when she says start, you start your song. Okay?"

"O-okay, miss," I quavered.

Even though I couldn't see the people in the audience, they seemed to fill the whole auditorium. As I stood on the stage behind the huge curtain, I heard them talking. I took a deep breath. "Jack was every inch a sailor," I sang to myself. "Four and twenty years a whaler, Jack was every inch a sailor. He was born upon de bright blue sea."

Then the curtain started to rise! As it lifted off the floor and I saw the heads of the audience, I froze. Ann began playing her guitar, then whispered, "Okay, Josie, start."

Suddenly, I couldn't remember the first word of the song!

"Start," Ann hissed.

I tried and tried, but I was speechless. Finally, right there on the stage, all by myself with all those people staring at me, I started to cry. They had no choice but to drop the curtain. I can't recall what happened next. I think everybody felt sorry for me.

"Josie, do ya remember when ya cried on de stage?" people asked me for years afterward.

At Easter there wasn't a lot of decorating as there had been at Christmas. Easter was more of a religious celebration. As the weather got warmer and the snow melted, it was a joy to be outdoors in the bright spring sunshine. I began hearing talk of the Easter egg hunt.

"Whass an egg hunt?" I asked one of the girls as we were playing on the see-saw.

"Tis when de Easter Bunny hides lotsa eggs all round de place and we gotta find 'em. An ya can keep all ya finds fer yaself."

"Oh, dat sounds like fun. When do we do dat?"

"Easter Sunday, an ya have ta move fast if ya wants ta get any!"

Good Friday was a sacred day during which we weren't allowed to do anything. "Don't pee outdoors, or ya'll be peein in God's face!" one of the girls yelled as we made our beds on Good Friday morning. I was gripped by fear for the rest of the day. I didn't want to pee in God's face, and I certainly didn't want to burn in hell forever.

Saturday was a warm, sunny day. It was so bright that I couldn't keep my eyes open. We were turning brown from the strong sunshine of a Labrador spring. The birds sang in the trees: *Chic-a-dee-dee. Chic-a-dee-dee.* My spirit soared.

Marcie, I, and some other students headed across the harbour to the store. As we crossed the ice, we sang songs: "The Bear Came over the Mountain," "Home on the Range," and "On Top of Old Smokey." When we arrived at the store, we were warned not to touch anything and to be good little boys and girls. It was a big place filled with interesting things. The delightful smells of apples and candy made my mouth water. I was mesmerized.

"Can I have some candies, Marcie?" I asked my sister.

"Have ya got any money?"

"Whass money?"

"Oh, Jos, yer some stun, maid! Money ... ya knows? Coppers!"

My heart sank, but at least Easter was coming.

On Easter Sunday we woke up early as the rooster crowed and we lined up for face washing, teeth brushing, breakfast eating, cleanup, and finally the egg hunt! I had no idea where the eggs had come from. But I had such fun searching for them that, for the moment, I didn't worry about who would find the most. All too soon it was over and everyone was counting their eggs to see who had gotten the most. I didn't do very well, but I knew better than to make a big fuss.

When the Easter holidays were over, it was time to return to school. The teachers pushed hard to get us through the last quarter of the school year. That meant keeping us around the big tables longer at night to study. The snow was melting quickly, and the ground around the dormitory and the school was drying out. It was time to retrieve the skipping ropes that had been tucked neatly away in our lockers since Christmas.

Spring brought new activities. For the little girls there were always competitions. Who were the best rope skippers? Who were the best rope jumpers? Hopscotch players? Jackstone players? Marble players? Even though I'd learned to do all those things and enjoyed them, I wanted to build a playhouse. I kept hearing the girls talking about building playhouses on the mud hill behind the dormitory. It soon became my favourite thing in the world. And it was my most personal competition.

The first thing you had to do was mark your spot. Painstakingly, I carved my place into the muddy hillside. Scrounging an orange crate from the cook, I ran to Fannie in the sewing room and begged her for a small piece of lace to decorate it. Now it was time to collect my tiny set of dishes that had been carefully tucked away in my locker since Christmas. The next thing I had to do was gather pieces of glass, tin cans, little boxes, or anything else I could use for my house. It was so much fun building that playhouse, and I spent all the time I could there. The idea was to see who could make the nicest one.

"Where'd ya get dat lace, Josie?" one of the girls asked me. "I bet ya stole it."

"No, I dint. Someone give it ta me." I didn't mention Fannie, not wanting to get her into trouble. I adored her.

The evenings got longer, and the weather became much nicer, but we still had to be inside at our regular time of 7:30 in the evening. That was agonizing for me. Once I was in my nightgown, I'd jump onto the windowsill and hang out the window. I'd scream, holler, and wave at the big children who were still outside roaming the grounds and having fun.

"Get down from that window and get to bed!" an aide yelled at me one time as she came barging into the dormitory.

"Okay, miss."

"If I catch you up there again, you'll be in big trouble!"

"Sorry, miss," I mumbled, returning to bed and feeling sad.

But spring fever was so strong and the need to be outside so great that as soon as the aide was gone, I hopped back up on the windowsill again. *I'll be a big girl soon,* I thought. *Then I'll be able to stay out longer.*

The sunset was magnificent from that window as it splashed the sky behind the distant hills and reflected across the water into our bedroom window. The sky was brilliantly lit with reds, pinks, and oranges. With the lights out, tears flowed freely into my pillow. "Please, God, don't let me pee in my bed tonight," I prayed.

At Lockwood we always seemed to be competing. The boys competed with one another when they played football outside. At school we had competitions for indoor and outdoor games, competitions for reading, chores, athletic abilities, and even a competition for who could keep their cod liver oil down. Schoolwork was competitive for me, as well. I worked hard to acquire those gold stars.

I was now reading well and enjoying it immensely. And though we had a shortage of books, I always managed to find something to read. I had a few comics in my possession. *Little Lulu*, *Archie*, and *Bugs Bunny* were my favourites. When I was buried in a comic or a book, I didn't have to compete with anyone or anything, didn't have to be homesick, and didn't have to feel like the smallest child at Lockwood.

Despite the torture I received for wetting the bed, the dunce cap in school, and the constant teasing from other children, I was beginning to enjoy life at Lockwood. One sunny day in early spring, Mrs. Forsyth came out during supper and told us we were going on an excursion.

"Whass a cursion?" I asked a girl sitting next to me.

"Dunno, maid."

"Whass a cursion?" I asked another girl.

"Tis jus a fancy name fer a long walk."

"Long walk?"

"Yeh, we get up early, get our chores done, pack a picnic, an walk round in de woods all day."

I didn't know what to expect, but I was excited, anyway, because I loved being in the woods.

On the day of the excursion the bell rang at seven o'clock as usual. Everyone got up, made their beds, and trundled into the bathrooms to wash. We hurried through breakfast. Then we did our chores, which were posted on the bulletin board and had to be done every Saturday. We scrubbed the floors, cleaned all the windows on the front porch, and scoured the stairways, our lockers, and the bathrooms. There was much hustling and bustling until finally we were all lined up and ready to go. Everyone had to go on the excursion. That was the rule.

We strolled along the path beside the hospital and into the forest, following the trail toward the dam. A storm had left so much snow on the boughs of the evergreens that they looked as if they were straddled by miniature white mountains. We sang all our favourite songs as we walked.

"She'll be comin round the mountain when she comes!" I belted. The sweet aroma of the spruces filled my nostrils, and the birds trilled as if trying to compete with our tunes. The trail was narrow, and as we delved deeper into the woods in knee-deep snow, we had to walk single file.

"Listen," Mrs. Forsyth whispered, stopping suddenly.

"*Sssh!*" a teacher hissed. "Be quiet! *Sssh!*"

The command came down the line to the end. Everyone halted, and then we heard the roar of water rushing over a dam. It got louder and louder. Soon the noise was like thunder, and then there it was!

The deep gorge was blanketed with heaps of pristine white snow. The river leading to the dam was a ribbon of black ink threading through ivory linen as it wound through the evergreen forest. A wide band of concrete spanned the river, and water cascaded over the top in a fast, even flow. In the distance the river disappeared into the forest. A little cottage was nestled in the trees.

The bigger children started across the dam with great caution, because even though there wasn't much water flowing over the barrier, the current was extremely strong. I followed them. When I got halfway across and felt the water pulling my feet out from under me, horror set in. I screamed for help.

One of the bigger boys hustled over to rescue me. "Don't lift yer feet too high. Shuffle 'em long an take small steps."

"Okay, but I'm scared. I don't wanna fall down dere. I'd die fer sure."

"Not if ya listen ta me, Josie. Don't move and do what yer told. Now hold tight ta my hand an don't look over de dam! Shuffle yer feet. Don't lift 'em."

Slowly but surely, we edged back. When we were on land, Marcie was angry. "Ya jus had ta go, dint ya? Tis too bad ya dint fall off an drown!"

"Don't bawl at me, Marcie," I snivelled. "I dint know de water was gonna be so strong."

But Marcie was still angry. "Tis a wonder yer not dead long ago!"

Even so we had a lot of fun on that excursion. I enjoyed the boil-up in the woods, and the smell of smoke billowing around us as it wafted through the trees into the clear sky. I felt warm and safe inside the fellowship of the group as we frolicked in the forest. With the waterfall as our orchestra and the birds our harmony, our songs echoed through the frosty air.

It was heaven. What could be better? No worries of peeing in my overalls or of being locked outside in the cold, no worries about punishment for wrongdoing. After dinner we sang more songs. By that time it was well into the afternoon, so we started back toward the dormitory. It had been an unforgettable day.

By early May, the snow was almost gone. Mrs. Forsyth announced during the supper hour that we would be going to Burdett's Brook on another excursion — this time a hike to a plane crash. I'd heard about the plane crash often enough, but I had no idea where or what it was.

"Weers Bird's Brook?" I asked Marcie later.

"Oh, Josie, tis not Bird's Brook! Tis Burdett's Brook, an I cant explain it to ya cuz ya wont understan. Jus try ta be patient an wait till Saturday comes. Okay?"

The week dragged by until finally the day of the hike arrived.

"Tis goin to be a nice day for a cursion," I piped up.

"Tis not a cursion," Marcie said. "Tis ex-cursion, dummy."

At last the promised Saturday morning came. *Cock-a-doodle-doo* crowed the rooster. *Ding-a-ling-a-ling* chimed the bell. The dormitory came alive again. The routine of breakfast, cleanup, and chores were soon behind us, and we got ready to go to Burdett's Brook. This time we took a different direction. We walked to the landwash, which brought back memories of roaming the rocky shore of Spotted Island freely. The smell of the landwash was a heavenly scent to my nostrils.

"Wass dat, Marcie?" I asked, pointing at a huge hulk in the distance.

"Tis de plane. It crashed in de war."

"A plane crash? De war?" This was exciting!

My curiosity was getting the better of me. How did it get here? Where did it come from? I'd never seen a plane before. It was huge. There was enough room to walk around inside. It was covered all over with scratches. On closer inspection I saw names.

"Josie, ya can scratch yer name on it, too, if ya wants ta," Marcie said.

"Can I, Marcie? Where'll I put it?"

"I scratched me name dere last year, see?" she said. "Wanna put yers nexta mine?"

"Yeh, I can scratch mine nex ta yers an it'll be dere ferever, hey?" Suddenly, I felt important.

I searched for a sharp object to scratch my name on the fuselage of the dilapidated wreck. JOSIE CURL, 1951, though barely readable, looked quite permanent to me.

We wandered around the beach for a while, but all too soon it was time to head back. Of course, we had another singsong. Several of the children talked about school ending soon, while others spoke about going home in a few weeks. As we trudged toward the dormitory, I thought of my name proudly scratched on the plane. It would be there forever!

Spring also brought May 24 celebrations. "De twenty-fourta May is de queen's birtday. If we don't get a holiday, we'll all run away," we sang as Victoria Day approached. It was the day of the races. It was Sports Day. And we were competing against St. Peter's School across the harbour. The competition would be fierce. The students at St. Peter's were bigger because they went up to grade eleven, while at Lockwood we only went as high as grade eight. There was immense rivalry between the two schools.

Sports Day was always held on the Lockwood School grounds. There were large green fields and all the facilities, equipment, and space needed to host the events. A few weeks before the big day we started practising. High-jump poles appeared, and broad-jump areas were created. There was a track for all the races: sack, potato, and three-legged. We also had a competition in the gym upstairs in the school.

I hadn't yet experienced a Sports Day, so I really didn't know what to expect. Being the smallest child at Lockwood, I tried hard to measure up during practices. Against everyone's advice, I decided to try the high jump. I loved it! I ran with all my strength and jumped with every fibre I had. I worked as hard as I possibly could and made the team!

"How much longer before Sports Day, Marcie?" I asked my sister for the hundredth time.

"Oh, Josie, will ya stop askin me dat!"

"Awright, Marcie, I won ask ya no more. I jus hope de weather's civil."

At last the day arrived.

"De twenty-fourta May is de queen's birtday. An if we don't get a holiday, we'll all run away," we chanted over and over as we ran around the grounds. Some pupils sang the Lockwood song as they skipped about in anticipation of the day's events:

> In Sandwich Bay there's a little fishing town,
> With its great wide harbour where the hills roll down.
> With a hock-hock-hedder-ho, look, boys, a big black crow.
> Sing a song for Lockwood, oh — our Lockwood School.
> By the harbour there's a school, and Lockwood is its name.
> It's the pride of the bay and great is its fame.
> With a hock-hock-hedder-ho, look, boys, a big black crow.
> Sing a song for Lockwood, oh — our Lockwood School
> Tis the finest school of the long Labrador.
> Let this song go rolling down its rock-bound shore,
> With a hock-hock-hedder-ho, look, boys, a big black crow.
> Sing a song for Lockwood, oh — our Lockwood School.

When Sports Day arrived, the weather was ideal — sunny and warm with a slight breeze off the harbour to keep us cool and to blow the flies away. The St. Peter's students began arriving from across the harbour at nine o'clock. The first thing I noticed was their clothes. They all wore different colours and styles, unlike us in our school uniforms of overalls with collared blouses and shirts. The Hudson's Bay manager, Mr. Massie (who I think was the St. Peter's coordinator), accompanied the kids, along with their teachers and a lot of other people to watch us compete. The events were well organized, with each age group competing against its peers.

"All set?" Mrs. Forsyth asked. "On your mark, get set, *go!*"

I ran as fast as my little legs could carry me down the track, almost losing my balance. *Stay on yer feet, stay on yer feet,* I kept thinking. *Don't fall, don't fall.* I was out in front. There was nobody beside me. I pumped my legs with all my might. "Stay on yer feet," I muttered to myself. Then I was at the finish line — and I won! I was thrilled beyond imagining.

"The first-place ribbon for the road race goes to Josie Curl!" Mrs. Forsyth shouted over the crowd.

I was thrilled. The ribbon was so pretty and shiny, and when they pinned it on my chest, I paraded around the grounds, bragging, "I got one! I got a firs prize ribbon!"

"Oh, Josie, I'm some proud a ya," Marcie said.

No one had ever said that to me before. I was so moved by that simple but powerful statement that I cried.

The prizes I received that day overwhelmed me. I savoured every glorious moment. The races went on all day, and there was a lot of chatter as to who was accumulating the most points. There was some bickering about tripping and bickering about who should have won a certain race or event. But all in all, the day exemplified genuine sportsmanship and good behaviour. I don't recall any yelling or fighting. Even though St. Peter's was our enemy, we were all taught manners, rules, and the importance of good sportsmanship. At the end of the day a big table was set up with refreshments, and we celebrated together.

After Sports Day, the students cleaned up the grounds and life returned to normal. I remember the calls of the St. Peter's children returning across the harbour echoing across the water, and thinking,

Dey're goin home to dere mommies and daddies. I couldn't get that thought out of my mind and started to cry again. In a few minutes they would be home! Desperately, I tried to recall what my home looked like, what my parents looked like, and what my brothers and sisters looked like. It had been so long since I'd seen them.

The last weeks of my first year at Lockwood passed quickly. We followed the school routine to the letter, no exceptions, no staying out later in the evenings even though it was springtime. It seemed that the school rules were engraved in stone and couldn't be broken no matter what happened to the weather.

Then one day when we went upstairs Fannie was busy sewing the clothes we'd brought with us the previous fall. It was so good to see our own things again. We all wondered if they'd still fit us. Had we grown? But we weren't allowed to go into the sewing room or interfere with Fannie's work. It made me realize how close we were to going home to freedom — freedom to roam the hills, freedom to play with my siblings and friends, freedom to play with my puppy, freedom to eat Mommy's delicious food, freedom from cod liver oil!

The men were working on the mission boats, *Loon* and *Maravel*, which had to be cleaned, scraped, and painted every spring. They were the boats that would take us home.

"Can I help, Mickey?" I asked, circling around the boats, watching his every move.

"Awright, little Josie, ya can help fer a bit."

I loved helping grown-ups. I felt important when I was doing it.

Soon the *Loon* was ready to be launched. I went down to watch as the boat was eased into the water. It floated beautifully in its new coat of shiny white paint.

That night at supper it was announced that we were going across the harbour to the store, something I loved doing, especially by boat! "*Wowwee!*" I squealed. "A boat ride!"

"Oh, be quiet, Jos," one of the boys said. "Ya sounds like ya was never in a boat afore."

It was our first boat ride since our arrival at Lockwood the previous fall. I skipped down the road and onto the long wharf. We weren't allowed on the wharf at any time, so this was an adventure. I peered into the water and saw seaweed as well as a few sculpins and sticklebacks swimming about. We clambered aboard the *Loon* and pulled away from the wharf. Although it was only a half-mile to the store, it seemed like a long way to me. When we tied up at the wharf on the other side, we were warned by Mrs. Forsyth, "Now, children, mind your manners. No wandering off. Stay together. And absolutely no stealing!"

I contemplated the consequences of stealing. When I walked into that store and smelled the candy and fruit, I had to fight an overwhelming urge not to take something. I remembered that Mrs. Forsyth has told me about property that wasn't mine. It was torture for all of us who had no money. Later, back at the dormitory, Mrs. Forsyth, who had bought candy for us, tossed the candies high into the air, and we had to scramble to get them. Since I was the smallest, I got pushed around mercilessly during a candy toss, but I still managed to grab some. I had learned a hard lesson about this activity months before.

As soon as we finished, the bigger boys always wanted to see your candy. "How many have ya got, Josie?" one of the boys asked slyly.

"I'm not tellin ya, cuz ya'll take 'em from me," I shot back.

I was a lot smarter now. Previously, I'd boasted about how many treats I'd gotten. Then I'd hold out my hand to display my luck. Swiftly, someone would bang my hand and send my candies flying into the air and onto the ground where they were snapped up by several older boys. So the trick was to keep sweets to myself — another valuable lesson learned!

With school just about finished, I yearned to go home more than ever to wander in the woods again. At Lockwood it was strictly forbidden to go anywhere alone. Sometimes I did venture onto the forest pathway when longing overcame me and I was unable to resist. On a number of occasions I'd risked being lost, or worse, being attacked by wild animals.

I hope we has nother cursion soon, I thought in exhaustion as I drifted off to sleep, thinking of the wild forest, the endless trees, and my tiny home in Roaches Brook.

16

Longing for Home

Even now, years later, it's difficult to recall what happened at the end of my first year at Lockwood. I remember the warm spring sun, the torture of going to bed in the long northern twilight, my joy when I heard we were going home for the summer. Just thinking of Mommy and Daddy and the summer we'd have on Spotted Island thrilled me. Soon my first year would be over. Soon I would be home!

It was the end of June 1951, and school exams were finishing up. I was high on the ladder, and even though I didn't make it to the top of the class as I'd planned, I'd accumulated enough stars to be satisfied. I worked extremely hard not to cheat or sneak a peek at someone else's answers. I was pleased with my reading ability, and I had begun to know that when I applied myself and concentrated on my studies I did well.

I found it hard to believe we were actually getting ready to go home. It was the last day of school, and I was so excited. Parents of children who lived closer to Lockwood were arriving to collect them. If a family didn't have a boat, the mission's vessels would take them home. There were teary goodbyes and people hugging one another. Calls of "See ya next year" and "I'll be back" echoed in the air. I watched children leaving with mounting excitement. Children from places farther south such as Spotted Island, Black Tickle, and Bateau had to wait for the *Kyle*.

"*Whoopee!*" I cried. "We's goin home real soon, hey, Marcie?"

My sister gazed at me strangely. "Yeh, Josie, we's goin home."

"I wonder how Sammy is," I said. "I wish he'd get some schoolin."

"Mom an Dad needs him ta help wit de wood an water an stuff."

I couldn't concentrate on anything. I didn't feel like being in my playhouse now that so many children were gone. There was nothing to do except wait.

At last the boat that would take us home rounded the headland and came into view. "De *Kyle*'s comin round de point!" several of the kids shouted.

"All of you can get dressed in your own clothes now," an aide said. Then she glanced at me. "Except you, Josie. You come with me."

"No, miss, I gotta get me clothes on! De *Kyle*'s comin!"

"Come with me for a few minutes," she insisted.

"But, miss, I gotta get me own clothes on!"

The aide practically dragged me into the staff quarters where Dr. and Mrs. Forsyth were waiting.

Mrs. Forsyth tried to soothe me. "Josie, calm down. You're getting all upset. We've written your mother, and she's given us permission to keep you here with us for the summer."

It took a few minutes for the words to sink in. What was she saying? I wasn't going home? I wouldn't see Mommy and Daddy? I was shocked. I couldn't be hearing that.

"No, no, no, miss! I gotta go home now! De *Kyle*'s here. I gotta go an get my own clothes on an go home wit Marcie!"

"Little Josie, you'll be all right here with us. You'll have fun. We'll take good care of you. Before you know it, the children will be back."

"But, miss, I gotta go now, see? De *Kyle*'s comin in de harbour! I gotta go home ta see my baby brother, Eddy, an my mommy an daddy, an my sister, Rhoda, an Sammy an —"

Dr. Forsyth tried to hold me tight, but I kicked and screamed at the top of my lungs. They tried to tell to me how much they cared for me. But I shut them out because what they were telling me was more than I could bear. They were keeping me for the summer. They meant what they were saying.

Slowly, ever so slowly, the message was sinking in. Somehow the Forsythes had made an agreement with my parents to keep me in the dormitory for the summer. No one had given any thought to what that would do to me. They hadn't even bothered to tell me until now. I was trapped in their plans.

"There are too many mouths to feed at home," Dr. Forsyth explained. "You'll be well taken care of here with us."

I didn't want to hear anything about mouths to feed. What did he mean? What was he talking about? "I wanna go home! I wanna go home!" I cried over and over again. "Please, miss, lemme go! Do Marcie know I'm not goin?"

"Yes, Marcie knows. We told her not to tell you for fear of upsetting you."

So that was why Marcie had had such a strange expression on her face. My own sister had known! How could she not tell me? I felt so betrayed and abandoned.

"Oh, come here, little Josie," Mrs. Forsyth said. "Don't cry. It's not all that bad."

Suddenly, I couldn't speak. I had nothing to say to her. I can't remember what happened after that moment. I don't recall seeing the children leave. I don't remember saying goodbye to my sister. I don't know if I went down to the dock or out to the *Kyle* with them or not. I simply can't recall any of it. I have blocked it out of my memory. I was devastated.

The loneliness I felt was deeper than any I'd ever experienced. Wave after wave of despair washed over me. I'd felt isolated and alienated many times at Lockwood when I was being punished and mistreated for bedwetting, stealing, or disobeying the rules, but I'd never felt anything like this. The blackness was indescribable.

The Forsythes moved me from the little girls' dormitory down to their living quarters. Although it was nice and cozy and fancier than anything I'd ever seen before, I wasn't happy there. I couldn't help but compare it to my little feather bed in the loft where I slept at home. The rubber sheet was still hard and cold, and I still woke up every night in a pool of urine. When I rolled over, I could hear the urine splash as if I were lying in a pond. I suffered immensely from this terrible affliction.

About two weeks later Dr. Forsyth decided to remove all of my baby teeth without telling me, of course. "You won't feel any pain, Josie," he assured me as he assembled his instruments.

When I woke up, my mouth was stuffed with cotton wads. I was swallowing blood, and the pain was excruciating. My whole mouth felt as if it were missing. Every single one of my teeth was gone. "Weers me teet, too? I mumbled, unable to talk properly.

"The doctor took them out," Mrs. Forsyth said. "He wants your new teeth to grow in nice and straight."

I didn't question the Forsythes after that. I never knew from one moment to the next what to expect. Nothing mattered. I was a non-person. I was their little Josie to play with for the summer, and my feelings, concerns, and happiness didn't matter.

At mealtime I was fed soft foods such as soups and ice cream. For the rest of the summer I ate soft foods. I loved ice cream, but I missed my teeth so much. I missed my sister. I missed my friends. I longed to see my family and Spotted Island. Almost every night I cried myself to sleep.

Eventually, I accepted my plight, and being naturally feisty, I just wanted to be outdoors. Since there was no one else, I began to play with Ann and Richard, Uncle Mickey's and Aunt Susie Bird's children. They lived at the bottom of the hill in a little house that I adored. It was a real home, and we played together for hours. Aunt Susie was always baking homemade bread that reminded me of my mother's.

I started following Uncle Mickey everywhere. He was very kind, patient, and understanding. His older son, Fred, was home for the summer. One day Fred was pulling me on the merry-go-round as fast as he could. The ride was constructed of a large steel pole with a big ring at the top from which hung six chains with two-tiered wooden handles to hold on to. As it spun faster and faster, I went higher and higher, trying desperately not to let go. Suddenly, my hands slipped, and I flew into the air, hitting the gravel with such force that the wind was knocked out of me. I was badly scraped, but luckily no bones were broken.

One morning I woke up to the smell of smoke. When I went outdoors, I saw that Uncle Mickey was setting the grounds around the dormitory on fire.

"Whass ya doin, Uncle Mickey? Yer gonna burn de whole place down."

He laughed. "It'll make de new grass grow better."

"What if ya catches de dorm on fire?"

"Den ya'll have no place ta live."

"Dey'd have ta send me home den, Mickey. Maybe ya should burn de whole place down."

I was standing too close to the fire, so I backed away and watched as Uncle Mickey kept lighting the dead grass, leaving charred, smouldering ground behind.

By mid-August my mouth was healing well and I was feeling a little better, so I skipped down the road to Aunt Susie's house. Without knocking I entered to find all the children sitting around the table, eating fresh-baked white bread, hot from the oven, with blueberry jam.

"Josie, want a piece?" Aunt Susie asked.

"Oh, yeh, miss."

"Ya don't have ta call me miss. Ya can call me ma'am 'stead."

"Yeh, ma'am, I'd love some," I said, pleased that I'd remembered my manners. Living with the Forsythes, I always had to remember my manners. Sit up straight. Don't put your arm on the table. Close your mouth when you chew. And every other manner that was ever invented.

"Awright den, sit der next ta little Harvey an I'll cut ya a slice," Aunt Susie said.

I had grown extremely fond of Aunt Susie and was happy that I had somewhere else to go besides the dormitory and into the clutches of Dr. and Mrs. Forsyth.

One late summer afternoon, as I was soaking a cookie in a glass of milk to soften it, Mrs. Forsyth called me into the kitchen. "Josie, please go out to the garden and cut me some nice fresh lettuce."

I knew what to do because I'd gone with her several times to gather vegetables from the garden. She handed me a large bowl and a huge knife. I bounded out the door and headed for the garden. It was fully enclosed inside a white picket fence on the right side of the school and reached to the edge of the trees. As I skipped along the road, I tripped and fell. I lay on the ground for a moment examining my scraped knee. Right in front of me was a large brown hose that wound its way into the garden. Without thinking I started cutting away at it. Suddenly — *swoosh!* I was swept off my feet with the tremendous force of water that burst from the hose. I was horrified. I would be punished for this for sure.

Running for the dormitory, I yelled, "Miss, miss, I done sometin bad. I done sometin real bad! I cut de hose an de water's squirtin ever'where!"

"Okay, Josie, settle down. What did you do?"

"Sorry, miss. I dint mean ta. I cut de water hose an water is goin all over de place!"

"Oh, little Josie, Mickey will fix the hose. Now don't worry your pretty little head."

I was confused. I'd done something really bad, and Mrs. Forsyth was saying it was okay? I didn't understand. She put a bandage on my scraped knee, and I raced back to Uncle Mickey.

The *Kyle* came and went every two weeks or so. Other than the normal delivery of freight for the store and the mail, nothing of importance happened. Then, one day in late August, Mrs. Forsyth invited me to go onboard. "Josie, the *Kyle* left Spotted Island this morning at six o'clock and will be here around noon. The little piglets and chickens will be onboard. Would you like to see them?"

"Oh, yeh, miss. Little piglets, hey? Dey must be some cute. Can I play wit 'em?"

Mrs. Forsyth wasn't sure. "Well, I don't know about playing, but you can hold them for a while. They're cute, but they wiggle and squirm, and with their sharp toenails they could hurt you."

"Oh, miss, I can handle a little pig. I play wit my puppies when I'm home."

Suddenly, I was sad thinking about my family on Spotted Island. If I was home, I'd be rollicking on the rocky hillside or clambering around the fishing stages. I might be sauntering along the landwash with the boat Sammy had made me, or I'd be sitting and listening to the surf crash against the rugged shore. Maybe I'd be hearing the dogs howl when the big bell rang at mealtimes, or be watching the boys play cricket behind our house. But for now, at least, I could hold piglets.

Mrs. Forsyth and I had a strange relationship. I loved her because to some degree she'd become my mother. She was the only person available to me in times of need. However, I did fear her. Although I don't recall Mrs. Forsyth ever hitting or beating me, I hated her constant nagging to be good. "Don't pee in your overalls. Don't be saucy. Mind your manners." I had no way of knowing at that time, of course, that she was negotiating with my parents to adopt me. I didn't know who I belonged to anymore. I didn't understand what was happening to me.

Slowly, it dawned on me that summer was almost over and the new school year would begin. I realized I wouldn't see my family for another whole year. I often cried at night, feeling misplaced and abandoned. Who was my mother? Where was my father? Where was home?

My permanent teeth were starting to grow in. However, they wouldn't be fully grown when the children returned in a few weeks. I knew the other kids would torment me for being toothless. Why did Dr. Forsyth have to take out all my teeth? Why did they have to pick me to be their plaything for the summer? Did they really love me?

The chicken coop and the pigpen were only a few yards from the dormitory, and each morning I went out and collected the eggs. I liked watching the chickens as they strutted around the pen. Every day Mickey slopped the hogs. It smelled terrible in the pigpen, but I loved the little piglets. They were adorable. I'd get in the pen and try to play with them whenever I got the chance. Then, as I got braver and they got bigger, I began riding on their backs.

"Can I feed the pigs, Uncle Mickey?" I asked one day as I joined him on his way to the pen.

"It can get mighty dangerous fer a little one such as ya."

"Naw, sir, I can do it. Dey don't bite, do dey?"

"Well, I don't know much bout dat. Dey never bit me, but dat's not ta say dey won bite ya. Depends on how ya treat 'em."

"I jus wants ta feed 'em. Can I, Uncle Mickey, please?"

"Oh, awright den. Here's de bucket. Jus dump it in de trough."

It sounded simple enough, but as soon as I entered the pen with the bucket and the pigs smelled the food, they came running. I panicked because I didn't want them to knock me into the muck.

"Uncle Mickey, Uncle Mickey, come quick! Der knockin me down!"

Uncle Mickey laughed. "Just drop the bucket and come out."

When he opened the pigpen door, I hurried out. As I turned to look back, I saw all the pigs trying to get their heads into the bucket and squealing because they couldn't get their food. "Boy, Uncle Mickey, dere some wild, hey?"

"Dey sure are, Josie, specially when dey're hungry. But I had ta let ya find out for yerself or ya'd pester me till I did."

Uncle Mickey seemed to understand me. Filled with adoration, I watched him work around the school and in the garden. Sometimes he let me ride in the mission truck. I tagged along with him as much as I dared. He never once yelled at me for being a pest or for getting in his way.

A few days later I spotted Uncle Mickey coming up the road in the truck with a load of paint. "Whass ya doin wid dat ol stuff, Uncle Mickey?"

"I'm gonna paint yer school."

"Thass a lot a paintin. Can I help?"

"Ya can help by stayin outta de way."

When Uncle Mickey used that tone of voice, I didn't question him. From a distance I watched him work. There was a lot of painting to do to freshen up the dormitory and the school for the coming school year. The other kids would be back in a week.

Whoopee! I thought. *De chilren is comin back real soon!*

Lockwood was suddenly alive with people getting it ready for the returning children. For now this was my home. I had to forget about Roaches Brook, Spotted Island, Mommy, Daddy, my sisters, and my brothers and try to be happy here. I was trapped in a situation I had no control over. To some degree, I'd grown to love Mrs. Forsyth as a mother, but I still felt misplaced. I'd lost my sense of home, of place, of belonging.

Did the Forsythes do the right thing keeping me in the summer? I don't think so. For me it was a trauma.

There's an indescribable ache to homesickness. It's aptly named, because you feel ill with longing. I lost the bond with my family. I still don't know them very well to this day, and I've always felt alienated from them. Recently, things are better and I feel closer to my family again, but it's taken 50 years.

17

The Children Return

A few days before the children came back I was dropping off to sleep after lights-out when an aide approached my bed and gently shook my arm. "Josie, Josie, I have something to tell you," she whispered.

"Whass de matter?" I asked, startled. What could be so urgent that she needed to wake me?

"I came to tell you that Mrs. Forsyth is gone."

"Whaddya mean she's gone? She can't be gone! She's me mommy! She can't leave me!"

"I'm so sorry, Josie, but they left for the United States this evening."

I didn't hear anything else the aide said. I just screamed and screamed. I went berserk and woke up everybody. It took several people to hold me down. It was such a shock. First my real mother had deserted me, and now this mommy had abandoned me, too. It was more than I could bear. Who was going to take care of me? There must be something terribly wrong with me.

"I wants ta go," I cried. "Can I go, too?"

"No, Josie, they've already gone," the aide said, rocking me and trying to silence my sobs.

I wept for hours. I'd never felt so abandoned, rejected, and alone before. Mrs. Forsyth had been good to me. "I thought she loved me," I wailed.

A few days later, when I thought things couldn't get any worse, I found out that Mrs. Forsyth had chosen another little girl to take with her. That made me crazy all over again.

Shortly afterward, I learned that Gladys, the kid who had explained valentines to me, had been chosen by the Forsythes. Gladys was now their new little girl, and I wasn't. Oh, how I hated Gladys. I didn't know at the time that I'd been the first choice, that Mrs. Forsyth had tried to adopt me, but Mommy wouldn't let me go.

At that point I retreated deeper into a shell. I didn't want to participate in anything and didn't care who tormented or teased me anymore. Even the prospect of the returning children failed to cheer me up.

A couple of days later our new house parents, Mr. and Mrs. Hank Shouse, arrived. She seemed to be a gentle person, but I was quickly intimidated by Mr. Shouse, who stood tall and straight in front of us that first day. He scared me.

The dormitory came alive with activity. And even though I was depressed, I still got caught up in the excitement. When I went down to the harbour to watch the schooner unload children, I shook my head in disbelief. There was Sarah, my little sister! Marcie was back, too. Although I was happy to see them, I was torn with jealousy at the thought of their summer with Mommy and Daddy on Spotted Island. We hugged and cried as we clung to one another. Sarah seemed scared and a little confused as she tried to recognize me. I marvelled at the thought of having my little sister at Lockwood.

The children were returning by many different methods of transportation. Schooners and small motorboats loaded with children of all sizes pulled up to the wharf, and the dormitory was soon crammed to capacity. I cringed when the little ones were stripped of their clothing and then deloused. Some of the new children were crying already, and my heart ached for them. When I saw the terror on their faces, I knew what they were feeling and understood the comments they made about how big the dormitory was and how huge the school was. Little eyes and mouths popped open at the sight of the colossal bathtub with the dragon feet. They were in awe of everything, just as I'd been.

I was dreading the teasing I knew would come as soon as my enemies found out I'd stayed on with Dr. and Mrs. Forsyth for the summer. They would also torment me about my teeth, which were barely showing through my gums. And I was right. As soon as the returning kids settled in, the mockery started.

"Jos tinks she's big now. Too good fer us. Too good ta talk ta even."

"No, I'm not! I din't ask ta stay here all summer! Miss jus kept me here!"

"Whass happened ta yar teet? Someone smack ya in de mouth or what?"

"No! De doctor took 'em out and twas some sore, too!" I said, trying to gain sympathy.

We weren't allowed into the big girls' room, but I desperately wanted to find Marcie and tell her how sad I was. However, all the courage I'd gained during the summer to be myself was gone. Now I was feeling alone and afraid once more. I wanted my mother, and the more I thought of not seeing my family for another whole year, the more such thoughts overwhelmed me.

I meandered down the wide staircase to the main floor, along the hallway, down the darkened basement stairs, and into the furnace room. Creeping behind the furnace, I started to sob. "Why, oh, why do dey have ta be so mean ta me? What'd I do ta get dis? I wan my mommy an daddy." My tears flowed freely for a while, then I wiped them away with my shirt sleeve and went to find my sister.

"Whass de matter wit ya, Josie?" Marcie asked suspiciously when I finally found her.

"I wanna go home!" I cried.

"Oh, Josie, it won be dat bad. Anyway, tings isn't so good back home. De fishin was bad dis year and der's not much food. At least here ya gotta warm bed an lots ta eat."

Warm bed? I thought. All I could think of was cold pee.

As the children continued to arrive and the dormitory filled up, I was right there to tell the new ones what to do and what not to do.

I was an old hand at dormitory living by this time, and it made me feel good to help them. It gave me purpose. I felt such compassion for the little ones that were arriving for the first time. I could hear them sobbing at night from the terrible loneliness and homesickness, something I could relate to.

After everyone arrived, the humiliating ordeal of delousing began. Each child was assigned a bed, a locker, a toothbrush, a face cloth, and mission clothing. Rubber boots and jackets were handed out, as well. Then everything had to be labelled. All our basic needs were provided. We were herded like cattle for wash-up, hand inspection, ear inspection, and meals. The absolute worst thing that we had to line up for on a daily basis was to take cod liver oil. We all hated it so much, and it often made us sick to our stomachs.

The rules and regulations that governed Lockwood didn't change when the house mothers changed. They were handed down from Dr. Grenfell and had to be followed to the letter. So everything was just as before. Every Saturday morning was chore day. A list was displayed on the bulletin board to tell us what to do. Then the children were paired up for the chores. A big girl worked with a little girl to sweep, dust, and scrub the floors. We were even assigned our own floor cloth and were responsible for keeping it clean. The bigger girls made the bread and mixed the klim (milk powder) at night. We helped out in the kitchen by peeling potatoes and carrots. The big boys were responsible for getting the wood and starting the fire in the school every morning. Some of them had rabbit snares set in the woods and got up early to check them. Fresh rabbit was always welcome at the supper table.

I'd become quite fond of Rachel, the cook, and tried to manipulate her by offers of help. My plan, of course, was to get my hands on the dried apples and apricots in the storeroom downstairs.

"Out de kitchen ... out de kitchen!" she yelled in her Inuit accent, pointing at the doorway.

"But, Rachel ... I jus wanna help ya peel potatoes," I wheedled.

"Not taday, Josie. Sides yer too slow."

"Can I get sometin from de storeroom den?" I asked, knowing how she hated going up and down those stairs due to her arthritis.

"Okay, den," she said reluctantly. "But don't steal anytin or ya be in big, big trouble."

I went down to the storeroom and got the few things she needed to make supper, cramming as much dried fruit into my mouth as I could and chewing it as fast as I could. I didn't dare put anything in my pocket for fear that Rachel would search me.

"Whass ya doin down der sa long fer, maid?" she shouted from the kitchen door.

"I'm comin now, Rachel. I couldn't fin de peas," I lied.

I had learned to read quite well by then and read everything I could get my hands on. I read stories about other people's lives. I fantasized about my escape into their world. I seemed to bounce back and forth between periods of joy and wonderment when I could be a little girl and an angry fist-flinging tyrant when I was pushed into a corner. My sense of adventure and competitiveness was strong, and that was where I excelled. But I got into a lot of fights and was sent up to bed many times. Other times I was made to stand in the corner or ordered to write out lines and lines of rules either in my scribbler or on the classroom blackboard in front of everybody. I was humiliated so many times that it probably seemed as if I was addicted to attention. But then maybe bad attention was better than no attention.

As soon as the children were settled in, the routine of school started all over again. *Cock-a-doodle-doo* cried the rooster in the henhouse every morning. *Ding-a-ling-a-ling* sounded the bell. Once more I climbed out of my pool of urine and proceeded to line up for the washroom.

"Pooh, Jos!" one of the girls taunted. "Ya stinks!"

"Yeh, she tinks she's big too cuz she stayed wit Miss all summer," another girl said.

"Yeh and she tinks she's better den us, too," the first girl said. "Don't ya, Jos?"

"No, I don't!" I cried. "Leave me alone!"

"Les see yer lovely teet," the second girl said, moving closer. "Ya haven't got much ta brush, have ya?"

Then they laughed, and I cried inside, not wanting them to see my tears.

As I pulled on my overalls and fastened my buckles, I thought of what I was going to do to those two girls once we got outdoors. We lined up for inspection before we were allowed down for breakfast. The porridge was stringy again. The klim was too lumpy, and the toast was cold and hard from sitting too long in the oven. I watched the new children gagging, so I decided to share my experience with them. I'd learned to just spoon the food and swallow really fast without tasting it. Anything was better than being sent to bed.

"Ya gotta eat it," I whispered to the girl sitting next to me.

"It tastes real bad," she whimpered. "I can't eat it."

"Do like this. Look. Jus swallow real fas, an ya won even taste it."

The little girl gulped the gruel down quickly, but still gagged a little.

"Dass good. Ya learn fast. In dis place you gotta do what dey say an you gotta listen, too. Ya learn real quick if ya do sometin ya not s'posed ta."

The school and dorm were now in operation, and I was trying to stay out of trouble. I remember how much I hated arithmetic problems, though. One day I couldn't figure how to do a particularly hard one, so I started pinching the back of my neck out of frustration. I pinched it for a long time, and even though it hurt terribly, I didn't care. How long could I stand the pain? I wondered.

Many times during that winter I felt sad, alone, and that nobody loved me. It was as if I were adrift and lost forever. One day as I was walking past the woodshed on my way to the playground, a group of boys huddled near the corner of the woodshed called out to me.

"Josie, come here. We got sometin ta show ya."

They called me Josie. That was different. They really seemed friendly. "Oh, yeh, whass it? I asked, not really believing they had anything. My curiosity got the better of me, though, and after a little more coaxing, I asked, "Where's it to?"

"In here," one of them said. "Come an look."

As I entered the semi-darkness of the huge woodshed, I noticed it smelled strongly of wood and wet sawdust. Wood was piled almost to the roof. For a few minutes, as my eyes adjusted, I took in my surroundings. Then, before I knew what was happening, I was grabbed and thrown to the ground.

I landed hard on the jagged junks of cut-up wood. Pain shot through my body. I fought like a tiger, but I couldn't stop them. Several boys, much bigger than I was, pinned my arms and legs. No matter how I struggled, they held me tight. The next thing I knew they were taking my overalls off!

I don't remember screaming. I don't remember crying. I just remember the terrible pain in my back from lying on the spiky pieces of wood. *What are they doing?* I wondered. Suddenly, several other boys lined up and unzipped their pants. Where had they come from? I figured they must have been hidden along the dark walls of the shed.

Then a boy grabbed me. I felt a stabbing deep inside as if something knife-like was ripping my insides. There was more excruciating pain as each boy seized and tossed me around like a rag doll, then forced himself into me, scraping and bruising my body, as I was thrust over the jagged wood. It happened so fast, and I was powerless to stop it. They were giggling and laughing and making fun of me.

I wiggled and squirmed but was unable to move as one after the other poked their thing into me. I didn't know what it was. I had no knowledge of sex. I didn't know about rape. I didn't even know what a penis was. I'd never seen a boy naked at that point in my life — until now. I was only nine years old.

"Poor little Josie," one of the boys taunted. "Not so big now, is ya?"

"Yeh, who's gonna save ya now, little Josie?" mocked another.

I was helpless and in shock. All the teasing I'd endured in the past was nothing compared to this savagery. The smirks on their faces will be etched in my mind forever. They were animals.

Finally, it was over, and they were gone. I couldn't move. I was in shock. It was as if I were glued to the spot. With my overalls still around my ankles, I lay there sobbing, my tears mingling with the damp, cold sawdust. I was numb and didn't know what to do.

After a long time, I sat up and tried to pull on my overalls. My legs were covered with blood, but I was shaking so badly it was difficult to clean myself. The school bell would ring at any moment. I knew what had happened was wrong and felt shame as never before. I couldn't face anyone, let alone tell someone.

Hours seemed to go by, but it was probably only a few minutes. Then the bell rang for school. How could I go? They would be able to tell what had happened to me. But I knew what would happen if I didn't get to school on time, so I slinked over to the classroom and slid into my seat, trying desperately to be invisible. I was sore and hurt inside. And there had been so much blood. I was terrified.

I can't recall much of the rest of that day except for the deadly fear I felt. The boys involved strutted around as if nothing had happened. They gave me smirks that tore into my very soul. I was trapped inside my own fear and shame. I felt dirty and degraded beyond description. Were they going to get away with this?

After several days, the teasing started. Some of the other kids said I was the "girlfriend" of one of the boys who attacked me. Taunts were made about a certain kiss or something happening. I recoiled from everyone and felt as though something were crawling inside me. I had no fight left. Like a whipped animal, I ran to hide, weep, and suffer in silence. I wasn't able to have any kind of conversation or join in any play activity.

Desperately, I tried to appear normal, though I certainly didn't feel that way. During the school day, I did my best to block the whole thing from my mind, but every night I had nightmares. I was losing touch with reality. Had it been a dream, after all? Had I imagined it? I hated those boys and wanted to kill them. But I couldn't talk about it because I knew no one would believe me. I was the invisible one, the piss-de-bed, the house mother's pet. Nobody wanted to be my friend.

Mrs. Shouse, the new house mother, was a kind and gentle soul. Although I wouldn't have dared to confide in her, she did provide me with a small way to save my sanity. Her daughter, Ann, was about my age, and we became friends. Sometimes I was allowed into the staff room to play with Ann.

As time passed, I got better at repressing the horror in the woodshed. Although I was very guarded, I slowly became once again the inquisitive, tenacious little Josie. I spent as much time as I could at Aunt Susie Bird's house and enjoyed the homey smells that drifted from her kitchen. The whiff of fresh bread, rabbit stew, and partridge soup reminded me of home.

During the Easter break when I was waiting for the snow to melt so I could start making my playhouse on the hillside, it happened again. Occasionally, the root cellar behind the dormitory was left unlocked and I would sneak in because it was warm and smelled of vegetables. I was near the door to the root cellar, enjoying the warm spring sunshine, when suddenly the boys from the last time grabbed me and forced me inside!

"Little Josie!" one of the boys jeered. "Sneakin round agin, is ya?"

"Yeh, poor, poor little Josie," taunted another. "Piss yer pants today?"

"No, I dint! An ya better get away from me, too."

"Yeh?" one of the bigger ones sniggered. "What if we don't? Ya gonna tell Miss, is ya?"

A lump of cold fear sat in my chest. Once again I was helpless to do anything to defend myself. They were just too big. It was the same horror all over again — the same taunting, the same grim jaws, the same curled lips, the same cruel pain and humiliation. I knew there must be something terribly wrong with me. There had to be, otherwise why were they doing this? Why did they hate me so? I had to quit fighting to stop the pain. Then I wasn't feeling anything. *It's nothing*, I said to myself. *It's nothing …*

As I lay there in the dark after they finished, I knew I wanted to die. I wasn't good enough to live. I was a bad, bad girl. Otherwise this wouldn't be happening to me. Slowly, I dragged myself out of the root cellar and headed to the bathroom to wash myself. There was no cloth or soap, but I scrubbed and scrubbed with my hands until I was raw. I cleaned away the blood, rinsed my panties, and hid in the furnace room to dry them. I felt so dirty and dead inside. Nothing mattered anymore. Did this happen to any of the other girls? I wondered.

"Why, oh, why couldn't Mrs. Forsyth take me with her?" I sobbed into my pillow night after night. I did love her, and she was the only mommy I'd had here. But she'd left me without even saying goodbye. She'd left me without having any idea how she'd contributed to the hell I was now living in.

That night, as I lay on my hard rubber sheet, I didn't even mind it. I felt safe and didn't ever want to leave the dormitory. I felt protected by the other children in the room. Finally, completely exhausted, I drifted off to sleep. In the nightmare I had that night I was falling off a high building into an endless black pit, into endless space, never reaching the bottom.

18

Learning to Cope

"Why're dose spots on yer legs, Josie?" Marcie asked one day when we were in the gym.

"Dunno, Marcie, but dey's not sore."

She reported the spots to Mrs. Shouse, and I was sent to the hospital behind the school. The next thing I knew I was stripped of my clothing and a nightgown big enough to fit Paul Bunyan was hauled over my head. I was ordered to bed — with a thick rubber sheet, of course.

"Josie, we're going to place this box over your legs and you can't remove it," the nurse said. "And you have to stay in your bed at all times and rest."

"But, miss, I'm not sick an I'm not tired. I don't wanna stay in dis ol bed."

"No, maybe you don't feel sick, but you still have to stay here. Doctor's orders."

There was an Inuit woman in the bed next to me, and even though she was older, we became friends. She had kind eyes and a tender manner, and when she smiled, she displayed strikingly white teeth. Her dark hair covered the whole pillow as she raised herself on an elbow and rested her head on a hand. She seemed pleased to have my company.

"Who is ya an whass wrong wit ya?" I asked her when I finally settled down.

"I am Emma Tulak, an I have tuberculosis." She pronounced every word carefully, even though she had a thick Inuit accent.

"Whass t-t-t … I can't even say dat."

"Dey call it TB for short. I don't rightly know what it is, but it takes a long time to get better."

"I hope I don't get dat ol stuff den," I said.

"Yes, cuz it will be awful hard on you. You have ta lie in bed all the time."

Emma Tulak laughed a lot despite her illness. I liked hearing her talk. Her pronunciation was beautiful to my ears, with the thick sounds of her people mingled with the grammar she had learned from the missionaries. It was good to have company. We coloured together and drew pictures and she told me stories.

"How long do it take ta get better?" I asked her.

"Months and months"

I stopped chattering. I didn't want to hear about months and months. I wanted to go outdoors now. The nurse's aide came into the ward with a big wooden box and placed it under the blankets to prevent them from touching my legs. It was impossible for me to lie still with my legs under a box.

When the backs of the hospital staff were turned, I soon discovered it was a fun place to hide and play. The nurses and aides couldn't keep me in bed, and I wouldn't listen to them at all. My classmates came and stood outside under my window. I couldn't resist climbing halfway out the window to talk to them, which frustrated my poor nurse to no end.

"Josie, get back to bed!" she yelled a dozen times a day. "What are we going to do with you? The more you get up the longer it will take you to get well!"

"But, miss, I'm not sick!" I cried. "I wanna go an play!"

"Well, you can't go! And if you don't listen, you won't ever get better!"

It was torture. It turned out that I did have TB, but it didn't seem to diminish my energy. I'd hide in the box and play peekaboo with everyone. It took a few months for the TB to heal, and it left a permanent scar on my lung that has given me trouble ever since. Today every time I get a chest X-ray I have to explain.

That same year, in the middle of winter, I came down with double pneumonia and was admitted to the hospital once again. Although I didn't know it then, I was extremely ill. However, as soon as I started feeling better, I snuck in to see Emma, who was still in the TB isolation ward. I had no idea that TB was contagious.

In the hospital there were books to read, and I read every one I found. I tried many of the adult books, magazines, and newspapers, and even glanced through the catalogues.

Finally, I was well enough to return to school. Even though I'd been give lessons in the hospital, I was lagging far behind in my schoolwork. It was necessary for me to work very hard to catch up, which was a challenge because I got tired quickly. As soon as an aide saw that I tired easily, I was slated for an extra dose of the dreaded cod liver oil.

"Miss, I don't wanna take dat ol stuff anymore," I protested. "It makes me sick!"

"Oh, Josie, it's not that bad. It'll make you well and strong."

"But, miss, I hates it!"

"Open up!" she ordered as I clamped my mouth shut.

"No, I'll get sick an throw up all over ya."

"Josie, open your mouth this minute, or you'll be in bed for a week!"

As soon as I opened my mouth and allowed the vile liquid to be poured down my throat, I began to gag. My stomach churned, and I raced to the closest sink. "I'm not takin dat ol stuff anymore I don't care what ya do ta me. An I don't care if I die. An ya can't make me take it, either!"

The winter passed quickly, and as soon as the weather got warmer, I wanted to be outdoors, especially after a major snowstorm. One day, after a storm that lasted two days, we were walking to school, but because the snow was so deep we had to practically crawl most of the way. In doing so, I noticed that a huge mound of snow had accumulated inside the hens' pen. I decided it would be fun to climb to the top and jump off.

Several others joined in. We scaled the wire fence to the top. I stood and marvelled at the huge mountain of soft snow. Then I jumped, never thinking for a moment that anything could happen to me. I sank way down — the length of my body! We were laughing and having such fun, enjoying the experience, when the bell rang for school. All the others wiggled free and headed to class, but I couldn't move. I was stuck! My oversized boots were jammed solid in the snow.

As loudly as I could, I called after the others to come back and help me, but they ignored me. They didn't want to be punished for being late for school to rescue me. After an exhausting struggle, and frantic at the consequences of being late, I finally broke free. But I was minus one boot! Terrified of being late, I hobbled on one foot and snuck into the back of the classroom just as everyone was sitting down. I slid into my seat, wishing the floor would open and swallow me up. Settling into my desk, I tried to hide my bootless foot behind me. But I was noticed.

"Josie, what trick are you trying to play this time?" the teacher demanded.

"Nuttin, miss."

She seemed bemused. "And where's your other boot?"

"Out der, miss. I … eh … I got stuck …"

"And where did we get stuck?"

"I jumped in de hens' pen, miss, an me boot got stuck in de snow."

Somebody giggled. Then another and another. Soon the whole class was laughing hard.

"Well, then I guess you'd better go back out and get it, hadn't you? And I'll send one of the bigger ones along to help you, but get back here as soon as you can. All right?"

"Sure ting, miss. I'll hurry. Tank ya, miss." I limped out of the room with the sounds of merry laughter ringing in my ears.

Because the door of the hens' pen had been barred shut since fall, there was no way to get in other than to jump from the top again. So we leaped into the deep snow once more. However, this time it was no fun. I was on a mission. I tried to pull my boot out, but it wouldn't budge. So we had to dig with our hands to clear away enough snow to free the boot. My foot was getting very cold by this time, because the snow was heavy and damp. However, I finally got my boot back and limped to the dorm for dry socks before returning to class. There was more laughing and snickering, but I ignored it and continued to my seat. The year before I might have started a fight, but now I didn't have it in me.

I tried to be normal with all my might, but it was hard. An exam was coming up, and I didn't want to go to school, so two of us devised a plan. We pretended we were sick and stayed in bed. Once the other children were gone, we jumped out of bed and had a wonderful pillow fight. At dinner an aide brought us some food, and by then we were feeling quite smug. We couldn't help thinking what a smart idea this had been as we played with our Jell-O and threw it at each other. The next thing we knew, the doctor and nurse were standing in the doorway.

"Well, well, well," said the doctor, "what have we here? You don't look sick, but I'll examine you just in case. We may have an epidemic on our hands, and we can't have that, can we?"

My partner in crime and I exchanged terrified glances. What had we done? How did he know?

The doctor checked our ears and eyes and peered down our throats. "Say *aaah*," he told us, then placed his ice-cold stethoscope on our chests. *Tap tap, tap, tap* went his fingers on our bodies.

"Nurse Diack, what do you think? Should we give them this needle now and keep them in for a week, or should we teach them a good lesson about honesty and the consequences of telling lies?"

I was very squeamish about needles, and this one was the biggest I'd ever seen. I didn't dare look at it. Instead I stared at the floor and held my breath for what seemed like forever, waiting for the nurse's answer.

"Well, Doctor, how sick are they?" the nurse asked. "Should we put them in the hospital?"

At that point the doctor and nurse couldn't contain themselves any longer and burst out laughing. But I knew better than to trust such laughter. The rules of the school were ironclad and had to be followed, so my friend and I knew there would be punishment. No amount of good humour would ever deflect the punishment that was prescribed. And sure enough, we were strapped. After that we were forced to stay in bed for the rest of the day without food or drink. Needless to say, I never tried that trick again.

In April of that year I came down with a second bout of pneumonia and was horribly sick. The doctor was puzzled as to why I had it so severely again. He said it was unusual for anyone to get pneumonia twice in such quick succession.

Somehow I managed to block out a little of the horror of those vile rapes so that I could live day to day without giving up. I became very wary of danger and never allowed myself to be in a situation where I could be victimized again. Sometimes I even felt good about myself once more and was able to accept my situation and experience a bit of joy like the pillow fight. I learned to move on from pain and live in the moment. What I didn't realize was how deep the scars were and how they would affect me years later.

My illnesses hadn't defeated me. The tuberculosis had been difficult. Having to lie in bed for several months without actually feeling sick was extremely hard. I learned from that experience the lesson of patience and discovered the value of friendship through Emma.

The bouts of pneumonia could have been caused from lying in pools of cold urine night after night. Being locked out in the cold weather for hours on end in wet clothing could have been a contributing factor, too. Whatever the illness, we were all cared for in the appropriate manner at Lockwood. Thank goodness there was a hospital and qualified medical staff on-site. Back home the TB wouldn't have been detected and I surely would have died from the pneumonia.

My little sister, Sarah, Sal as we called her, didn't like Lockwood from the beginning, yet I don't recall many dealings with her during that second year. I remember her being extremely shy as I had been in my first year. And I did try to help her whenever possible. Marcie was our protector, but she was older now and didn't always want to be burdened with two little sisters.

Being a reader, I constantly searched for new books that would take me away from the mundane life of dormitory living. Through books I escaped the restricted life of rules, punishments, and degradation while finding out things about the world outside Labrador. I had graduated from *Little Lulu* and *Bugs Bunny* comics to novels such as *Little Women* and *Huckleberry Finn*. I loved *Little Women*. The interactions of the girls reminded me so much of being home with my family that I cried while I read the book. Reading *Huckleberry Finn* and *Tom Sawyer* was sheer joy. I longed for the freedom of Huck Finn and fell in love with his courage and tenacity. I imagined being on the raft going down that great wide river, and enjoyed learning about his kindness and compassion for Jim. Their relationship gave me a feeling of great hope.

When I read *Tom Sawyer*, I related to his antics and attitude, especially his defiance of authority. I laughed out loud at his mischief and his ability to manipulate people. I daydreamed for hours about running away. I fantasized how I would live free, away from the embarrassment and punishment of my prison at Lockwood.

While rummaging through lockers one day, I found a comic called *Archie and Veronica*. It was about romance. My imagination was sparked as I read about school parties and proms. I loved Archie, and I wished I could be like Veronica.

"Whass a prom?" I asked Florence when I saw her soon after I found the comic.

"Never heard of it," she replied.

Later in my final year I encountered *True Story* magazines. I didn't know the meaning of some of the words, so I skipped them and still got the gist of the stories. I was in heaven when I had a new *True Story*. In them I read about people's feelings and relationships, but I couldn't comprehend their lifestyles. There were living rooms in every house. And everyone had bathrooms *inside* their homes. I wondered what a terrace was, or a patio. I couldn't comprehend things like nightclubs, cocktail parties, or happy hours. I didn't understand about travel, distance, or valet parking. Since I had never seen a car, I couldn't comprehend drive-in movies! Maybe some day I would go to a drive-in movie. It sounded like fun. I read about children taking the bus to school. What did a bus look like? I wondered.

"Whass a bus, Marcie?" I asked at the supper table one night.

"My, Jos, yer some stun, maid. A bus is like a big, big car only longer wit lots an lots a seats ta take people round in."

"Yeh, but why can't dey walk ta school like us?"

"Never mine, Jos," she snapped. "Ya'll learn someday."

The stories I read introduced me to a foreign world. I'd never heard the word *kids* before. We were always referred to as youngsters, children, or little ones. I also read about kids going to bed after dinner. That puzzled me. To me dinner was the midday meal. I didn't know about lunch. To me lunch might be a mug-up, not a midday meal. I couldn't believe that the kids had a bath every night. *Every night?* My mind couldn't comprehend people who partied and socialized, who bowled, curled, played tennis, or golfed. And I thought bridge playing had something to do with a bridge across a river, not a game of cards.

Then one day I found a western pocketbook and fell in love with the characters jumping out at me from the pages. The cowboys riding horseback and roaming the range were doing what I wanted to do. Although I'd never seen one, I was intrigued with horses. I didn't know anything about saddles, stables, bits, roping, or lassoing, but I knew what a harness was because we used them on our huskies. I didn't understand a lot of what I read, but I could relate to the outdoors, the freedom, and the wide-open spaces.

I yearned for the love and admiration of another human being. I could imagine galloping off into the sunset and camping under the stars. In the books the weather always seemed to be warm. I felt excitement as I became deeply involved in a gunfight or a romantic encounter. Then the bell would go and I'd be called back to reality — supper, homework, bed, inspection lineups … cod liver oil.

Once, while I was rummaging through the big girls' lockers, I found a Harlequin romance novel. This was a whole new experience for me. My body ached for the gentle touch of another human being, and I longed to hear a kind word of encouragement. Would I ever experience those intense feeling of love, I wondered, as I read page after page of romance? My eyes strained in the dim light filtering in from the hallway as I read of foreign lands and exotic people. The tall, dark, and handsome man capturing the small-town girl and transporting her to a world beyond her wildest dreams filled me with new desires. The long, lingering kiss, the gentle caress, was something I'd never experienced.

When I remembered that I hated boys, I always ended my day-dreaming. All they did was hurt me. But as long as I could live in the imaginary world of books, I had a way to cope with life.

I loved to sneak around the dorm and poke into secret places. I had my heart set on getting into the attic because it was always locked and had an air of secrecy. One day I found it unlocked and couldn't resist. I crept light-footed as a cat up the long wooden stairway and pushed open the door. A huge space yawned before me. I saw boxes and boxes of toys, books, clothing, and supplies. The attic seemed to stretch for miles. By this time, I knew better than to be caught in a secret place far from the eyes of supervising adults, so I tiptoed back downstairs and didn't go in.

Life at Lockwood was so predictable: breakfast, school, the morning crow of the rooster, collecting eggs from the henhouse, the terror of Halloween, Guy Fawkes Night, the slaughter of the first hog at Christmas, the Christmas concert, Valentine's Day, the Easter Egg Hunt, Sunday outings, early bedtimes, Sports Day … fights. It was so predictable and that made me restless. I wanted to bring my grades up in school so I could get another gold star, but I had difficulty concentrating. I couldn't sit for long without becoming agitated. I was a squirmy child and had little patience for sitting.

"Josie Curl, for the last time, turn around in your seat and get to work!"

"Yeh, miss. I will, miss."

"Do you want to stand in the corner again?"

"No, miss."

"Well, then, if you want to go upstairs to the gym with the rest of the class, you'd better get your work finished."

"Yeh, miss." I bent down to my work.

I hated the idea of missing physical education and loved going to the gym. I was still fascinated at how the apparatus descended from the ceiling. There was a trapeze and two big metal rings at the end of long ropes that were so high I had to be lifted up to them. Tumbling mats were laid out on the floor, and we played and wrestled until we were bruised black and blue. It was such fun.

Friday afternoon was art period, and drawing was one of my favourite things to do. I drew little sailboats floating in a sea of whitecaps with high hills on either side. I could imagine myself floating away in these boats. I also enjoyed drawing husky dog teams travelling to unknown places. Maybe they could carry me away to some unknown land. We had to draw the Union Jack often, and I enjoyed the challenge. The only thing I didn't like to draw were maps for geography class. So I often cheated and copied the map from one of my neighbours.

I was just trying to make it through every day. As time passed, I stopped worrying about my place on the ladder of success. The chart with the stars on the wall wasn't as important as it had been during my first year. I began to accept that I wasn't the smartest child in school. Therefore I didn't focus on doing well as much. School was just school. I responded to the bell, sat in class, and kept to myself most of the time.

As I think back to those days at Lockwood School, I recall the names of some of my classmates. But I don't think I made a real friend during that time, just acquaintances and companions. I liked Minnie Rose with her smiling face and sweet disposition. Peggy Dyson was a cute girl. I remember Jessie Dyson as a tough girl, and though I was afraid of her, I admired her, too. She was defiant like me, bigger than I was, and inspired my respect. Gladys Elson was quiet, as was Becky Dyson. They were attractive girls, and I felt inferior to them. I recall Rhoda Hopkins, Martha Davis, Gladys Morris, and of course Florence Turnbull, my fellow bedwetter. Then there was little Hazel Williams. I felt sorry for her, with her back so twisted she couldn't walk. She had an older sister named Martha. Some of my cousins were there — Olive Webber and her brother, Archibald. I can't remember much about the boys, maybe because of the terrible incidents in the woodshed and root cellar.

Strange things started to happen while I was in my second year at Lockwood. Loud blasts were heard from a distant hillside. Airplanes flew overhead, scaring us out of our wits. What was going on? we wondered. Something was invading our tightly knit, isolated community. I was fearful as I lay on my cold rubber sheet, hoping I wouldn't end up lying in a pool of cold urine again.

Odd things began happening to my body, as well. No one had ever talked about pubic hair or any other part of the body for that matter. My mind drifted to the beautiful women from my Harlequin romance novels as they roamed the fields of France or some other exotic land or snuggled in the arms of their lovers whose tall, dark, handsome male bodies were draped around theirs, hot blood surging through the women's veins as the men whispered words of love and encouragement. My body ached for a gentle touch like that. When I discovered self-fulfillment, all my worries were gone and only the pleasure of the moment existed. It was another getaway, another escape.

My parents, Tom and Flossie, in 1957, stand in front of their house in Cartwright.

Part Three

Return to Family

19

Getting Home

In the spring of 1952, while pestering Rachel in the kitchen one day, I asked to help peel potatoes, knowing she might need something from the storeroom and I could sneak a few dried apples or apricots.

"Oh, awright, Josie," she said surprisingly.

I climbed up onto the counter, with my legs swinging over the edge, and started peeling a huge mound of potatoes. While I was working, I glanced out the window and got the shock of my life. I thought I saw Sammy, my brother, in the yard filling up a water barrel from the outside tap. But it couldn't be. My family was in our winter cabin in Roaches Brook.

Jumping off the counter, I ran outside as fast as my short legs and oversized rubber boots could carry me. Sure enough, it was Sammy! I screamed with delight and hugged him.

"Ya don't have ta go slobberin all over me, maid," he grumbled, trying to hide his joy.

"Whass ya doin here? Where's Mommy? Where's me daddy?"

Sammy told me that Daddy had a job working at Black Head Hill building the road. Mommy and all the youngsters were up at someplace called Muddy Bay. Sammy went on to explain that since Muddy Bay was closer, he'd come to take Sal, Marcie, and me home for Easter.

All I heard was the word *home*. "H-home? I stammered, breathless. "I can go ta Roaches Brook wit ya?"

"No, Josie, we live up ta Muddy Bay now. Dad's workin outta de site."

I didn't know where Muddy Bay was. I didn't know about anything called the site, either. I was confused.

"Go get de girls," Sammy said suddenly. "We gotta get back fore dark."

I found Marcie and Sally in the dormitory, we collected a few things, and then we all raced out of the building. Sammy had delivered the water and was back to pick us up. As soon as we jumped onto the komatik, we were off across the snow, the dogs leaving a cloud of powder at their heels. When we approached the harbour, I noticed the ice was black in spots, which meant it was thin, something we all feared in the spring.

Sammy didn't hesitate, though. He told me later he thought he could make it. Out on the ice we flew, trying to avoid the black spots. But suddenly the runners of the komatik cut through, and we were falling through the ice!

"Get down!" Sammy screamed. "Lay out flat! Hang on tight!"

Frantically, Sammy cracked the whip as the dogs headed for the shore. I grabbed the rope and felt it burn into my fingers. But I knew if I let go I'd be lost forever in the dark water. Soaking wet, freezing, and terrified, we held fast with all our strength. The dogs instinctively knew we were in danger and did their job, running at full gallop inland to safety, literally dragging us, half hanging off the komatik, behind them. We had to go around the harbour then and travel for the rest of the trip huddled together to keep from freezing to death. It was the coldest trip of my entire life. Thank goodness it was only five miles.

When we arrived at our destination, I discovered that Muddy Bay was a tiny place with only two houses in the cove. Edward and Bessie Pardy lived in one, Henry and Violet Pardy lived in the other. Aunt Emma — our real aunt — lived farther out on the point.

Once I got warm, I was told we were living with Henry and Violet Pardy, who had a physically and mentally challenged adult daughter named Alvina. She drooled constantly, which left a large yellow stain on her dress. Her arms flailed about as if on springs, with long, bony fingers that crooked every which way. And though she scared me at first, I soon realized she was a harmless soul and a kind and caring person.

As soon as I could, I went outdoors to explore this new place. High hills covered in tall spruce, juniper, and birch trees surrounded the cove. The birds singing in the trees were music to my ears. What fascinated me most were the rabbits that ran through the thickets. I'd never seen live rabbits before. It was so exciting.

Memories of the few days I spent with my family over that short Easter break are vague. Although it was wonderful to see Mommy at first, I felt indifferent toward her. Sammy had grown up tall and strong. He even had his own dog team. Rhoda was still sickly, with terrible nosebleeds that seemed to last for hours. Brother Eddy was now three years old and very cute. Every time I looked at him I recalled when husky dogs in our porch at Spotted Island attacked him. The newest addition to our family, wee baby Winnie, was only fourteen months and simply adorable. However, after not seeing my family for almost two years, I was confused and felt like a stranger.

When everything was explained to me, I learned that Daddy had taken a job with the Americans who were building a radar site in Cartwright. And since Daddy was related to the sweet old lady who lived out on the point, we'd been brought here to Muddy Bay. Aunt Emma was a wonderful old soul, and I grew to love her quickly. I'd walk around the cove to visit at every opportunity. Then, on Good Friday, a most holy day, I saw my father limping home from the radar site.

"Daddy's home!" I cried, running into the house. "Whass ya doin, Daddy? What we doin here?"

"Gotta job," he said, hugging me.

"How'd ya get here?" I asked after he let me go.

"Walked, Jimmy."

He called me Jimmy! How wonderful it was to hear that name again. With tears streaming down my face, I clung to him. I marvelled at how he'd walked the five miles from Cartwright with a lame leg.

Only those small memories come back to me. I can't remember what we ate for Easter Sunday dinner or anything else about the feast. I felt disconnected, out of place. The sense of abandonment and the adult trickery of the previous summer had severed something precious in me. I wasn't at home here. Muddy Bay was just somewhere they were staying.

When my sisters and I got back to school, the rituals of spring unfolded as they did every year. The ground was bare enough to play hopscotch. Skipping ropes were grabbed from lockers. The playground came alive with field games.

Several of us were exploring the far reaches of the grounds one day when we came upon a wooden box, similar to a large square doghouse with a lid on top. It looked as though it were coming out of the ground. I tried the lid. It was big and heavy, but I had to see what was inside. So together we pried it off. The smell was foul. I leaned over the side, trying to see what was causing such a terrible stench, when I lost my balance and fell into the sewer. One of the girls tried to pull me out, but I was too slippery.

"I'm smotherin!" I screeched. "Hurry. De maggots is eatin me!"

Some of the bigger boys heard my screams and came to my rescue. By the time they pulled me out, I was choking. It was so horrible that I threw up my dinner from the stink of the sewage filling my eyes, ears, and mouth. Stumbling, I managed to get to the basement to shower the worst of it off with the hose Mickey used to wash the pigs. Then I soaked in the huge bathtub for a long time and scrubbed my skin raw. I had nightmares for days after that experience.

Since it was spring, it was time for Sports Day again. We practised every day after school. Everyone who saw me was surprised that someone as small as me could do the high jump. During the races, I ran myself right off my feet. Chanting to myself all the way, I made it to the finish line and fell to the ground, exhausted. Like the year before, I won.

The weather grew warmer and the evenings got longer. We spent the bright nights hanging out the windows as we did every spring, hollering at the bigger youngsters still out on the grounds. Suddenly, I noticed strangers walking toward the dorm. They were black! Was I seeing things? What kind of people were these? I had never seen a black person before. I jumped back from the window and pointed. I was speechless.

"Oh, my glory, der some black, hey?" Florence said.

"Where dey come from I wonder?" another girl asked.

Gladys, who knew everything, said, "Dey comin outta de site. Der comin ta visit somebody. They won hurt ya."

The dormitory was in an uproar, with every girl commenting about this amazing thing. Finally, Mrs. Shouse came up to explain. We didn't understand about the outside world. Our minds were filled with amazement. Questions tumbled out. What were they like? Where did they come from? How did they get like that?

"They were born that way," said the house mother. "Yes, they can speak English. No, they don't peel. Yes, they stay that way forever. Yes, they're real people like you and me, just a different colour."

At last the aides got us away from the window and settled us down. As time passed, we got to know the black men. They were nice people and occasionally gave us money, maybe only a few pennies or a nickel, but still money!

American military personnel were arriving in Cartwright by the dozens. Since Cartwright was so close, a lot of things started appearing in the dorm that we'd never seen before — games, puzzles, books, magazines, records, and candy. The most exciting thing of all was the movies. The Americans brought films for us to watch on Saturday afternoons!

Mrs. Shouse rounded us all up for the great event. "All right, boys and girls, go into the great room and sit quietly. We're going to watch a movie."

I was puzzled. "Movie, miss?"

"Yes, Josie. Just do as you're told and you'll soon see."

It was a western movie. All the worlds I'd dreamed of in my books seemed to flicker across that screen. I'd read about cowboys, and there they were right in front of me! Totally absorbed, I fell in love with Hopalong Cassidy that day.

The mission boat *Loon* was launched and ready to take us across the harbour to the store. I could hardly contain myself. I had a few pennies the Americans had given me, which meant I could buy something of my very own. I was elated as we marched, skipped, and ran down the hill onto the long wharf to the *Loon*. We clambered into the boat and off we went across the harbour. It was only a few minutes' ride, and soon we landed at the wharf where the men were getting ready for the busy fishing season ahead.

Men were hustling around the buildings, repairing, painting, and hammering. I sprinted up the wide boardwalk that led from the wharf all the way to the store. Inside people were shopping for oilskins and rubber boots, cod jiggers, oil and gasoline for their boats, and nets. There were jars and jars of candy lined up on the counter, and I made a beeline for the sweets.

"Got me own money, sir," I mumbled as I approached the counter.

"Have ya now?" the storekeeper said. "Well, well, well, where'd a little person like you get money?"

"Strange man give it ta me. Can I have a peppermint knob, please?"

The storekeeper handed me a tiny brown bag, and I scurried for the door, opening the bag as I went.

It was shortly after that trip that we started getting ready to go home. School was drawing to a close, and the teachers were busy administering tests. I found it difficult to concentrate because I was preoccupied with thoughts of finally going home.

"Josie!" the teacher yelled, bringing me back to reality. "What are you daydreaming about this time?"

"Nuttin, miss," I mumbled.

"I'm telling you for the last time, you have to finish those exams and hand them in if you want to pass grade three!"

My mind was too crowded with worry to care very much about my marks. All my desire to be at the top of the ladder seemed to have evaporated.

Certain things had to be done around Lockwood to close it up for the summer, but I couldn't stop worrying about my family. What was going to happen to us now? I thought about our old home on Spotted Island, and that made me sad.

The other children had only been away from their families for 10 months, but even though I'd had that brief visit at Easter, I'd actually been away from my family for two years. Deep down inside, I was terrified.

I couldn't forget what had happened a year ago. I couldn't forget how excited I'd been to go home and how crushed I was when Mrs. Forsyth told me I couldn't go. I couldn't forget my sense of betrayal and the knowledge that my feelings didn't matter to anyone. I couldn't forget that people had lied to me, planned things behind my back, and taken away all my rights. As a result of that deception, I didn't trust anyone.

This year no one had said anything to me about whether I was going or not. Finally, unable to hold back any longer, I decided to approach Mrs. Shouse and ask her straight out. Worried sick, I made my way to the staff quarters and knocked on the door. Barely able to breathe, I waited for what seemed like a long time, then suddenly Mrs. Shouse was there in front of me.

"Josie, little Josie, what can I do for you?" she asked, startled.

"Miss, am I going home, too?"

She laughed. "Yes, Josie, of course you can go home. Why would you think you weren't going home?"

I stared at her. Thoughts tumbled through my head. *Why are you laughing? Don't you know what happened to me last year? Don't you know my heart was broken?* But I said nothing, turned around, and bolted off to find my sister.

"I'm goin home, Marcie! I'm goin home wit ya!" I cried when I located her. Then I dashed to the sewing room and shouted, "Fannie, Fannie, where's me clothes to? I want me clothes. I'm goin home wit me sisters!"

I stood over Fannie's shoulder as she searched for the little bundle with my name on it. She seemed to take forever, so I pushed past her. "Right dere. Look," I said as I reached past her and pulled a bundle out. "Me own clothes!" I squealed with delight.

When I got the bundle back to my bed, I untied the knot holding it together. As the worn homemade garments tumbled onto the bed, I examined them, smelled them, and hugged them. Then I started to cry. I was filled with so many pent-up emotions. Would my clothes still fit? I wondered. After all, it had been two years.

I pulled on the flannelette underwear that Mommy had made for me all those months ago. They were snug, but I could get into them. Then I pulled on my little skirt and blouse. Lastly, I stuck my feet into my very own rubber boots. They fitted! They weren't two or three sizes too big anymore. I had grown into them, after all.

I left the room and wandered outside, looking at Lockwood's grounds and thinking about everything that had happened here. I thought of the good times with Mr. and Mrs. Forsyth. I still couldn't believe she'd left me without saying goodbye. I'd loved her so much. I thought of the bedwetting and the punishments, the teasing, the ridicule, the bad food and clothing. I thought about what I'd learned — my reading, the manners I'd been taught … and the rapes. Sagging to my knees, I sobbed. Would I miss this place? Would I miss Mr. and Mrs. Shouse? After all, they'd been kind and occasionally had even allowed me into the staff quarters to play with their daughter, Ann.

Throughout this time, reading had been my escape. I was particularly fond of *Black Beauty*, a book written from a horse's point of view. In this book the horse told the story of his life. It was so believable. The horse talked about his feelings, how the hard, cold bit felt in his mouth, like the bathtub I'd had to sleep in many times, like the floor in the hallway where my caretakers forced me to sleep.

Black Beauty explained how tight the harness felt on his body, something like the stiff overalls we had to wear. At Lockwood our overalls never fitted comfortably. The straps were too tight or too long, and I always had to pull them back over my shoulders. The horse talked about how he felt when passed from owner to owner — like me when Mommy sent me away, when Mrs. Forsyth abandoned me and broke my heart all over again. I had completely forgotten that I was the one who had begged Mommy to send me here in the first place.

In *Black Beauty* the horse told how he felt about the kind and caring owner who treated him well and how he felt happy and high-spirited then. After that he was sold to another owner who treated him cruelly. Black Beauty talked about his despair, his loneliness, and his hunger for days on end because the owner was too drunk to feed him. He spoke of his spirit being broken when he was confined to his stall, of the pain of being whipped and kicked endlessly for no apparent reason.

I'd come to the conclusion that the story of that horse paralleled my own life. His was a tale of being passed around like a piece of property, with no regard for his feelings. It seemed just like the school's systematic breaking of my spirit to comply with its rules without considering my feelings. I felt as if I'd been whipped into submission just as Black Beauty was.

Sitting on a swing on that last day and thinking about everything that had happened at Lockwood, I was startled when someone shouted, "Yer brother's here, Josie!"

"Goodie, I'm goin home now," I babbled, excitement overtaking my worries.

Homecoming would be bittersweet for me because I wasn't going back to the home that I loved. Even though I would finally be with my family, I felt that I hardly knew them anymore. To me home was Spotted Island and Roaches Brook. Home was those beloved islands where Daddy fished all summer and then moved us to our hunting and trapping grounds in the fall. My mind whirled with memories.

In the boat I emerged from my confusion long enough to notice the beauty all around me. As the vessel bounced through the choppy waters, I studied the jagged cliffs of the coastline crowned with green berry bushes and patches of stunted trees nestled in the crevices among the rocks. Tall, magnificent trees with tips like spears poked skyward in the shelter of the hills, away from the cutting winds of the North Atlantic. I squinted at the distant landscape garbed in shades of grey, green, and purple and felt my spirit soar as I took in the vibrant blue of the ocean that sparkled like diamonds. Then, looking out to sea, I drank in the luminous white of faraway icebergs. It was a sight that took my breath away.

Just as quickly, though, my mood darkened. We were bound for Muddy Bay. I couldn't imagine that we were going to live there and that I wasn't going home to Spotted Island. When we arrived, I clambered out of the boat, scrambled over the slippery rocks, and headed for Uncle Henry's house. I was sad, empty, and lost.

Would I ever see Spotted Island or Roaches Brook again?

20

Muddy Bay

In Muddy Bay we were back with Henry and Violet Pardy. To me they were strangers. Living with another family made it impossible to reconnect and bond with my own family. Not only had I lost my sense of place, I no longer had a feeling of belonging. At Lockwood I'd lost my sense of self.

My family's poverty seemed more obvious in Muddy Bay. The next-door neighbours, Edward and Bessie and their children, had a two-storey house. Two of their pretty daughters, Marie and Louise, had gone to Lockwood with us. When Edward, Bessie, and their kids came over to Henry and Violet's to greet us, I felt so humiliated. *What must they think?* I wondered. They had a home of their own, not like us, with nine people crammed into the house of complete strangers.

Although it was extremely kind of Henry, Violet, and Alvina to take us in, I didn't want their charity. I cried for hours, feeling lost and afraid of the future.

I took my things into a tiny bedroom where there were two sets of bunk beds and hung my dolly on the wall. She was like new because she'd been stored in my locker at Lockwood for almost two years. "Don't ya dare touch her, either," I warned my sisters.

"What if I do?" snapped Sal.

"Ya better not if ya knows whass good fer ya," I warned.

Mommy was busy trying to get us settled in. We were quick to learn that we had responsibilities, but I didn't want anything to do with work. I wanted to find the rabbits I'd seen running through the thickets. We had to fetch water, though, so off we went to the brook. I was proud of the tin can buckets with the string handles that Daddy had made for us. Once the paper on the cans was removed, our buckets were shiny and bright. Sammy chopped the wood, and the girls had to bring it into the house.

Not long after our arrival in Muddy Bay, my sisters and I went outside after a rainy evening to discover that wild mushrooms had sprouted overnight. I'd never seen anything like them. Aunt Bessie said they were good to eat, so Mommy told us to pick some.

"Don't pick de wormy ones," Aunt Bessie warned. "Dey gets full of worms real quick."

"I'm not pickin em if der full of worms den," I insisted. "I hates worms."

Mommy ordered us to go, anyway, but I cringed whenever I spied worms in a mushroom and dropped it as if it were a burning coal. However, most of the mushrooms were okay, and we soon had our tin cans full of them. Mommy fried them up for supper, but I didn't like them at first. Eventually, though, I acquired a taste for them. Strangely, we never ate that kind of mushroom again after we left Muddy Bay.

One day Marie and Louise took us to a special place — a huge concrete foundation about four feet high and wide enough to walk on.

"Whass dis place called?" I asked Louise.

"Twas de ol Muddy School. Burned down long time ago."

I was intrigued by the size of the foundation as we clambered on top and walked all around. "Twas some big, hey? Twas like Lockwood?"

"Yeh, twas," Marie said. "Lotsa kids wenta school here, an one of 'em burned in de fire."

I felt sorry for the child who got burned because I'd been burned badly once and knew how much it had hurt. I couldn't comprehend burning to death, though. That was too painful to think about.

Muddy Bay Public School was one of the first schools in Labrador. Reverend Henry Gordon and Dr. Harry Paddon, who had been on the Labrador coast for several years, saw the need for a boarding school. Reverend Gordon travelled to Great Britain and throughout Canada to raise the money necessary to start the school. It was built as a boarding school, but after the devastating flu of 1918, which left so many children homeless and without parents, Gordon decided to run it as an orphanage instead. Muddy Bay Public School officially opened in 1921 with 30 children and operated successfully until 1928 when a fire destroyed it. After Muddy Bay burned down, the International Grenfell Association established Lockwood, the new boarding school in Cartwright.

Those school ruins became one of our favourite places to play. We roamed the hills and swam in the brook — out of sight of Mommy, of course. She would never allow us to go swimming.

"Les go see Aunt Emma," Louise suggested one day.

We all agreed, and as we walked to the point, we noticed smoke.

"Whass all de smoke from?" I asked. I could see it billowing from a tiny hut near the water.

"'Tis a smokehouse," Louise said. "Aunt Emma's smokin salmon or trout or sometin."

"Oh, I tought de house was burnin down," I said.

So we walked around the cove to Aunt Emma's house. I fell in love with her all over again. She was so happy to see us. Aunt Emma was a short woman with wisps of hair cradling her round face. Soft brown eyes and high cheekbones complemented her warm, toothless smile. She gave us a piece of smoked salmon that was unbelievably delicious. As we strolled back around the cove, I thought that maybe this would be a good place to live, after all. We had family. We had playmates. We had freedom. And from Aunt Emma we got unconditional love.

Muddy Bay was infested with mosquitoes and blackflies. We were always covered in bites, and the agony was awful. Mommy got a spray gun from somewhere — I think Daddy brought it from the military site

— and every night after supper she told us to go outdoors, then sprayed the whole house with DDT. We had no idea then that it was a deadly chemical. It was the only thing available to us at the time, and Mommy thought she was doing us all a favour. I'll never forget trying to go to sleep with enough fumes in the house to choke us. It did get rid of the mosquitoes and blackflies, but at what cost we'll never know.

On Monday mornings huge pots of water were heated for the washing. Mommy showed me how to use the washboard and how to hold the garments to scrub collars, cuffs, the knees of overalls, and the feet of socks. Our knuckles were skinned raw from rubbing so hard on the washboard. Mommy taught me how to hang clothes on the clothesline properly and how to iron. I had to help her clean the house, too, including scrubbing the floor. She also taught me how to make bread and how to take care of my younger siblings. And I had to do everything right!

"Tis too hard, Mommy!" I cried frequently. "I don't wanna do all this!"

"Ya gotta do it, Josie," she said. "Ya gotta learn an das all der is to it!"

One morning I was sweeping off the bridge when I spotted a huge black-and-green-striped caterpillar covered in long fuzzy hair crawling along the step. I picked it up and placed it in the palm of my hand. After examining it for a while, I decided to show it to Mommy. To my horror she panicked and stumbled in her haste to get away. She had a look of terror on her face that I'll never forget.

"Get dat ting outta here, Jos, ya little blood-of-a-one!" she cried.

"Mommy, look at it. Tis some pretty." I'd never seen my mother like this. She was shaking. I couldn't believe that my tenacious, tough mother was actually afraid of a little caterpillar. I left the house with my fuzzy friend and decided to say no more about it.

One afternoon Sammy took me with him to hunt for partridges. I was overjoyed. We made our way through the woods, pushing aside the thick brush and blazing a trail as we went. Sammy was a fair piece ahead of me, so I didn't notice when he hid behind some trees. I glanced up suddenly, and he was gone. I called out to him, "Sammy! Sammy! Where is ya?"

There was no answer.

"Sammy!" I shouted louder this time, now a little frightened.

I looked around the deep wilderness with a sinking feeling. Then ... *whack!* A branch smacked right into my face!

Sammy had held it and let it go just for a joke. He didn't realize it would hit me in the face. It hurt a lot, and I began to cry, though I didn't want to. When I was with my brother, I wanted to be tough.

"Didden mean ta hit ya in de face, maid," he said.

"Dat's awright, Sammy. Ya didden mean ta hurt me, hey?"

Sammy was such a good brother. He had nicknames for all of us. He called Sarah "Ol Ding Derry," and Rhoda was "Little One." Despite having no schooling, he was smart, learned quickly, and was very responsible. Even though he was only fourteen and too young to work at a regular job, he was quite capable of taking care of us when Daddy was away working.

One day Sammy took me birding in the punt. We rowed to a tiny island and landed in a cove. When we reached our destination and laid our gear on the rocks, he told us, "We gotta build a blind."

"Whass a blind?" I asked.

"Oh, Josie, yer some stun, maid. Get some rocks an start pilin 'em up on top a each udder."

"Awright, Sammy, I can do dat," I said, eager to please him.

We finished making the blind and hid behind it. I soon realized it was also a good windbreak. The north wind off the Atlantic cut right through to the bone. It wasn't long before we heard a flock of ducks approaching. As they came closer, Sammy raised his gun. *Bang! Bang!* Two birds fell to the ground. I was ecstatic.

"Wow, Sammy, yer some good shot!" I cried.

"Lotsa practice," he said modestly. Sammy was a person of few words.

We waited a little while, then heard honking behind us. These birds were bigger than the first ones.

"Wha kind are dey?" I asked.

"Dey're geese," Sammy said. "Now keep still. An keep quiet."

He took aim. *Bang! Bang!* The noise was so loud. Several geese hit the ground so hard I thought it shook. We stayed for another hour or so, but he was aware that I was getting cold, so we got ready to leave. He tied the birds together and slung them over his gun barrel, just like Daddy did.

"Ya got lotsa birds, hey, Sammy?" I said, proud of my brother.

"Yeh, we'll have a good meal tomarra."

"Where'd ya learn ta shoot so good?"

"Been shootin since I's small," he said. "Practice is all."

"Daddy'll be proud a ya, hey, Sammy?"

"Spose he might. I tries hard ta please him."

"I'm proud a ya, too, Sammy," I gushed as he pushed the punt back into the water and lifted the oars into the cradles.

Since I was a tomboy, I wanted to do everything Sammy did and be just like him. Even at that young age he could do almost everything Daddy did. He handled a boat and dog team with great skill already, and that day I realized he was an excellent marksman, too.

As we rowed out of the cove, I was a little disappointed that we hadn't had our mug-up. Sammy was too busy shooting, and I was too cold. On the way home, while he was trying to jig a few codfish, I reached into the grub bag and pulled out a lassie bun. After jigging for a little while, we started toward home, satisfied that we had killed some birds and jigged enough fish to last for a few days. I glanced at the birds in the bottom of the boat and thought how delicious they would taste cooked Mommy's special way.

The move to Muddy Bay was a mystery to me at the time, but I have some fond memories despite my unsettled feelings. We chased rabbits through the forest, wandered the high hills, played on the old school foundation, and found new ways to have fun. We had to make the best of it. I'd grown quite fond of Aunt Emma and the others in the tiny community. It was extremely challenging living in such close quarters with people we hardly knew, but Violet and Henry Pardy and their daughter were very gracious and kind to us.

Still, I wanted to go home.

21

The Move to Cartwright

W hen Daddy got the job as a dynamite blaster at the military radar site in the spring of 1952, the life of my family changed forever. No longer would we experience the semi-nomadic existence that fishermen and trappers had lived for centuries, and that my aboriginal ancestors had known since the dawn of time. Never again would Daddy have to move his family twice a year from the fishing grounds each spring to our trapping home each fall.

This change represented a turning point for Labrador, too. Strangers were coming to our shores. We didn't know anything about a defence agreement between Canada and the United States. We were hardly aware of the Cold War. What we saw were strangers. What we heard was dynamite blasting. What our people realized was that there were new ways to make a living. Hunting and trapping had always carried with it the risk of starvation. Now my father saw the possibility of something a bit more secure for his family.

Daddy's new job took our family to Cartwright, which had been founded by George Cartwright in 1775. With the opening of the Hudson's Bay Company trading post in 1873, Cartwright had quickly become a bustling community. Located at the head of Sandwich Bay, the town is sheltered on three sides by hills that include Black Head Hill and Flag Staff Hill.

My father was one of many men hired to construct the road from the top of Black Head Hill down to the dock, to be forever known as High Road. It was part of the construction of a military base that in turn was part of the three lines of early-warning radar stations built across Canada in the 1950s during the Cold War. While working on the base, Daddy met Bill Hawe. Bill felt sorry that Daddy had to walk five miles to Muddy Bay and back every weekend with a bad leg and agreed to let our family move into the rear of his new home in Cartwright. The house, which was still under construction, was the second-last home along the harbour in a small sandy cove. Daddy and Bill erected a partition that split the house in half. Bill, his wife, Joyce, and their three children — Beatrice, Millicent, and Michael — lived in the front half, which would one day be their living room. Our family of nine crammed into the back half, which would one day be their kitchen and bedroom. There were no ceilings yet, so the Hawes' two little girls played peekaboo over the wall at us, which was very stressful for my mother.

I hated that family from the start, though I didn't know why, other than envy. Perhaps it was their appearance of being a perfect family. Bill Hawe was very tall, with one eye that looked as though the bottom lid was inside out, exposing the pink under lid. He seemed angry all the time. Joyce Hawe was a gentle soul of average height, nice-looking, with fair skin and soft blue eyes. I'd developed such an inferiority complex that I felt I couldn't play or even talk with the Hawes' children. They were so far above us, so much better than us. They dressed differently and had fancy spreads on their beds and lace on their dressers. They even talked differently than us. I didn't like the situation my family was in. Too many changes in too short a period left me afraid, confused, and furious.

Cartwright looked much the same as most settlements on the Labrador coast back then. Surrounding each home was a vertical woodpile shaped like a teepee. Each house featured a saw lying on a sawhorse, an axe securely anchored in a chopping block, a dog-feeding tub, a komatik, a coach box, and a barrel for collecting water. However, unlike Spotted Island, dogs weren't free to roam. Most Cartwright dogs were tied up, while others were put on an island for the summer where they were fed fresh fish.

The well-kept clapboard houses that dotted the perimeter of the harbour opposite Lockwood School were sandwiched between two roads — the Low and High Roads. Several homes had an outhouse and a shed perched precariously on the bank above the high-water level. Small boats were tied to the wharfs scattered along the cove, while others were moored offshore in the harbour. At low tide the boats, marooned on the sand, settled onto their sides waiting for the next tide.

A huge marsh stretched from the harbour inland to Black Head Hill. Berry bushes covered the soft mounds of earth. Between the mounds were bogs that could swallow a person. Sprinkled throughout the marsh were several ponds, some big enough to skate on. Big Brook meandered along the far side of the marsh and emptied into the harbour. There was only one house past the Hawes' place — the Petten family home out on the point. The Pettens had children about the same age as us, but we didn't play together because they bullied us. There was nothing beyond that except the marsh, the brook, and a long walk around the harbour to Lockwood School, where few people ever ventured unless they were on business.

There were two stores in Cartwright. The Hudson's Bay Company one was known to the locals as simply the Company Store. It had started out as a simple trading post and had eventually evolved into an old-fashioned general store. By the time my family arrived in Cartwright in 1953, the Company Store was well stocked. The merchandise was kept in box-type shelving along the walls behind the counters. The Hudson's Bay Company employed people to work in the warehouses and fish storage facilities and as crew on the schooners and boats they owned to harvest salmon. The S.B. Fequet and Sons Store farther up the harbour toward the point was set up much the same way. It had been started by Sam Fequet in the early twentieth century and was handed down to his sons.

Even though most of the village's men worked at the radar station, a large number still clung to the old ways and shifted outside to their fishing grounds at Grady, Hare Harbour, Dumplin, North River, Eagle

River, Smokey, and other places close to Cartwright. But the old way of life had been changed forever. Our lives were punctuated by explosions night and day as workers blasted through Black Head Hill. Gigantic machinery roared through the once-peaceful village. We'd never seen anything like it, and it was terrifying.

"Whass dat ol ting?" I asked Sammy one day, pointing at a large yellow machine rumbling along the newly constructed road.

"Tis a bulldozer!" he yelled over the sound of the engine.

I watched as the giant machine left deep tracks in the muddy ground behind it. "De blade's bigger den me!" I piped up. "An tis some noisy, too, hey, Sammy?"

"Stinks some, too!" my brother said.

The machine turned, and I bolted into the woods, terrified it was going to run me over.

A short time later I was even more frightened when an enormous freighter entered the harbour. After that several of the ugliest gigantic hulks I'd ever seen steamed into the harbour. These things didn't look like boats, because there was no pointed bow. They were like huge floating boxes. And one of them came right into our cove and onto our shore! We watched in horror as it beached itself and the front dropped down. The monster was maggoty with men dressed in ugly green suits who marched out of its mouth onto our beach. Huddled together, we peered out the window, afraid to show our faces. It must have been amusing to the visitors to see petrified little faces peeping out at them from everywhere.

All summer long helicopters rumbled through the skies, colossal machinery tore up the ground, and American soldiers swaggered through our village as if they owned it. One day my little brother, Eddy, hid behind the corner of the house, pointed at the sky, and said, "Ders a plane wit ponametooners comin."

We all laughed.

Marcie grinned. "Der not ponametooners. Der pontoons."

It seemed as if war had come to Labrador. When I went to the store to buy bubble gum cards, the magazine racks were filled with gruesome pictures of war — ships burning, planes on fire, soldiers manning big guns with flames coming out of the barrels, and men dead and dying on bloody ground. I was terrified of the planes with two tails that swooped overhead constantly, and was particularly alarmed when they flew at night. I would lie in bed, convinced they were going to drop bombs on us.

Mommy lost her temper frequently. Because of the way she treated me, I began to wonder if I was evil. She didn't have any particular belt, strap, or paddle to hit us with. Most of the time it was just something easily available — the back of her hand, the front of her hand, a knuckle to the top of my head, a piece of bank line, or a willow. I knew for certain there would be dire consequences if I tried to rebel or sass her. It never occurred to me that she might be pushed beyond her ability to cope. She was living in a noisy, fearsome world, trying to look after nine people in makeshift accommodations, and she missed my father all week long.

"Mommy, can I go ta de store wit ya?" I asked one Saturday. Mommy always went to the store on Saturdays.

"Get yer work done an ya can come," she said.

"Whass I gotta do?"

"Ya gotta wash de dishes, bring in de clothes, an do de ironin. Der's lots ta do if ya'd look round ya."

"Who done all dat fore I came home?"

Crack! Her hand came across my face so hard it stunned me. I ran outside crying, not wanting Mommy to see me. If she noticed me bawling, she'd give me a real beating. I hated living with these strangers. I hated this person who was my mother. I hated the noise, the machines, the strangeness of everything, all the responsibilities I had. I felt trapped with nowhere to turn.

When I settled down, I went to take the clothes off the line. I really wanted to please Mommy. I wanted her to hold me and love me. Shoving my face into the clothing, I let the fresh smell penetrate my being. It calmed me and gave me new courage to return to the house. After I folded the clothes, I got up the nerve to ask Mommy again. "Can I go ta de store wit ya now?"

"Whass ya wanna go fer, Jos? Ya got no money."

"I know. But can I go? Please, Mommy?"

"Oh, awright den, but ya better behave yaself."

I was happy walking to the store with Mommy. It was such a big thing for me to go to this store, because at Lockwood it had seemed so far away. The great distance hadn't been real, of course. The rules and restrictions placed on us at the school just made it seem so. The freedom I had now to wander around Cartwright simply overwhelmed me.

On another day I found myself heading up the road by myself after escaping from the little ones at home. As I glanced across the harbour at Lockwood, I thought of how trapped I'd been there, and suddenly I started skipping. "Dis is de biggest place in de world!" I cried, stretching my arms over my head, feeling free from the confinement of Lockwood, free from the rules and regulations that had strangled me there, free from the constant teasing and bullying.

The people next door to where we lived were actually Joyce Hawe's parents, Austin and Betty Pardy. They lived around the cove a little way with their other daughter, Cynthia, who I befriended. One day Cynthia invited me to her house.

"Come in, come in," Aunt Betty said in a voice that sounded like Dr. Forsyth's at Lockwood. I was afraid to enter her home because it seemed way too fancy. The wonderful aroma of fresh-baked bread and homemade soup wafted out to me. Looking in, I spied Aunt Betty. She was a short lady who wore a pinny tied neatly around her well-padded waist. Aunt Betty was bent over the stove, putting in some wood. Without stopping, and after gently lifting the damper back into place, she turned to peer at me. "Oh, hello there. And who might this be?" she asked in a strong English accent.

"Mommy, this is Josie Curl," Cynthia said. "Her family's livin with Auntie Joyce for a little while until her daddy gets his house built."

Cynthia's place was too nice for me to be in, I thought. Her family had to be rich. There were lace-covered shelves with trinkets on them and pretty little cushions on the settle. There was a radio on a shelf in the corner and a pantry full of fancy dishes just off the kitchen. I couldn't help but think of the battered tin cup I'd used in Roaches Brook, and was glad to get out of there because I was afraid I'd break something.

One day, not long afterward, Cynthia took Marcie and me to one of her friends' homes, which had a parlour. The parlour contained an elegant sofa, lace-covered tables, and flowers everywhere. There was even a carpet on the floor that looked so clean! Before I saw this parlour, I had never imagined going into a room like that, let alone living in one.

"Whass a parlour?" I asked Marcie after we left and were strolling down the road.

"Dunno, maid. Tis like a sittin room or a livin room, I tink, but no one's allowed in 'em. Yer not sposed ta use 'em."

That was more than I could comprehend. I didn't see any sense in the idea. Why would anyone have such a beautiful room and not use it?

More and more I was beginning to enjoy roaming around Cartwright. One day I ventured beyond the Company Store, past Fequet's Store, past the Marconi Station, past houses where the really swanky people lived — the Davises, the Martins, the Fequets, the Moores. Eventually, I ended up on the point. As I crested the hill, the graveyard unfolded in front of me, and beyond it stretched the ocean. I was in awe of the splendour surrounding me and could see for miles across the dark sea dotted with little islands.

Sitting on the ground, I wept. It felt as if I were back on Spotted Island. I could close my eyes and pretend I was there. I thought of the graveyard directly behind our house on Spotted Island, the fishing boats and stages, the lovely rocky hillsides, and continued to cry. Strolling back along the road while the tide was low, I decided to poke about in the landwash for a bit. That had become one of my favourite pastimes. At low tide all kinds of tiny creatures were trapped in the pools of water among the rocks and seaweed. Beachy birds bobbed up and down as they fed on millions of sea lice scampering around. Thornbacks or sticklebacks were tiny fish that when alarmed raised very sharp thorns on their backs. Of course, I got pricked trying to catch them. My spirits lifted as I frolicked in the seaweed, though I screamed every time a flatfish wiggled out from under my feet.

On May 17, 1953, we finally moved into our new home. Daddy was busy working at the radar site, or hunting for food, cutting firewood, fetching water, and caring for his dogs. Yet somehow he found time to build us a house. Sammy, of course, was a great help. I had no idea how

Daddy acquired a piece of land beyond the marsh, but before long a group of men were helping to lay the foundation on it. The house, 12 by 20 feet, was on a bank about 150 feet from the high-water level near the harbour. With a lot of help from our neighbours, the walls rose quickly.

A few weeks after the walls were finished, Daddy came into the Hawes' house and said, "Awright, Mammy, I speck ya can start packin up our stuff."

"We can move in, Daddy?" I asked with excitement. "I'm some glad, too. I hates livin here."

"Shut yer lip, Jos," Mommy said. "Be tankful ya gotta place ta lay yer head atoll."

We all worked together to move our belongings. Although the house was tiny for a family of nine, we were absolutely delighted after sharing homes with other families for the past year. Our house had been built with only two rooms and a loft, but to us it was a mansion. The front door faced the marsh that ran down into the cove, separating us from the rest of the community. Two windows looked onto the harbour, one in the kitchen and one in the bedroom. There was also a window facing the marsh at the back.

Although much of the house was built with scrap wood from the dump, when you entered it, you inhaled the wonderful smell of new wood. As you walked into the main room, a shiny new stove that had arrived on the *Kyle* graced the opposite wall. However, that was the extent of anything store-bought. Immediately to the right, spanning the whole front wall of the room, Daddy built a locker to sit on. It served as furniture and also gave us needed storage.

Daddy also made a settle, which Mommy covered with a handmade feather-filled mattress. At the end of the settle Daddy constructed a table and made two benches to fit neatly under it. We sat along those benches at mealtime and pushed them under the table when we were finished. Two old chairs, found at the dump or kindly donated by somebody, graced each end of the table during meals. Daddy used one and Sammy took the other. In the corner above the table, and on the same wall as the entrance door, Daddy built a wall cupboard to store our dishes.

The floor was bare wood. Suspended from the ceiling around the stove were racks to hang clothes on. Behind the stove a cardboard box held woollen socks and mitts. As they were drying, the socks and mitts filled the house with a terrible odour. My parents' bedroom held the slop pail we all used, which created a constant stench in the house. We had to take turns emptying it into the slop hole just down the bank a little, and were all pleased when Daddy finally put up an outhouse.

At the end of my parents' bedroom just below a tiny window Daddy installed something that looked like a huge bin. An overstuffed feather mattress and a long feather pillow fashioned from bleached flour sacks were fitted into the bin to serve as my parents' bed. Handmade quilts added the only colour to the room. Above the bed and close to the ceiling was Mommy's private shelf, which we weren't allowed to snoop into.

In January 1953 I turned 10, and reading was still my escape. I craved books but didn't get much chance to read at home because Mommy thought reading was a waste of time. I learned to sneak in my books when my mother wouldn't notice.

Mommy was getting big again, and there were whisperings that a new baby might be found soon. Sure enough, on May 20, only three days after we moved into our new house, Mommy went to the mission hospital and soon returned with a brand-new baby girl. Wee Dora was born with blond hair and blue eyes like me.

Next to my parents' bed Daddy set up a tiny crib for baby Dora, a bed for Winnie, and another small bed for Eddy on the opposite wall. At the foot of Eddie's bed he built a ladder leading to the tiny half-loft where my sisters and I slept. Our beds were nothing but 12-inch-wide planks placed on the floor, just long enough to fit our bodies. There were no legs on our beds, since it was a very small crawl space. Feather mattresses made from bleached flour sacks were fitted snugly into each bin, along with feather pillows. Homemade quilts added colour to our pitiful sleeping arrangements. I don't remember bedsheets at all. Marcie, Sal, Rhoda, and I made up our beds in the loft. There was a tiny window facing the brook, and we all wanted that spot, of course.

Mommy was delighted with our new home and took pride in dressing it up. At the end of the locker closest to the door she placed a washstand with a basin, and above the basin on the wall she nailed a small mirror. An empty detergent box cut in half and fastened to the wall held combs and shaving things. Another nail on the wall held a towel. Mommy bought a piece of oilcloth to cover the table and fitted one end neatly underneath the cupboard. On the top shelves of our new cupboard she proudly displayed her antique cups, while on the lower shelves she placed our everyday dishes. Dishes were scarce at first, so Daddy made us cups from tin cans. Shortly afterward we actually got store-bought cups and saucers. Mommy bought Daddy a large white cup with a saucer and a special cup for herself, as well. We, of course, fought over who got the remaining cups. Daddy found a piece of brown linoleum in the garbage dump and nailed it to the floor. Mommy was so proud of her linoleum floor — no more scrubbing wood and getting splinters under her fingernails, which seemed such a luxury to her.

Not long after we moved in, Daddy and Sammy added a bedroom for Sammy and a porch facing the marsh to the end of the house. Sam's room contained a tiny bed with a spring mattress. However, the bed and the room were really too small for him. As soon as that was finished, Sammy and Daddy covered the house with grey brick siding. Soon after that they added a second porch and verandah that spanned the whole front of the house.

In Labrador the closed porches of a home were important. By pulling a rope handle to release the latch, you could enter the outside porch and walk onto the verandah. Along one wall neatly stacked firewood was always drying. In our house the other walls were studded with nails where Daddy slung his dog harnesses, animal traps, ropes, fishing jiggers, and twine. Mommy's washtub and washboard were also suspended on those walls. Since the porch was unheated, we kept fresh game out there, as well. During the winter, the game stayed frozen and fresh until it was cooked. Often ducks, rabbits, porcupine, or venison hung from nails in the ceiling.

Using the same type of rope handle, you entered the inside porch. It served as a second kitchen with an old comfort stove, a counter, and a cupboard to store fresh bread and store-bought food. Wooden planks along the cross beams of the ceiling also provided storage. Next to the cupboard was the wood stove used to heat water and to cook cornmeal for the dogs. Opposite the door a counter made from a piece of plywood attached to the wall served as a place for Mommy to prepare food. In the summertime, if she was lucky gathering food that day, there would be fresh cod, salmon, trout, arctic char, rounders, or capelin in her big pan. On a bad day we might have to settle for salmon spawn, cod britches, cod heads, or cod gills. I didn't like eating fish parts, but we had to or go hungry. When hunting season arrived in the fall, there were rabbits, seal meat, ducks, and turrs in her big pan. Anything was better than living on bread and tea.

Even though Mommy and Daddy were poor, they were smart and very industrious. Once Daddy got his job as a dynamite blaster, we began to eat things we'd never seen before. There were tins of Vienna sausage, canned fruit, fresh eggs, and even packages of cookies in the new cupboard in the porch. I was flabbergasted the first time Mommy brought home a whole bologna, and spent the next few days stealing chunks as it dangled from a nail on the porch.

As cramped as our new home was, it was heaven to us. Everyone had a little space to eat and sleep. Mommy loved to gaze out the window at the harbour and soon recognized all the boats and who owned them. There was lots of room to roam and play, and when Daddy built the outhouse, we felt civilized. Behind the house Mommy tilled a little garden. And even though it was difficult to grow anything, she enjoyed trying.

September was hunting season. Dog harnesses had to be made, and bridles had to be braided and readied before the first snowfall. Cod for dog food had to be jigged, salted, and stored. Firewood had to be cut. Everything was done methodically and in its own time.

Our new home was small, crowded, busy, and smelly, but we didn't have to live with other people anymore. There were no curtains on the windows, no fancy furniture, no lace-covered bureaus, but it was our own. We had a stunning view of the harbour, and the huge marsh yielded berries, which I loved picking in late summer. The marsh also had wonderfully big ponds that we could skate on in winter, providing, of course, I could manipulate Mommy into getting me a pair of skates.

I began to think Cartwright might not be so bad, after all.

22

St. Peter's School

"Got ya signed up fer school," my mother said one afternoon in the late summer of 1953.

"Don't wanna go ta dat ol school!" I cried.

"Ya gotta go, Jos, an dat's all der's to it."

"But, Mommy, I'm scared."

My crying fell on deaf ears, though. As the time approached, I began to feel physically ill. I knew all about the horrors of school and the kids who would be my enemies. Only one thing pleased me even slightly: I was given a brand-new shiny brown leather school bag, with two buckles and a plastic handle.

Marcie, Sarah, and I meandered across the soggy marsh and along the footpath past Aunt Betty's house, past Uncle Jim's, and past several other homes. My heart pounded, my palms were sticky with sweat, and I was light-headed. I tried to reason with myself: *Whass ya really fraid of, Josie? Ya can take care a yerself. Lockwood taught ya how. Ya gotta go! Ya gotta go!*

As we trudged up the little hill to St. Peter's School and Church, I noticed a group of girls laughing and talking. I recognized some of them from Sports Day at Lockwood and knew they were gossiping about me. Not only that, they were making snide remarks about the clothes my sisters and I were wearing. Who knew what they were saying about my bedwetting? And I was certain the odour of urine wafted from my body.

The bell rang, and we crept to the doorway and stepped inside, noticing that the school smelled musty and old. The wooden floor was painted ash-grey, and a potbellied stove stood in the centre of the typical old-fashioned classroom, which had several rows of desks, one behind the other, and the teacher's desk at the front. A large blackboard was fastened to the wall behind the teacher's desk. The original St. Peter's had been built in 1930 and was one of the first village schools in Labrador. Prior to that, Labrador had had itinerant teachers who spent four months in each community, always travelling on when their term was finished.

Because so many families were moving into Cartwright to work on the radar site, the tiny church and school were bursting at the seams and had to be replaced. When a new church was built, the old one was used for Girl Guides activities and other social events. A new two-room school opened in 1954, the year after I started at St. Peter's. There was no indoor plumbing in the old school, and two outhouses served as toilets. The front of St. Peter's faced the harbour, its large windows providing a clear view of Lockwood.

As we entered the classroom, I shook all over. I wanted to turn and run but said to myself over and over: *Jus keep goin, Josie.* I was terrified I was going to collapse.

Then the teacher spoke. "Good morning, class."

"Good morning, miss," all the students chimed.

"I'd like you to welcome the Curl family this morning. This is Marcella, Josephine, and Sarah." The teacher indicated my sisters and me.

I felt shame and humiliation as I took in the snide glances from my new classmates. There were stares and snickers as we settled into our seats. I heard a few grunts and kept my eyes on the floor. *Why do they hate us?* I wondered. Was it because we were poor? Had they heard what had happened to me at Lockwood? Was it because we were new in town, or because we had gone to the residential school?

As I looked around the room, I noticed most of the students were wearing store-bought clothes, and some even had store-bought shoes. I recognized some of the faces from Sports Day at Lockwood, though I didn't know their names. I tried to imagine being able to go to the store and buy new clothes and a pair of new shoes.

A little later, when the recess bell sounded, it startled me. Because I'd been so preoccupied I almost jumped out of my seat. I didn't want recess and was terrified to move. As I rose from my seat and headed toward the door, I saw children dashing up the road to the Company Store, something I could never do at Lockwood. I realized then that I could go anywhere I wanted to as long as I was back in time for the bell. I had never had freedom at school like this. My spirits lifted a little as I ran to the store and drooled over the candy stacked on the counter. I envied the children who had money. When I couldn't stand the tantalizing aromas any longer, I hurried down to the wharf where I stared at the water, wishing I could be a sculpin or a flatfish. Sitting by the harbour soothed me a bit and gave me a sense of peace. Gradually, my courage returned. I didn't have to be afraid. I could take care of myself. If anyone crossed me, I'd simply beat them up. But as I approached the school, my courage melted away and fear overcame me again.

After the first few days of classes, I got a little better at coping with my panic. I was sensitive to criticism, and because of the rapes, I hated boys. I wasn't ever going to be their victim again. One day two boys named Irving and Claude started teasing me. Before they uttered another word, I was on the ground attacking them both with full fury. I felt as if I were fighting for my life. In desperation I pummelled and punched to show them they couldn't pick on me and get away with it. Despite my smallness, I was blessed with good upper-body strength inherited from my family. I gained a little courage after that and felt better about myself. However, it took time before I gained the respect and acceptance I longed for.

We were allowed to go home for dinner at noon. Whenever my sisters and I arrived at our house, I'd barrel through the doorway to be greeted by the smell of rabbit stew or homemade soup with fresh bread. Coming home to my family and eating Mommy's homemade food comforted me beyond telling. It was the bright spot of my day. Everything was difficult for me at school, so noon hour was especially important. I was even struggling with my schoolwork, though I knew I wasn't stupid. It was impossible to do homework properly in our crowded house. My inability to catch up always put me at a disadvantage in class, so I took refuge in daydreams.

St. Peter's had about 30 students that year. Back then I thought the up-the-harbour crowd — the children from the Company Store all the way to the point — were stuck up. I was especially envious of Kathleen and Allison Moores. They were so beautiful that I couldn't take my eyes off them. Their father was the Marconi operator in Cartwright and was a prominent member of the community. Also up the harbour were the Davises, the Martins, the Reeves, the Hopkinses, and the Burdetts. Howard and Chubby Fequet's parents owned the other store in town, and it seemed to me that they were too good for us, as well. I often wondered if the new children felt as terrified as I did. Even though the Pardy and Bird children started St. Peter's around the same time as my sisters and me, to my mind they, too, were superior to us.

Mr. Massie was the Hudson's Bay Company store manager. He had a number of children and lived in a big house connected to the Company Store by a long wooden walkway. His house was halfway along the harbour and was the dividing line between up and down the harbour. Somehow I concluded that they had status and were much too good to bother with me.

To heighten my feelings of inferiority, one of the houses we had to walk by on the way to school belonged to a family named Petten. The father was a Newfoundlander with six children. For no reason that I ever understood, they hated us. Every day when we passed their house they obstructed our walk, threw things at us, and attacked us for no reason. I was terrified of them. They made me feel ashamed and degraded. I wanted to be liked and accepted, not talked about and ridiculed. How well I remember how I felt. I was an unhappy, frightened, lonely little girl.

At Lockwood we had regular bathrooms with toilets that flushed and sinks with running water, but at St. Peter's there was only an outhouse. It was smelly, and I was afraid of falling into the big hole. It always reminded me of the time I'd fallen into the sewer at the mission. Maggots, which I hated, crawled around the outhouse opening.

One day when the bell rang for class I reluctantly shuffled into the class and slithered into my seat only to get a pleasant surprise. I remember thinking that at least it was Friday, which I liked because we had drawing class. On this day we were asked to draw the Union Jack, and there were rumblings about a holiday.

"Today is a special day," Miss Stuckless announced, rubbing her hands together and sounding more excited than I'd ever heard her. "We're going to have a celebration."

"A celebration, miss?" I asked.

"Today is Coronation Day, a holiday," she told us. "We'll be going across to Lockwood to receive gifts from our new queen."

I was mystified. "From de queen, miss? Who's de queen?"

Almost too afraid to get excited, I thought for sure they'd leave me behind, so great was the scar left by that betrayal two years before when I was abandoned at Lockwood for the summer. I held my breath as we were herded to the boat waiting at the Company wharf. To my great joy I was allowed on with the other children. As I strolled up the familiar road to Lockwood, I watched for any mission children I might know. I recognized many of them but didn't know what to say to anybody. I was afraid to speak because I felt so awkward in their midst. I wondered what they thought about me.

The Lockwood staff came out carrying boxes of ribbons and surprises for us. The bigger children had to attach ribbons to the flagpole. We had to hold a ribbon and walk around the pole, winding them around and around while singing "God Save the Queen" over and over. Dr. and Mrs. Whittaker, Mr. and Mrs. Bird, and a lot of other people from both sides of the harbour attended the celebration.

The teachers told us about the death of King George VI, about Queen Elizabeth II, and about the elaborate festivities in England. We found out that the coronation meant the crowning of our new queen, which was beyond my comprehension. Then we were called up to accept gifts. Each of us received a shiny gold medal attached to a red, white, and blue ribbon, and a box of candy in a British tartan tin about four by six inches. There was a picture of Queen Elizabeth on the lid, and the box was filled with delicious toffee wrapped in shiny paper. Since it was the first box of candy I'd ever received, I was delighted. At the end of the day I carefully hid my treasures from my little brother and sisters.

My start at St. Peter's wasn't really a good one, largely because of my feelings about myself rather than the actual situation. I couldn't mingle with the children and stayed away from everyone as much as possible. For the first few months I was busy exploring my new surroundings, so recess and noon hour became my favourite times in the day. When the first year came to an end, I did poorly on the exams, because my mind was so scattered. I still missed Spotted Island so much.

And in my dreams, as always, I was falling, falling … never reaching the ground.

23

Life in Cartwright

I woke up early to the glorious smells of wood burning, tea brewing, and toast cooking on our very own stove. It was wonderful to have our own space and be able to get to know my family again. After scrambling around to get dressed, I climbed through the tiny hole and down the ladder. I could see that Mommy and Daddy were much happier. They were grateful for Daddy's job but were exhausted. No wonder. They had been moving from place to place and had built a house while Mommy was pregnant.

"Jus another ol maid," I heard my mother say shortly after she was back from the hospital with the new baby. Hearing her say that cut me to the core. I'd heard her speak many times of *old maids*. It seemed to me she didn't like girls as much as boys, and that made me feel unwanted and unloved.

Our first winter in Cartwright was coming to an end. Spring was fast approaching, and the harbour ice was breaking up. The ice moved in and out with the tide a few times before it finally drifted seaward. Some families couldn't decide whether to return to the coast and their fishing homes or stay in Cartwright and continue working for the Americans. Fishing and hunting had been our way of life for centuries. Although the stability of regular jobs was tempting, the pull of the sea for seasoned fishermen was even stronger. So we watched as off they went to Grady, Dumplin, North River, and other prime locations for a summer of fishing.

Mommy seemed to bounce back quickly after having her babies. Dora was her eleventh birth, but only the eighth surviving child, having lost three infants up to that point. I marvel now at how much she did and how smoothly she wove pregnancy and childbirth into her daily routine.

One day I came home from school and saw pieces of sealskin cut into odd shapes on the table. "Whass dis, Mom?"

"Tis industrial work. I gotta sew 'em together an bring 'em over ta de mission store."

The cut-outs were the pieces of baby slippers, coin purses, and wallets to be fashioned from sealskin. It was the beginning of Mommy's life work. Someone had found out about her excellent sewing abilities while she was in the hospital and had offered her the job. I admired her work but didn't know we were going to have to help her. Our job was to chew the edges of the skins to make them supple enough to sew. Sealskin tasted foul and burned my tongue. I hated it.

Shortly after she started sewing, I came home one day to find a huge box of clothes in the middle of the floor. "Where'd dat come from?" I asked, throwing my book bag onto the locker.

"Tis what the mission paid me fer doin de sewin."

The whole family was delighted. We dived into the box like dogs at a feeding tub.

"Oh, dis is nice," Marcie said, pulling out a sweater. "I'm gonna take dis one."

"I like dis," Sally said, holding up a dress.

"I'm havin dis blouse," Rhoda piped up.

Nothing was folded. It was just mixed up in the box.

"Mommy, tis too big," I said, showing her a lovely skirt. "Can ya fix it fer me?"

It was such a joy for our family. We didn't think of what the other children would say or if they would even notice. Besides, Mommy was so skillful with her sewing machine that nobody could tell she'd made it over. At least that was what I thought. Unfortunately, the up-the-harbour crowd certainly did notice and taunted us mercilessly, giving me yet another reason to detest them.

Sammy made me a slingshot that spring, and I had fun shooting at tin cans, bottles, and sometimes little birds. We made parachutes out of hankerchiefs and rocks, and Sammy fashioned bows and arrows for us. We had lots of room to play outdoors but didn't have anyone to play with yet. We certainly weren't going to have anything to do with the Pettens, our only neighbours across the marsh.

Just below our house, between the bottom of the hill and the landwash, was a flat area where we played tag and football. We went barrel-walking on an old barrel we'd found and tottered on stilts that always sank too far into the soggy ground, tossing us into the muck.

That spring a small boat chugged into the harbour, bringing a huge pile of lumber that was deposited next door. This was exciting. My entire family was fascinated as we watched the new two-storey home go up at the mouth of the brook. It was twice as big as ours and was finished in no time.

A new house meant new neighbours. I was anxious to meet them. Manuel and Alma Clark were from down the shore and had small children our age. The oldest was Dick, then Dora, Roland, Pleaman, and Bobby, the baby. I gravitated toward Alma's house right away and grew to love being there, taking care of her babies, washing her dishes, and sweeping her floors, even though I resented doing these things in my own home.

Alma and Mommy had known each other for many years. It turned out that Mommy had actually taken care of Alma when she was little. They rapidly became best friends and remained so for the rest of their lives. They got pregnant every year and had their babies close together, as if they planned it that way. And they also became the village cleaning ladies and laughed constantly as they strode across the marsh with cigarettes in one hand, scrubbing buckets swinging in the other.

"How come yer always so pale, Josie?" Alma asked me one day shortly after settling in.

"Dunno."

"Ya reminds me of Nellie Pale Face. So from now on I'm gonna call ya Nell."

And she did. I had no idea who Nellie Pale Face was, but I liked the nickname Nell.

It wasn't long after the Clark house was finished when another new home went up next door to them a little farther down the brook. Before I knew it, Aunt Sabina Learning moved in with her family. She was a jolly little old lady with dark hair and laughing eyes. Aunt Sabina had a couple of bigger boys — Don and Lloyd — and a younger girl named Dora, who became my friend.

One of the places Dora and I loved going to was the Company Property, a term that referred to the wooden steps and walkways surrounding the Hudson's Bay's store. In the evenings, after the hustle and bustle of the day when the men had gone home, it became a playground for us. We delighted riding on the Company trolley and played on it for hours. Night after night we'd frolic around the Company steps, then I'd hear Sammy behind me talking to his friend and would brace myself, knowing what was coming.

"Time to go home now, maids," he'd say.

And we'd have to go. There was no arguing with Sammy. When he commanded something, we did it. Mommy and Daddy had given him the authority.

Victor Curl, affectionately nicknamed Uncle Bucky, was Daddy's brother. He married Aunt Dulcie, who was Mommy's sister — two sisters married to two brothers! They had four children: Arthur, the oldest, away in hospital at that time; Susan; Harriet; and wee baby Jimmy. I hadn't heard anything about their arrival, but suddenly they were there and were building a house across the marsh from us. It was a good feeling to have relatives nearby. We weren't alone anymore in this strange new place.

I began to enjoy the summer. Sammy made me a little wooden boat and put a string on it for me. I was proud of it and played in the landwash for hours, careful not to get my new store-bought rubber boots wet again.

In the spring I'd made the same mistake I'd made all those years ago on Spotted Island — wading out too deep and getting a beating when my new boots filled with water. Finally, I'd learned my lesson.

"Can I go fishin wit ya, Daddy?" I asked one day that summer.

"Spose, Jimmy, ya can come, but ya better ask yer mudder first."

Instantly, I got uncomfortable. *It's not Monday,* I thought, *which is washday. It's not Saturday, which is cleaning day. It's not a scrubbing day, so I don't have to babysit.*

I began to hope. As I entered the house, Mommy was putting a junk of wood in the stove and tending to her bean pot. Tuesday was bean soup day, and she was skilled at keeping the wood stove at a certain temperature to maintain a slow simmer. I took a deep breath. "Mommy, can I go fishin wit Daddy, please?" Good manners always impressed her.

"Awright, maid, but be careful and don't fall overboard."

I was surprised, but wheeled around and bolted for the door before she could change her mind. "I can go, Daddy! I can go! Wait fer me!" I caught up with him limping down to the boat, his foot flying outward at each step.

We had to bring the boat in from its mooring and load the gear onboard. Daddy didn't have an engine, so we had to row through the harbour. I gazed at all the little houses dotting the shoreline and felt proud of my little home. It looked nice with the grey brick siding Daddy had put on it. Then I turned to the left and glanced at Lockwood. Memories flooded my heart with sadness. I shook myself. That was over. Now I was happy. I was going cod jigging with my father!

As we rowed out past the point and into the run, I noticed the tide was so strong that it made the water swirl. *I sure wouldn't want to fall overboard,* I thought. *I wouldn't last long.*

When we approached Earl Island, we were sheltered from the wind and tide. The reflections of the trees along the shoreline mirrored in the calm water seemed serene. Daddy pulled the paddles in and got two jiggers ready. He didn't talk much except for answering my barrage of questions. We were just comfortable together.

"Drop yer jigger over de side and let it down, Jimmy," Daddy said.

The metal cod jigger was heavy, and the twine burned my fingers because I released it too fast. As soon as the jigger reached the bottom, I pulled it up a little and started jigging. The jigging motion was important. It was the jerk of pulling the jigger upward that dug the hook into the fish's body and speared it. If you felt the jigger coming up solid, you had a fish. Now my jigger was tugging, and I knew instantly I had one! Pulling hand over hand, I got the fish into the boat quickly. I was ecstatic. Daddy unhooked it for me, and I dropped my jigger back in the water. Suddenly, it brought up solid again, almost causing me to lose my line.

"I gotta big one dis time, hey, Daddy?"

He grinned. "Das good, Jimmy. Now haul it in."

"Can't! Tis too heavy an wiggly an de line's burnin me fingers."

Daddy grabbed the line and hauled it into the boat for me. The fish was huge. The cod were plentiful that day, and I soon got tired and my hands were burning from the twine, but I paid no attention because I was having so much fun. It didn't take us long to get enough fish for the dogs and several meals to come.

Daddy pulled in the jigger. "We better go now, Jimmy. Mammy'll be sore if we're late fer supper. An we gotta drop some fish off to de dogs, too."

As we got closer to the island where we kept our dogs, we could tell they knew they were going to be fed. When we hit the shore, they sped toward us, wagging their tails and yelping. They had been on the island since the ice had melted. During the summer, they had gotten fat and now looked healthy and clean in their thick, shiny coats. The dogs were really hungry and gobbled up the fresh cod in seconds. We, too, had fresh cod for supper that night, and it was delicious.

One Saturday, Mommy and Daddy went to the store in the boat. Daddy didn't usually go unless there was a plan to buy something too big or too heavy for my mother to carry. I was curious. When they returned, they had two big boxes. One of them looked extremely heavy.

"Whass dat, Daddy?" I asked.

"Das a radio, Jimmy." He was puffing as he struggled to carry it into the house.

"A radio fer us? Is it our radio?"

"Tis, Jos," Mommy said. "Now get outta de way."

Daddy quickly constructed a shelf to accommodate the radio in the corner over his settle. He then strung a wire to a pole outside, and sure enough, we had a radio! We actually had music. At first the contraption emitted weird noises that made us cringe, screw up our faces, and cover our ears. I just couldn't believe it — a radio in our house! *Wow!* That night Mommy got the Gerald S. Doyle news from West Virginia. We were really coming up in the world!

How was I supposed to sleep when I could hear the radio making strange sounds as Mommy turned the dial back and forth? I wanted to be down there with her. Every night I crawled to the stovepipe hole and strained to hear the radio. For the first time I heard songs like "Old Shep," "There Stands the Glass," and "The Cat Came Back." Every night I'd lie in my smelly urine-soaked bed in the half-loft and listen to the music filtering up through the stovepipe hole.

For special occasions Mommy made homebrew in gallon bottles and stored them in the loft by the stovepipe to keep them warm. The foul smell of fermentation filled the tiny loft. Once in a while friends, and sometimes strangers, lined up along the locker and drank homebrew. On those occasions Daddy sang songs and played his accordion as they sipped.

Those were the times we children loved. The next thing we knew there was a dance going on at our house. Sammy was a terrific dancer. There were a lot of excellent dancers in Cartwright, but the most exuberant one of all was Uncle Bucky. With the sweat rolling off his face and his shirt dripping wet, he kept going all night. He was the party man, the funny man, and made everyone laugh. Uncle Bucky liked homebrew a little too much perhaps, but he certainly enjoyed himself. His wife, Aunt Dulcie, was the opposite — very quiet and subdued.

Another activity that intrigued me was the card games played around our homemade table. Usually, a four-person team and sometimes teams of six laughed and argued and banged on the table. The card games could last well into early morning. Nobody seemed to care that there were five or six small youngsters trying to sleep. If Uncle Bucky got a good score and won the hand, he'd take the last card between his thumb and forefinger and smack it on the table so hard that he shook the entire house. I was allowed to watch the games until bedtime and the dreaded words from Mommy, "Time ta go ta bed now, maids."

One day I found my mother in a fluster as she got clean clothes ready for us. "Whass ya doin dat fer, Mommy? I asked as I watched her pull clothes from the pile she'd just brought in from the line.

"Ya gotta go fer a checkup. De *Christmas Seal* is comin."

I looked out the window. "Where? I don't see anyting."

Mommy was so in tune with her world that she could glance out the back window of our house through a narrow strip between Black Head Hill and Flag Staff Hill and spot the spars of schooners passing by before anyone else noticed them. "She'll be comin round de point any minute now." And sure enough, a schooner came around the point, flags flying, horn blowing, letting everyone know it had arrived.

The *Christmas Seal* was the mission hospital ship. It sailed the Labrador coast each summer and was equipped with everything needed to care for the sick, injured, and dying. Because Mommy had lost three babies, she wanted to make sure we all had medical care. Fishermen from Newfoundland fishing on the Labrador coast for the summer, and local people, too, appreciated what the hospital ship's staff did — checking our health and giving us needles for polio, diphtheria, and whooping cough. We also had to have scratches for tuberculosis. Whenever the boat came, Mommy brought us to see the doctor who inspected all the nursing stations and hospitals along the coast.

Marcie moaned. "Don't wanna go. Fraid der gonna give me a needle."

"Ya gotta go, Marcie, an ya gotta help yer sisters, too, specially Rhoda," Mommy said.

"But, Mom, I knows I'm gonna faint," she whined.

Of course, there was no arguing with Mommy. So all of us had to go whether we wanted to or not.

As soon as we were cleaned up and presentable, we trudged to the *Christmas Seal* to get our scratches. That was the primary purpose of this trip along the coast — to make sure children in Labrador got their tuberculosis scratches. When my turn came, the nurse asked me to lean across something, and I felt four scratches on one side of my backbone, then four on the other side. It hurt, too. The nurse then placed a small bandage on the pricks and said, "Now, Josie, if you see pimples or a red rash, you'll have to go for more tests."

So for the rest of the week we all studied one another's backs to check for rashes, but none appeared. Thank goodness!

The end of summer was fast approaching, and that meant berry picking. Dora Learning and I went up Flag Staff Hill to pick blackberries. As we reached the top of the hill, we flopped onto the soft berry bushes and breathed in the fresh sea air. It was a clear, sunny day, and I could see for miles out to sea. Several islands and small icebergs interrupted the sun-splashed waves of the Atlantic as it stretched into infinity. I studied the clouds drifting across the blue sky. They looked like toe (cotton wool). Eventually, we filled our jugs with blackberries and talked about the good jam our mothers would make to put on our bread.

As far as food went, one of the things that changed when the Americans came was the dump. Daddy and Sam went to the dump almost every day and were continuously bringing home their finds. The Americans threw out so much that was useful. Huge tins without labels appeared in the kithen, and we were always excited to see what they held. They brought home powdered eggs and milk, concentrated orange juice, and sometimes canned fruit. It all tasted so good. With no labels to guide us, it was a wonder we weren't poisoned.

One day Sammy fetched home a strange-smelling substance. We kept sniffing it because it was so different from anything we'd ever encountered before. It was powerful, too. After a while, a neighbour came in and told us what it was.

"My God, dass ether!" yelled the neighbour when she saw what we were doing. "Don't sniff dat stuff. It'll kill ya!"

"Whass ether?" Marcie asked.

"Tis what dey put ya ta sleep wit in de hospital fore dey open ya up."

"Oh, my, oh, my!" Mommy cried.

We barely made it through supper when we started getting sleepy. Then we began passing out. Marcie, Rhoda, and Sally sprawled across their dinner plates. The rest of us were moaning and groaning but were thankful to be alive. Needless to say, we didn't have trouble sleeping that night. From that time on we were more careful when we opened things from the dump.

By the end of the summer, my family had adjusted to our new town and our new neighbours. Most important for me, I had a new friend. Because of the work on the radar site, Cartwright was growing. The picturesque community of several hundred people would never again be the same. It must have been difficult for the lifelong residents of that once peaceful village to have to choose between the old and the new lifestyles. For my part, I had learned to live in a family setting again and had gotten to know my brothers and sisters truly for the first time in my life.

To my great surprise, I even got to know some of the up-the-harbour crowd.

24

A Joyous Winter

With Daddy working at the radar site, it was crucial for our survival that Sammy do the essential jobs. Sammy was now 14 and handled the everyday chores of getting wood and water and feeding the dogs. He acquired his own dog team, and Daddy showed him how to make new harnesses, traces, and bridles. Sammy had several new puppies to break in that fall and worked hard with his team. He had to get them ready for hauling wood and water. My brother had become a good hunter and went into the woods daily to check his rabbit snares and to hunt for partridges and porcupines.

When autumn came, Daddy and Sammy got the house ready for winter. They built a shed to store the axe and saws and to keep the wood dry. In the shed they put the barrels for berries and anything else that had to be protected from the dogs. Everyone worked hard. Mom had her cleaning jobs and her sewing for the mission store across the harbour. Marcie, being the oldest girl, had to do most of the household chores while Mommy was working.

Sarah and I were fairly close, but I was envious of her because she seemed to get along so well with Mommy. Rhoda was weak and sickly and always getting nosebleeds. I felt sorry for her. Winnie was a stunning little girl — quiet, pleasant, and happy. Little brother Eddy was spoiled rotten because he'd been born after my parents lost two babies in infancy — Janet at three months and Wilfred at seven months only a year later. No wonder Eddy was spoiled. Baby Dora was adorable, as well. Even though I loved my baby sister, I resented having to walk the floor with her at night when I wanted to go out and play.

The Americans threw so much food away that sometimes Daddy and Sammy let the dogs loose at the dump. It was a cheap and easy way to feed them. When the dogs returned, they flopped down and started cleaning themselves, content with the long run and the food. Many times they came back with their noses full of porcupine quills. Then out came the pliers. The dogs whimpered as the quills were pulled out one by one. That was a cue for Mommy to take down her .22 rifle and go out looking for the porcupine. She rarely came back without it. She'd always been a good hunter. Porcupine stew with duff was one of our favourite meals. The meat was tender and sweet.

On the days the dogs didn't feed at the dump, my after-school job was to stir the huge dog food boiler on the inside porch stove. It stank, but I didn't mind the odour, because it gave me an opportunity to be alone with my thoughts. I wasn't fighting with my siblings or competing for attention or listening to Mommy ridicule me. Stirring the smelly boiler in the dark with only the light from the flames dancing around the room gave me a sense of peace.

The ponds were freezing over, and soon we could skate on them. Of course, I still didn't have skates. I begged Sammy to let me wear his. They were four sizes too big, but I didn't care. I simply had to go skating.

"Please, Mommy, please can ya buy me some skates?" I pleaded.

"No, Josie, where in de name of God do you tink de money is gonna come from?"

"Dunno, Mommy. Can I do some work fer de store, or help ya clean, or sometin?"

I was beside myself and cried and begged for hours, enduring the odd slap across the face with whatever Mommy could grab. I didn't even feel those slaps. I wanted skates that badly.

The next week Mommy came home with a new pair of skates just for me. They were boy's skates, but at least they fitted. I was overjoyed. My very own skates! I couldn't wait to go down to the pond. After school a group of us ran across the marsh with our skates over our shoulders. Several of the girls held hands and skated in circles. The speed caused the girls on the end of the line to break away and fly across the ice. My feet hurt as we limped back across the marsh, our toes numb from the cold. But it was worth the pain.

On windy days, just as we did in Roaches Brook, we held our jackets over our heads like sails and let the wind blow us across the pond. After skating, it was heavenly to walk back into our warm house and be greeted with the aromas of supper cooking on the wood stove. My place for meals was on the little bench next to Sammy, who sat opposite Daddy at the other end of the table.

When December arrived, I wanted to go to the Christmas concert at Lockwood. Even though it wasn't very far away, to me it seemed so. I wanted to see it again, to get up on the stage where I had cried when I was supposed to sing "Jack Was Every Inch a Sailor." I wanted to see Hazel and Rhoda Hopkins and little Martha.

"Please, Mommy, can I go?" I begged.

"No, Jos, ya can't."

"Please, please, Mommy. I'll be good an won't be any trouble. I promise."

"No, yer not goin, an dat's all der's to it."

As she was leaving, I clung to her coattail. She smacked me off. I chased her halfway across the harbour, but she wouldn't let me go. I screamed and cried until I was exhausted, but she was immovable. Finally, broken-hearted, I returned home.

Christmas was approaching, and I was looking forward to getting a few candies and maybe even a toy. That particular year everyone was buzzing about the Americans making a toy drop.

I was devastated, though, to hear that the toys were for the youngsters at Lockwood, not for us. But one day while I was at the Company Store, which was the only place to hear anything going on in town, Marcie, Sally, and I heard that the toy drop was going to be on the marsh behind our house.

"Behind our house?" Sally piped up. "I thought twas only fer de mission children."

A neighbour anwered Sally kindly, "They decided ta have it fer us, too."

"That'll be handy fer us, hey, Marcie!" I said as we ran along the harbour.

We burst into the house and cried all at once, "Mommy, der's gonna be a toy drop!"

"Whass a toy drop?" she asked.

We had all the information from the store. "Ya know, Mom," I said, pointing at the marsh through the back window. "De air force is gonna drop toys from a plane out der."

Mommy shook her head in wonderment. "My, oh, my, whass they gonna do next atoll?"

The little ones got very excited and chorused, "Will I get one? What bout me? Me, too?"

Later, we heard the plane come from behind Black Head Hill. It flew low over the community a few times to let the children know and to give them time to get to the marsh. Youngsters came running from all directions as fast as their little legs could carry them. Then the plane swooped low and dropped several large packages on the ground. We were excited as we gathered at the lodge to receive our gifts from Father Christmas.

"Ho, ho, ho!" he rumbled as he handed a gift out to every child. My mind spun, trying to figure out how he could do it. He must be very, very, very rich, I thought.

When I got back to the house, Mommy was baking delicious-smelling Christmas fare — sweet molasses bread, bakeapple tarts, and red berry pies. But because it was all for Christmas Day, she wouldn't let us sample anything. She even made molasses candy.

I remember Christmas clearly that year because it was when I found out there was no Santa Claus. I was watching Mommy as she hastily wrapped Christmas gifts one evening after supper. While I watched her, I chattered about Santa.

Finally, Marcie blurted, "Oh, Josie, der's no such a ting as a Santa Claus!"

"What?" I cried. "No such a ting?" I was crushed.

"Mommy and Daddy gotta buy all dis stuff for de little ones, ya know," Marcie continued.

I remember the shock. No Santa? There had to be a Santa! But I didn't make a fuss. I'd learned enough about my family by this time not to make a big deal over things, so I kept my feelings in check. The loss settled in the pit of my stomach like a hard lump.

Even so, Christmas Eve was exciting because I thought I might get something in my stocking on Christmas morning. And I couldn't help but be delighted for the little ones. After some hurried gift wrapping and romping around the house in nervous anticipation, we hung up our stockings. Then our little house filled up with family and friends. Daddy started playing his accordion. Homebrew was topped up in the tumblers, and the merriment began. I danced and sang, trying to avoid Mommy and the dreaded command for bedtime. But it came as it always did.

"Time ta go ta bed now, maids."

"Ah, Mommy, can we stay up a little longer?"

"No, deed you can't. Now, maids, go ta bed or ya'll get nuttin in yer stockin dis night."

I climbed up the ladder and crawled over to the stovepipe hole, listening to the joy and laughter filtering into the loft. Eventually, I got tired enough to crawl into bed and finally drift off to sleep.

Upon waking Christmas morning, I was glad to see the fresh orange and apple in the toe of my stocking. I didn't get a toy, though. Mommy prepared a wonderful dinner — fresh venison with pastry on top and a big hole in the middle. Glorious smells filtered through the house as she made a bakeapple duff, redberry pudding, bread pudding, and lots of gravy to soak up with our bread. Our tiny kitchen was packed with 10 happy faces as homemade tarts, pies, cookies, and candies came from hiding places all over the tiny house. The last pleasure was homemade molasses candy.

It was during the Christmas season that the jannies (mummers) came. They were scary people dressed in weird outfits and masks who danced around the house and acted crazy. The trick was to try to guess who they were and expose them. Being almost 11, I wasn't as frightened as I'd been when I was small. This time I enjoyed them.

On January 15, 1954, I turned 11. In midwinter it became extremely cold, with temperatures between minus 25 and minus 50 degrees for three solid months. On the rare days when the temperature rose to minus 10, we considered it warm. For us it was warm enough to randy. We went whizzing down the hills on anything we could find.

To go randying properly, Sammy and Marcie took the big komatik and headed for the hill, which was the well-beaten wood path the men used for hauling timber with a dog team. It was wide and had a long grade that went all the way to the harbour. And it wasn't far from our house, just past Big Brook and around the cove toward Lockwood. Every youngster in the neighbourhood came: the Clarks, the Learnings, and us. It was a big event. Pulling the big komatik uphill could take a while, but playing on the way up was half the fun. Once at the top, we all piled on, arms and legs flying in every direction.

"Hang on tight, maids!" Sammy hollered.

The large komatik was fast, and Sammy had to keep it straight on the path. Sometimes we got scared when our ride was too speedy. After a big snowfall, if there were lots of fluffy snow, Sammy purposely let the komatik run into a tree or stump and throw us all off, laughing and giggling. The cold, crisp air and the scent of the forest were heavenly. With our cheeks red from the frigid temperature and our lungs full of fresh air, we arrived back home stiff and sore but happy.

It was so cold in midwinter that it was difficult to stay out very long, and at times the weather literally took my breath away. I hated having to go to the Company Store. Leaning into the wind and marching as fast as I could to keep warm, I headed straight across the ice where it was even colder due to the wind gusting off the sea. I walked forward for a while, then backward, then forward again, trying to prevent my face and legs from freezing. On the way back while carrying the bags, my fingers almost froze. I felt my thighs getting numb, and when I got back into the house, the pain of my fingers thawing out was excruciating.

The icicles hanging from the house were long, and we broke them off and had sword fights. I stuck my tongue on them more times than I care to remember. I'd tear the skin right off my tongue and wonder why I kept doing it.

On extremely cold mornings the air was very still, and smoke billowed skyward as straight as an arrow. Windowpanes were etched with beautiful pictures as the frost formed perfect fern-shaped foliage that resembled a tropical forest. Day after day the frost built up so thick that we had to blow and blow to get a hole big enough to peep outside. On stormy days, though, our tiny house was crowded, making me feel trapped.

March always brought new snow, and for the youngsters that meant fun. We all bundled up and went out to build snow houses or tunnels. Once away from the wind, it was warm in the tunnel. Other times we'd jump off roofs into the snow, or make our way to the riverbank and leap into the mounds of white stuff.

Such was life in the dead of winter in Labrador's pure white wonderland.

25

Spring Adventures

Each spring the famous Cartwright Easter Fair was the biggest event of the year. Locals simply called it The Time. Spring 1954 was no exception. Friends, foes, and family arrived by dog team as early as Wednesday and Thursday from up and down the shore to participate in the Easter festivities that always took place on Easter Monday. Good Friday was a sacred day. We couldn't even throw out the slop water then, because we'd be throwing it in God's face.

Out our back windows we saw a steady stream of dog teams come along the marsh. They hailed from as far away as 60 or 70 miles to take part in The Time. Mommy kept glancing out the window to see if she recognized any of the dog teams from Spotted Island. Most of the competitors had been participating in The Time for years and had a relative to stay with or a favourite place to lodge at.

On Saturday the homebrew started flowing. Some of the up-the-shore fellows even had rye or Scotch. In our house it was homebrew.

Mommy had homebrew cooking in the loft beside the stovepipe. There were dances and card games in some of the houses and a lot of reminiscing about the previous year's races — who won and who should have won.

Around eight o'clock each evening, except for Good Friday, Daddy picked up his accordion and began playing while the homebrew slithered down the parched throats of our friends. More and more guests arrived and lined up along the locker. As soon as there were enough people, everyone jumped up and danced a Labrador reel. I scuffled around the floor in the corner of the room with a friend until Mommy sent me to bed. For the rest of the evening I got a crick in my neck as I tried to watch the fun from the stovepipe hole.

Easter Sunday always achieved the biggest church attendance of the year. St. Peter's Church was overflowing. There was praying for all manner of things, including the hope for fine weather during The Time.

When Easter Monday arrived, our little community came alive with activity. Our prayers had been answered. It was a marvellous sunny day. All the contestants got their dogs ready for the race. Resplendent in new harnesses with colourful wool tassels, Sammy's all-white team was in fine form. He'd been practising and training them for weeks. I knew they listened well, but were they experienced enough? Would they have the stamina?

The race was timed … and long. The dog teams began at Lark's Harbour around the point and went all the way to Woody Island near Muddy Bay, about five or six miles away. Silence fell as we watched the teams line up. With tails curled over their backs and breath billowing into the frosty air, the dogs strained at their traces and yelped in a frenzy to go. *Bang!* sounded the starting gun, and they were off, galloping across the frozen ice, drivers cracking whips and shouting "Auck, auck" or "Edder, edder," trying to keep the dogs from tangling up in one another's traces. It was a sight to behold. The last thing a team owner wanted was a fight; it would leave a jumbled mess that caused long delays.

Then there was the wait for the winner. By this time, more people had recovered from the previous night's parties and had gathered anxiously in front of the Company Store to see who the winner would be. While they killed time in the frosty air, they chatted about the teams.

"Who's dat wit de black an white dogs?"

"By gar, I tink dat's young Sam Holwell."

"No, dat looks like Gip Dyson's team wit de little black cracky."

"And who's dat one wit all de white dogs?"

"I believes dat's young Sam Curl. He gotta fine little team der, haven't he?"

Once the dog team race was over, we went over to the shooting matches. There were men's, women's, and boy's competitions, and sharpshooters in every category, including my own mother. She'd never entered a competition before, since this was our first year in Cartwright, but we'd heard about other contenders such as Rhoda Davis and May Learning, who were excellent shots. While we were watching the shooting, preparations were underway for the snowshoe and obstacle races and the tug-of-war.

In the afternoon, about one or two o'clock, the Orange Lodge had their big sale. People had been busy with sewing machines and knitting needles for weeks. All manner of baked goods and crafts covered the tables in the hall. The Orange Lodge was packed with curious people because the most exciting part of the day was about to take place. After the sale, the winners of the various events were announced. The room got louder and louder as people debated who won what or whether they should have won or not. Excitement soared.

Immediately after the announcements, the auction commenced. What everyone was waiting for was the Easter baskets. Each basket had been made by a single, unattached young lady. The baskets were magnificently decorated with brightly coloured crepe paper trimmed with flowers, ribbons, and bows. Goodies such as a pair of knitted socks, a jar of rabbit stew, homemade cookies, jams, cake, or candy might be found in the baskets. But the biggest secret of all was the identity of the baskets' owners. Tension was stoked by auctioneer Bill Morse as he peeked inside the baskets, commented on their decorations or their mouth-watering smells, rotated the baskets slowly, pranced around the stage, and uttered subtle hints. The young men's attention was on the bidder. Who was it? Who owned the basket? Did the bidder know her? Curiosity was at its peak, because whoever bid the highest and won the basket got to go to the owner's house for dinner. Many a Labrador marriage started out with an Easter basket.

Chatter continued throughout the hall.

"Ah, he knew all long twas her."

"Someone tol him twas hers. Dat's fer sure!"

Finally, when all the baskets were gone, the hall was cleared and the tables were set up for the big supper. All manner of meats and bakeapple pies and redberry pies were put out to be served around six o'clock. There were some very skilled cooks in Cartwright.

When supper was over, it was time to clear the tables away for the dance. Homebrew that had been cooking for weeks flowed freely. There was no shortage of accordion players in Cartwright. Daddy and our neighbour Manuel Clark played, as well as Lal Turnbell from Spotted Island, who was an excellent musician. Soon there were two Labrador reels happening simultaneously, each one lasting a half-hour or more. You needed a lot of stamina to get through it all.

It seemed to me that Uncle Bucky never missed a dance. "Dass nough! Dass nough!" he yelled through his toothless smile. With sweat pouring off his face, he stomped on the floor so hard that he shook the whole building.

The Orange Lodge was packed by this time. Sometimes fights broke out, usually the result of too much homebrew. Perhaps a few of the up-the-shore fellows wanted to fight some of the Cartwright fellows. Maybe there was a dispute about who really won the shooting match that morning. Possibly something might have happened during the dog team race. Or perhaps a young man was upset because he didn't get a certain basket. There was lots of talking and arguing, but all in all things went well. We'd laugh at the ones stumbling about and the ones who got sick from too much homebrew. The amazing thing was that there was no police presence, and everyone worked out their problems and kept law and order among themselves.

Of course, I didn't get to see everything during The Time. There was always the matter of small babies at home who had to be looked after. I cried and cried when I couldn't go. Mommy was in the shooting match, so she had to be there. I missed a lot of the festivities, but when I did get a chance to go for short periods, it was a lot of fun. During the dance, teenagers crowded onto the dark porch. Out of the darkness there were lots of giggles as boys pinched and kissed the girls passing through. All too soon it was over.

The next day people departed from our little community. We watched the dog teams leave in a steady stream, one behind the other, crossing the marsh for the long trip back. They wouldn't return until next Easter. We were sad to see them go but also glad to get our house back.

After The Time, life returned to normal at home. One early spring morning when it was still cold and dark outside, my parents and I were warm and cozy as we huddled beside the stove and enjoyed the heat and smell of Mommy's kingwaks. Daddy sat at the end of the table, sipping tea from his saucer. I could tell he was going out to the woods soon because his ninny bag and gun were on the locker ready to go.

"Can I go, Daddy?"

"Awight, Jimmy, but ya better ask yer mudder."

"Can I go in the woods wit Daddy, please, Mommy?" I asked.

"Awight, Jos. Ya can go, but ya better wear nough clothes."

"Oh, yeh, I will." I couldn't believe my good fortune.

Being a tomboy, I thoroughly enjoyed going with Daddy or Sammy whenever I could. Mommy knew I loved to go with the dog team and that I could be a great help to them. I was in heaven as I tore open my piping hot kingwak and slathered butter all over it. Then I poured tea from the large pot that was always brewing at the back of the stove. Sliding onto the bench, I munched my breakfast and enjoyed this quiet time with my parents while everyone else was still asleep.

Then Sammy came out, rubbing his eyes. "Marning." He looked at Daddy. "Wher's ya goin today?"

"I'm cuttin a new wood path jus under Big Hill. Ya can come if ya wants ta."

"Awright, den. I'll be in later. I gotta get barrel water first."

I knew that Sam went to the mission for a barrel of water, and I wanted to go with him. However, I decided to go with Daddy for a lot of reasons. Going with my father meant a boil-up, hunting for partridges, and checking his rabbit snares. It also meant I'd be out of the house for most of the day. Besides, I thought, Sammy would be going for water again in a few days and I could go to the mission then.

We finished breakfast, and I dug out my warm clothes from the locker and my warm socks from the cardboard box behind the stove. When I stepped outside into the cold, crisp spring air and gazed across the frozen harbour, I was awestruck. The pre-dawn light of the sunrise cast the sky in brilliant orange, pink, mauve, and blue. Dog teams crossing the harbour and navigating through the belly craters (ice mounds on rocks) stood out against the first blush of morning. The vertical woodpiles silhouetted against the sky looked like a teepees, and the smell of burning wood tickled our noses. Daddy brought out the harnesses and showed me how to fasten the dogs.

"Pull this over his head," he said, holding the front of the harness between his thumb and forefinger and pulling it over the dog's head. "Now take his paw an pull it up trough. Den take de udder paw an pull it up through de other side. Den give it a yank an straighten it out."

"Okay, Daddy, I can do dat," I said over the yelping of the dogs.

My father hitched the traces to the bridle and then to the komatik, and we were ready to go. It was difficult to hold the dogs back because they were barking and jumping so much. Daddy lifted the drag chain from the nose of the komatik, and we raced across the frozen ground, the dogs galloping at full speed. All I could do was hang on as tightly as I could until they slowed to a comfortable trot. Then I could relax and enjoy the ride.

"Auck, auck!" Daddy cried, and the dogs turned right.

They knew exactly what to do at each command. The lead dog, usually a female, knew what the master wanted even before the command came. Once we arrived at our destination, the dogs stopped and rolled in the snow for a while, then lay down to rest.

That morning there had been a new snowfall, so we stepped into our snowshoes and walked into the woods. I savoured the moment and breathed in the frosty air. The fragrance of juniper, spruce, and birch trees filled my nostrils and lifted my spirits. Except for the birds chirping in the snow-laden trees, the silence was deafening … until the *chop, chop, chop* of Daddy's sharp axe echoed through the forest.

I was big enough to chop off the limbs of the trees and was delighted to help. After about an hour of chopping, it was time for our mug-up.

"Whass ya got, Daddy?"

"Mammy made some pork buns las night. See?" He showed me a cotton bag tied with string.

"Oh, goodie. I loves buns."

I watched my father as he cut dry sticks, skillfully built a fire, set up a tripod to hang the tin kettle on, and laid down boughs where we could sit. He didn't let his crippled leg stop him or slow him down. I flopped beside him. Soon the kettle was boiling, and he poured our tea.

After our mug-up, Daddy chopped trees for a while and I limbed them. It wasn't hard work, but I wasn't used to it and was soon tired. Daddy decided to look for partridges. They were plentiful, so he wasn't gone long before I heard shots.

Shortly afterward, Daddy limped out of the woods, birds hanging from the rifle across his shoulder. After loading the komatik, we headed home. The dogs were rested by now. With tongues lolling and tails between their legs, they pulled us along at a comfortable pace. It had been a great day.

Every year the snowbirds came in early spring. That year I decided to catch as many as I could and cook them for supper. I asked Daddy to make me a trap. He put together a simple wooden frame and nailed a piece of fishnet onto it. Each day more and more birds landed in the feeding spot on top of the snowbank beside the house. After a few days, I put out my trap and watched through the window. Once a few birds were gathered together, I simply pulled the stick out and *wham!* They were trapped under the net.

I had used Daddy's dog team a few times to go to the store or to fetch a barrel of water. They were experienced and understood from what was loaded on the komatik or what direction Daddy headed them exactly where to go. For instance, if my father had the water barrel on the komatik, the leader knew they were off to the mission for water. Or if

Daddy had his horn junks on, they knew he was going to his wood path. So I felt safe taking Daddy's team for a short run.

For a long time I'd wanted to try out my brother's dog team but didn't dare ask him. Then one day his dogs were lying around on the snow, all harnessed and ready to go. I climbed onto the komatik and pretended to drive them. They took off at a full gallop across the marsh, heading for Black Head Hill, most likely for the dump. They didn't respond to my commands, so all I could do was hold on with all my strength. We whipped across the marsh and raced for the huge hill, which terrified me.

I managed to keep the komatik on the track going up the hill. Once the dogs reached the dump, they foraged through it for a while. I couldn't go until they were ready. At last they were finished, so I turned around the komatik, straightened it out, and headed home. It was starting to get dark, and I was becoming more nervous by the minute. As we hurtled down the hill, I tried to keep the speed under control. However, the path was quite steep and I had to constantly push the komatik with my left foot to prevent it from sliding into the trees. As we rounded a sharp turn, I lost control, smacked into a tree, and flew out into the snow. The dogs halted, sat on their haunches, and stared at me in puzzlement.

Crawling back through the snow to the komatik, I pulled it back far enough to free it from the tree. The dogs didn't want to co-operate, so I had a battle on my hands. They were a lot stronger than I was. Eventually, though, we were on the way again. The dogs seemed to know something wasn't right and kept looking back at me. I had to work fiercely to keep the komatik on the path. I was so relieved when we got down the hill and back out to the marsh.

Sam was waiting for me. Needless to say, I got a few smacks from him and from Mommy, with a stern warning never to try that again. Not with his precious dogs, anyway. I really didn't mind. I knew it was a dangerous thing for a girl of my size to do.

One day, as my friend Dora and I approached High Road, we saw a huge machine heading toward us. We'd never seen anything like it. It had a gigantic square front with what looked like huge drills running horizontally across it. The machine was absolutely terrifying. We thought it was going to eat us! The machine blew a plume of snow high into the air, leaving the roads clean. We didn't have to crawl and roll through the snow anymore. We'd never seen a snow blower in our lives. The walls of snow it left behind were as much as 10 feet high and smooth as glass.

Spring snow kept falling. Soon it was so high that we could swing on the wires that ran from the base to the dock and along the road in front of the school. We didn't know what they were. It was a good thing they weren't electrified. Snowballs flew around the school grounds like bullets. We'd stand beside the trees and sink into the snow past our heads. If the snow was heavy, we got stuck for a long time and someone would have to get help to dig us out. It could be very dangerous, but of course we didn't care. It was so much fun.

Another springtime joy was ice sailing. During the day, the hot sun melted the surface of the ice, then a frosty night left it as smooth as glass and thick enough to bear our weight. The only other element needed for a day of ice sailing was a strong wind. This combination of conditions lured us out in droves. Some of us had little komatiks to sit on, and after hoisting our coattails, we were soon flying across the harbour. Others used pieces of cardboard or skin boots and jackets as a means of slithering across the ice.

In late spring, when the ice broke up and little pans of ice floated in the cove, the activity that landed me in the most trouble was panning (jumping between ice floes). Even though it was forbidden, it was simply irresistible. I did it whenever possible. Mommy seemed to be always watching us. However, when she had to do a cleaning job or went to the store, I saw my chance. First, we had to get a long stick light enough to handle. Then we hopped from pan to pan, using our poles to manoeuvre around the cove. It was risky, but we didn't know or care about that.

While panning one day, I thought I was leaping onto a second pan when it turned out to be just foam on the surface of the water. Down I went into the icy drink. I came up underneath another pan and groped madly to find the edge of the ice so I could pull myself up. I was sure I was going to drown. Thank God the water wasn't over my head. I got a huge beating that day ... and maybe I deserved it.

As spring progressed, the snow melted rapidly, but there was still enough on the path to go to the pond at Table Bay for a day of ice fishing.

"Can I go, Mommy, please?" I begged.

"Okay, Jos, ya can go. Marcie'll look after de youngsters."

What appeared to be a wonderful excursion was actually another source of badly needed food. We needed the spring smelts. I sorted out our hooks and lines, while Daddy and Sammy got the team ready and Mommy packed the grub bag. My mother usually made fresh pork buns, and there was always molasses bread and tea.

When everything was ready and Mommy was sure we had enough clothes on, we piled onto the komatik, with Sally joining us. Daddy lifted the chain, and the dogs were off. The pond at Table Bay was deep in the woods about five miles from Cartwright. The path took us between Black Head Hill and Big Hill and beyond.

After a long ride, we came out of the woods onto a huge pond. The dogs led us to the end so we'd be close to the woods at mug-up time. The first thing to do was to chop the holes. We didn't have augers, so it was *chop, chop, chop* with the axes until finally, *swoosh*, the water gushed through the holes as if released from a pressure tank. Sammy cleared the slush away, and it was time to get out the fish hooks and lines.

"I'm gonna have de firs hole!" I squealed.

"No, ya can't!" Sally piped up, and the fight was on. "I'm havin it."

Sammy had to straighten us out before Mommy got a whiff of what was happening. Otherwise everyone's day would be ruined.

"Der'll be anudder hole in a minute," Sammy said. "Can't ya wait?"

Eventually, we all got our own fishing hooks and hole. The smelts were plentiful and started appearing on the ice all around us.

"I got one! I got anudder one!" I pulled up my line and watched the tiny fish glisten in the brilliant afternoon sunlight. It was particularly exciting if we caught a few trout, as well.

"Awright, tis mug-up time," Sammy said as he marched off to cut firewood.

We helped gather twigs and broken branches. Daddy cut a large tree as a bench for us to sit on and set up twigs to hang the kettle on. Absolutely nothing could beat a mug-up in the woods.

After we ate, it was back to more fishing. When we got home, we had to clean hundreds of smelts. I found cleaning fish nauseating, but we were starving and had to clean them so Mommy could fry them for supper.

In May the Americans held Armed Forces Day at the radar site. A notice was posted in the Company Store, and talk among the neighbours started. None of us knew what to expect. When the day came, we walked up to High Road and waited for a big stake truck to pick us up. As soon as the truck arrived, we clambered aboard and proceeded up Black Head Hill.

The whole town and the harbour all the way out into the run, with Earl Island in the middle, were spread before me. Lockwood's buildings on the left were a picture of serenity. The large white structures nestled under the hill against the dark green forest. On the opposite side of the harbour, the Hudson's Bay Company buildings, also white, dominated the smaller family dwellings scattered among the trees and alder bushes.

When the truck reached the military base, I was astonished at how many buildings were actually there. We were led through doors at the end of one of the buildings. The hallway seemed to go on forever. As we walked to one of the display rooms, I noticed other long corridors running perpendicular to the one we were in. Then we entered a room where the walls were covered with pictures of planes.

The men who greeted us were dressed in well-pressed uniforms. They explained their planes' capacity to fly, shoot rockets, and track enemy planes. We were a peaceful people and weren't interested in hearing about planes and blowing things up. The men took us to the motor pool and showed us their bulldozers, road graders, and snow removal machines. There, in front of me, was the huge snow blower that had terrified me earlier. Then they took us to the mess hall for food and snacks.

At four o'clock it was all over and we were driven back down the hill. We were happy and excited with the candy and treats we'd been given. It was the first Armed Forces Day for us and the beginning of an annual military open house, a tradition that continued for many years afterward.

Spring has always been my favourite time of year. My world was coming alive again. The birch and balsam trees were budding with baby leaves. Little birds sang in the willows and gladdened my heart. Streams of water ran everywhere from the rapidly melting snow, carving tiny creeks through the soft earth, perfect to float little boats on. Strong breezes whistling through the trees and the crash of the surf were music to my ears. It wasn't too hot yet, so there were no pesky flies to bother us.

Springtime in Cartwright — friends, fun, freedom, and adventure, the things that brought me joy.

The Curl family in 1990. Back row left to right: Sarah, Linda, Flossie, Rhoda, Winnie, Dora. Front row left to right: Phillip, me, Marcella, Edward.

Part Four

Later Life

26

My First Job

In spring 1954, Mommy was pregnant again, but that never stopped her from working. At least once a week her best friend, Alma, sauntered into our house, scrub bucket in one hand and a roll-your-own cigarette in the other. Alma was a jolly woman, taller than my mother and quite a bit bigger. She stood beside the stove while Mommy rolled a cigarette and pulled on a pair of pants, and got her cleaning supplies ready. While she waited, Alma told us a story. Soon the woman had us all in stitches, especially my mother, who tried to compose herself as she gathered her cleaning supplies. Then off they went across the marsh, cigarette smoke billowing into the air, scrub buckets swinging.

Life in our house wasn't easy. I didn't understand my own behaviour. Why did I have to rebel against my mother at every turn? Why was she always picking on me? Why did I feel so alone and insignificant? I tried desperately to get some kind of approval, but it seemed the harder I tried, the more I got yelled at, slapped around, or beaten. What did I have to do to please her?

I often lay awake at night thinking about what I was going to do when I grew up. I wanted to marry a tall, dark, handsome man and have a lot of babies. I was going to treat my children lovingly and with respect. I wouldn't be impatient and cruel. I'd never have my children fight over rags from a bag. I didn't ever want them to come home from school hungry and crawling with head lice. I would get away from Cartwright and go to a big town, to a place I'd read about in Marcie's *True Story* magazines. In those magazines there were stories of children with their own bedrooms, lots of food, and clothing bought in department stores.

"Whass a department store?" I asked Marcie one day. She knew everything.

"Dunno, Jos. I spose it's a big store where ya can buy lotsa stuff."

"Is it bigger den the Company Store?"

"I spose, maid."

At school I wasn't doing well. It must have been an indication of how I felt about myself. The constant bickering at home was affecting me, and I stayed away as much as possible.

Even though Mommy kept trying to clean me up, the head lice problem continued to be a nightmare. We were powerless to do anything about it. Fighting with the Petten family was also relentless. They taunted us until I was enraged and a fight broke out. When I ran to Mommy, I got no sympathy.

"Good nough fer ya, if yer foolish nough ta go fightin," she'd say.

"But, Mom, they say I stink!"

"Praps ya do. And stop cryin, or I'll give ya someting ta cry fer."

When summer began, Mommy found Marcie a job working on weekends for the wife of Bill Morse, the Marconi operator.

"Ya better work hard. Do what yer tol an do yer work right, too. And I don't wanna hear any complaints, either," Mommy told Marcie.

"Awright, Mom," Marcie mumbled, looking scared and unsure.

Marcie was an excellent worker, and Mommy was pleased. But Marcie's job created a bigger burden on me at home. I had to babysit more often and do more work around the house. *Poor me,* I thought constantly. I was angry at the whole world. I didn't have a lot of patience with the little ones. One day I was babysitting, and Eddy, who was now four, was playing in the landwash and waded in over his boots. I pushed his head underwater and kept him there, furious and panic-stricken about what Mommy would do to me for allowing him to get his feet wet. I almost drowned my little brother because of my fear and rage.

Despite my anxieties, I was thrilled to have the summer off and the freedom to roam the beaches and swim in the pond at Lark's Harbour. Summer meant many things — stabbing flatfish in the landwash, catching thornbacks and scullies, picking mussels, digging for clams, and cod jigging with Daddy and Sammy. My mind raced in anticipation of the long summer ahead. I could spend time rollicking on Flag Staff Hill, playing on the Company trolley and around the Company Store. I could play tag and hide-and-seek with my friends and hang out in the long twilight.

Mommy came home from cleaning the Company Store one day and was putting some bologna in the frying pan for supper when she said calmly as though it were nothing, "I gotta job fer ya, Josie."

"W-what?" I stammered.

"I gotta a job fer ya workin fer Mrs. Massie. She'll pay ya $10 dollars a mont."

I froze. I didn't want to go to work. I was only 11 years old and wanted to play with my friends. "But, Mommy, I's too small ta go ta work yet. I don't wanna go!"

"Ya gotta go now cuz I awready tol her ya would."

I couldn't say anything. I was speechless. She'd made up her mind that I was going to work and that was that. I heard the determination in her voice and knew I had to do as I was told.

My thoughts whirled. Where was the summer of fun that I longed for? How would I get to know my family, my home, my community? What about trying to find out who my friends would be? What about getting to feel at home inside myself? I knew, even then, that it was too much too soon. I was already doing more at home than any 11-year-old should have to do.

I ran from the house and headed for the landwash. Flinging myself over a big rock, I watched in tears as sea lice scurried in the seaweed. I felt so sorry for myself. What would I have to do in this job? Would I be able to do it? Would I even know how? I was terrified.

As I calmed down, something occurred to me. I'd be making my own money. I was going to get $10 a month and would be able to buy my own clothes. I hurried back to the house just as Mommy was putting the teapot back on the stove.

"What'll I hafta do?" I asked.

"Dunno, maid. Take care of de youngsters, I spose."

"How many she got?"

"Lots, but whatever ya gotta do, you'd better do it right."

On my first day of work, a Monday, I got up early, washed my face, and wiped it with the filthy towel that hung on the nail. Then I took the comb from its holder and pulled it through my long, wavy hair. It was tangled and my head was tender, though there were no more lice. Mommy had worked hard to clean me up before the job started.

Gloomily, I trudged up the harbour to Mrs. Massie's big white house, which was connected to the Company Store by a long wooden walkway. The size of the house intimidated me. I scuffled up the dirt path from the main road to the back door and stood paralyzed. I hardly had the courage to knock. But I knew the consequences if I didn't. I'd seen Mrs. Massie in the Company Store several times but didn't actually know her. I would never have dared speak to her. She was a woman of status, too important to talk to someone like me. I knew her sons, Don and Lloyd. They were my schoolmates. I wondered what they thought. Did they know yet? I knew there would be much teasing once everyone knew. That was what I was thinking when the door finally opened.

"Hello, Josie, come in," Mrs. Massie said softly.

"Okay, miss."

"You don't have to call me miss."

When I entered Mrs. Massie's house, I noticed how big the kitchen was. Off the kitchen was a large bathroom with a toilet and running water. I hadn't seen that since I'd left Lockwood. In the other half of the house there was a large dining room and living room, but I never went in there. From what I could see in passing, it looked like the ones in the houses I'd read about in magazines.

My duties were to make the beds, wash the dishes, clean the bathroom, and mop the kitchen and bathroom floors.

"You can start by making the beds," Mrs. Massie said as she showed me upstairs.

"Awright, ma'am. Any particular way ya want 'em made?" I asked, hoping she'd show me how.

"No, just as long as the sheets and blankets are smoothed out and the bedspread is tucked neatly over the pillows."

I went around making the beds. Because Mrs. Massie had six boys home at that time, there were a lot of beds to make. The store clerk, Arch Munn, was also boarding there, so I had to do his room, as well. The six children, from eldest to youngest, were Jim, then Donald, Lloyd, Wayne, Douglas, and baby Rickie, who was about a year old and still in diapers. Mrs. Massie was trying to potty-train him but was having a difficult time. She would spank her baby son sometimes, and I felt sorry for him. Spanking was an accepted punishment back then.

Mrs. Massie was a short woman with dark hair and a medium complexion. She had one arm that was slightly but permanently damaged, though I never found out how it had happened. Her build and size were similar to my mother's. I used to wonder if having a lot of children gave women a bit of a belly in front because that was the way both Mrs. Massie and Mommy looked. What I remember best about Mrs. Massie was the way she spoke to me — kindly and with respect. I found that strange.

I didn't see Mrs. Massie much except when she was cooking meals. Unlike in our house, the Massies ate well. I know my own mother was a good cook, but her struggle to find the food to cook was constant. I especially liked the way Mrs. Massie made mashed potatoes. She added lots of butter and milk to make them creamy. We never had mashed potatoes at home. We could never afford all that butter and milk, anyway. I ate in the kitchen with the children, while the rest of the family took their meals in the dining room. I was afraid to even look in there. Mr. Massie came home for every meal, and I was frightened of him.

It didn't take me long to learn my job, and I became confident that I was doing it well. Marcie and I compared what we had to do and how we had to do it. She had to fold and iron clothing. I didn't have to do that. She said that Mrs. Moores was very particular and had to have everything done just so. Every morning I got up and trudged to work. I made the beds first. Then I washed the dishes, cleaned the kitchen and bathroom, and scrubbed the floors. It was hard work for a little girl. There were times when I had to watch the children so Mrs. Massie could go somewhere, maybe for tea in the afternoon or to visit a friend.

Lloyd and Don were close to my age, and since they were my schoolmates, I didn't know what to say or how to act around them. I felt ashamed to go into their bedrooms and make their beds. It made me feel inferior and degraded. I was afraid to touch any of their things, but when I went into Arch Munn's bedroom I did a bit of snooping. I was interested in him because he was from far away, so I was intrigued and curious to find out who he was. I sniffed his shaving lotion and clothing. Everything smelled fresh and good.

I got Saturdays and Sundays off and was always delighted to have free time. Just to be able to go out and explore was heaven to me. With my work at home and my work for Mrs. Massie, I wasn't getting a chance to be a little girl. I woke up one Saturday, though, to discover that Marcie had to work for Mrs. Moores. She was very upset, and I was dismayed, too, because now I had to stay in and help Sally do all the work at home. In Mommy's words our job was to "dig the shack out."

Each Saturday, Mommy put pea soup on the stove, and when it reached a comfortable simmer, she visited Alma while we cleaned the house. We had to dig everything out from underneath my parents' bed, the settee, the stove, and the locker. After cleaning under all the other beds in the house, we had to scour behind the stove. I hated the smell of the sock box. It was a cardboard box piled high with stinky socks and dirty mittens and mixed with wood chips from the firewood, which was also stored behind the stove. There was never-ending clutter. Our last job that Saturday was to scrub the floors before dinner at noon.

We were still cleaning when Mommy returned from Alma's. She quickly added onions to the pea soup, made dumplings, and put the kettle on to boil water for tea. At 12:00 sharp we had to pull out the table and slap the old dishes onto it, some of which had been collected from the dump. Mom cut the bread and called everyone in for dinner. With

10 of us around the table the pea soup didn't last long. We gobbled it up, and the little ones went back outside to play. Looking at one another, we wondered who was going to wash the dishes. No one still at the table wanted to, of course, and Rhoda was too small and sickly.

"Tis Josie's turn!" Sally piped up.

"No, tis not," I protested. "Tis your turn."

"Never mind whose turn it is, maids," Mom said. "An stop fightin."

"But, Mom!" I cried. "I did them last time!"

As usual, though, it was no use arguing, so I lifted the lid off the hot water tank attached to the end of the stove and began washing the dishes. When I was done, I dumped the dirty dishwater outdoors. After our noon Saturday dinner, Mom and Alma always went to the Company Store, leaving me to babysit once again on what should have been my day off.

Activity on the American military base increased, providing even more work for our people. Huge planes continued to land in our harbour, and more and more men in U.S. military uniforms roamed about town. A huge oil tank was being erected just under Flag Staff Hill, not far from our house, with a high fence around it. As a result of all the work, a lot of new people moved into Cartwright. John Hamel and his family were the first to settle across the brook. The Mullinses, composed of Fred and Linda and five children, came from Happy Valley–Goose Bay and were the first to build a place on High Road. Charlie Lethbridge and his wife, Jane, moved in with their family around the cove next door to Uncle Jimmy Pardy's house. And many more families arrived and built houses up the harbour.

That summer Sammy got a job on the salmon collector boat with the Hudson's Bay Company. His left at four o'clock in the morning, cruised around to all the fishing settlements, and collected the day's salmon catch. The collector boat returned every day at about four in the afternoon.

My brother was extremely helpful to Mommy and Daddy and was kind and considerate to us except for poor little Rhoda, whom he pestered mercilessly. He spent a lot of time visiting his buddies and didn't spend much time at home, so I didn't have that many lengthy conversations with him, but I respected him and loved him dearly. Sammy was a man of few words, and though he liked to tease us, he never deliberately hurt us. When he got home from the salmon-collecting job late in the afternoon, Mommy filled the wash pan with water and cleaned his back to get the fishy smell off his body.

Soon after receiving his first few paycheques, Sammy ordered a brand-new guitar from the Eaton's catalogue. I was amazed at how quickly he learned how to play. When he heard a song he liked, he'd ask Marcie, Sal, or me to read the lyrics over and over until he memorized the words. Soon he taught himself a repertoire of songs, mostly country and western. I loved to hear him sing and play and spent as many hours in his room listening to him as I dared.

The summer of 1954 was all work for my family: Daddy at the radar site; Mommy cleaning all the prominent buildings in town and sewing for the mission store; Sammy on the Hudson's Bay Company salmon collector; Marcie at Mrs. Moores's house; and me at Mrs. Massie's. That left poor Sally to look after all the youngsters. She was only 10.

Thanks to the combined earnings coming into our house, we were able to buy store-bought clothing, boots, and shoes for school that fall. We were also able to get canned fruit, fresh fruit, and even fresh eggs sometimes. For the first time in my life, Mommy made potato salad, and the occasional cake started appearing on our table for Sunday supper. It was so exciting! We still got the bag of rags to dig into every time my mother had done enough work to warrant her receiving one. And we still fought over the contents.

The Company Store was a gathering place for everyone. There were no telephones then, so the store was the place where we heard the news about who was sick, who died, and who was doing bad things. There was one story about a girl from around Paradise who was living in the woods and had returned from working in Happy Valley–Goose Bay with some kind of terrible illness. It was a mystery. It turned out to be a sexually transmitted disease, but of course I didn't know what that was at the time. It was all very hush-hush. The whispering at the store went on for days.

Summer twilight in Labrador is long. When I was able to enjoy the lengthy evenings with my friends, it was sheer joy. We walked along High Road hand in hand, stretching across the whole street, singing songs, and talking about certain boys we liked or hated. Or we played around the company wharf and watched teenagers holding hands and kissing, and laughed and giggled at them.

I sometimes think moving to Cartwright was a good thing for our family, if not for me, than certainly for my parents. They now had their own little house, and even though it was small, they seemed content. Mommy and Daddy had struggled so much, living off the land and packing up the family twice a year and moving to find food. We had to survive with no help from the outside world. There was no way we could improve our lifestyle. If we couldn't find food, we simply went hungry. If we didn't have money to buy clothing, Mommy had to make it from bleached flour sacks or whatever scraps she could find. In Cartwright we had five members of the family working, each earning their own bit of money to buy clothing. I would have had to work at home, anyway, so doing it for someone else and being paid wasn't that bad. At least Mrs. Massie didn't yell or swear at me or call me terrible names. And I did like helping people.

27

Challenges

In August 1954, Mommy gave birth to Phillip, a boy. He was adorable, with jet-black hair and squinty eyes. Adults always told us that babies were found somewhere. Now I was 11 years old and was beginning to doubt he'd been found behind a stump, in the landwash, in the woods, or anywhere else. I'd never heard the word *pregnant*. Therefore, the process of Mommy having her babies remained a mystery to me.

Mommy was extremely busy with daily chores and tried to hold on to the old ways of making soap, hooking mats, and sewing our clothing. However, with the availability of cash, she eventually dropped some of the old ways. She made her last batch of homemade soap that year and decided to buy Sunlight from the Company Store from now on.

"It don't do so good a job as mine," she grumbled.

One of my daily chores was to clean and fill the oil lamps with kerosene, which I hated to do. The glass chimneys were black and were very hard to clean. Then one day Mommy came home from the store with a new mantel lamp. It had a long, skinny chimney and was three times brighter than the kerosene oil lamps we had always used. At first Mommy wouldn't let us touch it. However, I eventually got used to cleaning and lighting it. One night I turned it up too high and it caught fire. The whole thing went up in a puff of smoke!

"Ya bloody little fool!" Mommy screamed. "Don't ya know dat cost money?"

"Sorry, Mommy. I dint mean ta burn it." I kept my voice very respectful, but for the first time I was laughing inside. I now saw a funny side to my mother's rages.

Mommy tried to teach me many of her skills, and now I wish I'd paid more attention. But being a tomboy I wanted to tag along with Daddy and Sammy. I wasn't interested in learning household things. I wanted to be outside. During the winter, I asked Daddy to teach me how to make dog harnesses, how to splice rope, how to lash the komatik box onto the komatik, how to mix the dogs' food, and how to command the dogs and handle them at feeding time. Occasionally, my pestering paid off and Daddy let me take the team out for a barrel of water. I discovered that the trick was to let the dogs know who was boss.

In the spring and summer, Sammy taught me how to use a slingshot, how to walk on stilts, and how to play football or soccer. Daddy showed me how to knit a fishnet, how to string the twine needle used for knitting fishnets, and how to row a boat. When we eventually got an engine, he taught me how to change the sheer pin. The one thing he wouldn't teach me or even let me touch was his guns. But I loved to watch as he cleaned and loaded them.

Daddy was very good with a pocket knife, as well, and deftly cut sealskins into thin strings of babbish to fill his rackets. And I observed intently as Sammy set his rabbit snares, and soon learned how to set my own.

Although Daddy had his polio infirmity to contend with, he limped around effortlessly, his breath puffing into the frosty air as he prepared the dog team for the many chores necessary to keep his family warm and fed. After supper, it was even a joy to watch him cut the shavings used for lighting the fire each morning.

"How do ya do dat, Daddy?" I asked one evening as I sprawled on the floor beside him.

He spread his legs in front of him. "Well, Jimmy, if ya gotta know, tis like this."

Daddy picked up his draw knife and placed it on the split wedged securely between his legs. Then he put the blade two-thirds up the wood, which was slanting away from him. With a clean, smooth stroke he pulled the knife toward him. A neat coil of wood formed each time he did it, producing curly wood shavings still attached to the wood. With great patience he showed me how to do the job. Since I was inquisitive and a willing learner, I mastered many of Daddy's skills and thrived on the challenges. Although more than 50 years have passed, I still remember how to do most of the things my father taught me.

Around this time I heard about the Pentecostal church, which was something new in our region. At that time there was only the Anglican church in Cartwright. There was a small village behind Black Head Hill called Goose Cove where all the "saved" people lived. They were strange people. I'd heard rumours about them rolling around on the floor in some kind of trance.

"Whass a trance?" I asked Marcie one day.

"Dunno. They praises the Lord and rolls around shoutin, 'Hallelujah, hallelujah!'"

"What fer?"

"Cuz they's saved."

"Whass they saved from?" I pestered.

"Sin! Don't ya know what sin is?"

"I wanna go ta Goose Cove an get saved den," I said.

So I got up the courage to ask Sammy to take me to Goose Cove to find out for myself what all the chatter was about. "Will ya take me to Goose Cove?" I asked my brother one Sunday shortly afterward.

"Awright, I'll take ya, but ya'd better be good an don't go laughin in church."

As we entered the little church, people glared at me. They obviously didn't take kindly to a stranger in their midst. Then the pastor started preaching. My mouth dropped open as he got wound up. I was mesmerized and had the fright of my life. If I didn't repent right then and there, I was going to burn in hell forever! People waved their arms as they sang over and over: "I am saved. I am saved. Jesus bids me go free!"

For days I couldn't get the voice of that preacher out of my head. He talked about Oral Roberts, and I thought that man was God. We were handed pamphlets and told to repent and that our lives would be changed forever. Even though I was tempted, I didn't have the nerve to walk up to the front of the church. Later I occasionally went there to enjoy the songs and to make fun of the people testifying, speaking in tongues, gesturing weirdly, and praising the Lord.

In the fall of 1954 another school year began, and once again I didn't do well. I wasn't interested in applying myself to my studies. Instead I daydreamed of escaping St. Peter's. Sixteen, which was the magic age for escape, seemed far away. Filled with longing to roam, I dreamed of the exciting places I'd read about. I wasn't afraid to try anything as long as it was outside my house with someone else's family or with my friends. I'd start a fight in an instant if someone rubbed me the wrong way, so I had few friends. I could never bring anyone home, anyway, because of the state of my house and all the little ones crawling about.

My challenge was to devise ways to escape the house, so I lied to my mother about everything. I cherished every moment I was free. When I dreamed, it was of falling, falling, falling … never reaching the ground.

On January 15, 1955, I turned 12. I can't recall a cake or candles, a card or a gift. Being a natural early riser, I woke up before my parents, and just before my father, to light the fire every morning. The aroma of the fire starting soothed me, and besides, I cherished every single moment I could share with Daddy before a half-dozen other youngsters sauntered into our tiny space. Mommy was next to join us around the stove. Small talk was to the point.

"Marnin, Mammy," Daddy would say to Mommy.

"Tis gittin starmy," she'd comment.

"Tis. I'm goin huntin tomarra mornin."

"Where ya goin?"

"Out roun Hare Harbour somewhere — me an Vic an Henry John."

"How long ya goin fer?" she'd ask.

"A couple or tree days, praps."

"Be careful."

Early in the summer of 1955, I kept getting a sore throat. It worried Mommy, so she decided to make one of our rare trips across the harbour to the mission hospital. As it turned out, I had tonsillitis, and my mother was informed that I'd have to go to St. Anthony Hospital in Newfoundland to get them out. Mommy, it seemed, had to go with me.

"Where's Sin Anthony?" I asked my mother as we strolled down the familiar mission road.

"Dunno, maid."

"Where's Newfundlan den?"

"Dunno that, either. All I know is we gotta fly there."

"Fly? Ya means in a plane?"

"How else is ya gonna fly? Yer not a bird, is ya?"

"Oh, Mommy, I hope we don't crash. There's a plane crashed over in Burdett's Brook."

"Go on, Jos. Leave it ta you ta come up wit someting like that. Anyway, we gotta go, an dat's all dere is to it."

I fell silent, thinking about what had just transpired. I had to fly to some foreign place and have an operation. It would be my first time out of Labrador and certainly my first time on a plane. I couldn't wait to tell my friends.

The day the plane was expected I was all eyes and ears as we searched the sky. We were told to go across the harbour and wait. Suddenly, the plane was flying right over us! There were a couple of Indian children onboard. I'd never seen real Indians before. They laughed and pointed at us, which made me feel really uncomfortable.

I squeezed into the tiny seat and struggled with the seat belt. The propellers started up and went so fast I couldn't see them turn. We taxied out into the harbour, with the engines revving. Then we were in the air!

The houses got smaller and smaller, and then the aircraft began to shake. That terrified me. I grabbed Mommy's hand and looked at her. She was white as a sheet, her face rigid with fear. I was shocked. I couldn't imagine my mother being afraid of anything except caterpillars.

It was a brilliant sunny day, and I was entranced as I gazed out the window. The rugged coastline stretched for miles. *The world's some big,* I thought.

While flying over the coastal mountains, I spotted hundreds of small ponds that resembled mirrors. As we crossed the Strait of Belle Isle separating Newfoundland from Labrador, the sun glistened so brightly off the water that I struggled to keep my eyes open. From high up the icebergs looked like white dots. Then the plane flew close to the water and the majestic ice mountains displayed their true beauty. They kept changing form as we soared by them.

"I was always fraid of dem ol tings," Mommy said suddenly.

"Why, Mommy? Der beautiful."

"Yeh, till they founder down on top a ya."

Once we reached the Newfoundland shore, the plane dipped so low that I could see sheep in the fields. I was ecstatic. I'd never seen farm animals before. I shook my mother and pointed at the sheep. She was too sick to care, but made a slight attempt to look. Shortly afterward, we landed at St. Anthony Airport. We were picked up by the mission truck and brought to the hospital, a huge brown brick building on an embankment surrounded by fencing. It was the largest building I'd ever seen. As we entered the front door, there was no doubt in my mind that it was a hospital. The smell reminded me of the time Sammy had brought ether home from the dump.

We were admitted and brought to a huge ward with other women. The row of beds reminded me of the little girls' dormitory at Lockwood. I was happy that Mommy got a bed next to me, because I would have been scared without her. We settled in for the day and waited for something to eat.

When our meal came, I eyed the plate of food suspiciously. "Whass this supposed ta be, Mommy?"

"Ya never mind now, Josie. Jus eat it an be quiet."

My mother didn't call me Josie very often, and I liked the sound of her saying my name. Maybe I would get to know her a little better here. After all, being away at the hospital when I was attacked by husky dogs, away to boarding school, and away from home working for other people, I'd never spent much time with her. At around eight o'clock that night a nurse's aid came in and gave everyone a back rub. They applied an alcohol solution that felt wonderful. When the aide left, the women in the ward started telling stories. It was a revelation to me. I discovered that my mother was funny. There was a lot of laughter and I was having a wonderful time. I didn't even think about the operation until the lights went out at ten o'clock. The women in the ward continued to talk and laugh well into the night.

I was scheduled for surgery the next morning. I was scared and said so.

"Try not ta worry, Josie," Mommy said softly. "Yer gonna be awright."

"Okay, Mommy."

Despite my worries, I was enjoying this experience with my mother and finally drifted off to sleep. The next morning I was wheeled into a room, but my mother was left behind. I was lifted onto an operating table with a huge light above me. A mask was placed over my face. It smelled exactly like the stuff Sam had brought home from the dump. *Oh, no,* I thought, *I'm gonna die!*

I was told to count and only got to three. The next thing I remember I was coming out of the anaesthetic and feeling groggy. My throat seemed to be on fire. Several nurses were laughing and joking around me.

Then I heard someone say, "She's a feisty little thing."

"She certainly is and she's strong, too," someone else said.

As I listened, I learned that while I was coming out of the anaesthetic, I had hit one of the nurses in the face with my fist. I was horrified. It was the talk of the hospital for the rest of the trip — how little Josie Curl had ploughed a nurse in the face.

When I look back now, I realize this was such a unique experience. At home I didn't get along with my mother and felt I had no connection with her. Yet when I was alone with her for a whole week, I discovered that she was really a nice person. She was extremely polite, and according to the nurses, she was kind and considerate and had a wonderful sense of humour. I was so proud of her.

An amazing thing happened after I had my tonsils out. I stopped bedwetting. I was delighted as, of course, was Mommy. She made me a new feather mattress. I cleaned up my bin, scrubbed the floor, placed my new feather mattress in it, sprawled across it, and sobbed. This was a turning point for me. It started me on a different journey, one with a little more confidence and a better attitude toward life. I didn't smell like pee all the time. But my new confidence was short-lived.

Now that it was summer again I had to go back to work for Mrs. Massie. I also babysat for several other women during that summer. There was a very traumatic side to babysitting. Many times I was sexually abused. I was only 12 and so little for my age. In many families the men would come home from work drunk and molest me. I was defenceless against them. I felt powerless and terrified to do anything about it. There were many incidences of sexual abuse during that time. All the confidence I'd gained was soon replaced by shame.

Financially, my family was managing much better with everyone working. I didn't have to give my money to Mommy that year and was allowed to keep it for myself. Carefully, after getting hold of an Eaton's catalogue, I made out an order for two dresses at $2.98 each, a wide leather belt with two interchangeable buckles, a pair of black-and-white saddle shoes, a crinoline, and two pairs of bobby socks. I was elated. At the Company Store I sent my order out, and two weeks later, when the *Kyle* was expected, I trudged back to the store to see if my order was in. I was getting anxious because the new school year was starting soon and I needed the clothes.

Finally, they came! I ran all the way home, tore the package open, and gazed at my things, unable to believe my eyes. The dresses were beautiful. The shoes shone, and the belt fitted me perfectly. I loved my crinoline and my bobby socks. I was going to be the best-dressed girl at St. Peter's this time.

"Get away from that lookin glass, Jos," Mommy said when she spotted me. "That ol Jos is some conceited," she told the rest of my family.

I was crushed. Why couldn't Mommy say something nice to me? Why couldn't she be thankful that I had money to buy my own clothes?

Marcie, Sally, and I got confirmed before we started school that year. Mommy ordered confirmation dresses from the Eaton's catalogue for us, and we had to learn the catechism. I was lazy and didn't want to learn it. I hated church, anyway, and was terrified of the bishop who was expected to arrive on the *Kyle*. It turned out to be a good experience. We had to attend Holy Communion, and I felt grown up as I knelt to receive the body and blood of Jesus. The wine tasted awful and the bread stuck to the roof of my mouth, causing me to gag. Once we were confirmed, we had to receive the body and blood of Jesus every Sunday.

Summer was passing quickly, and everyone was busy. Daddy and Sammy went cod jigging every chance they got. I always wanted to tag along, of course. One day Daddy took Sally and me out fishing. He'd gotten an engine for our little boat, and it was wonderful not to have to row against the strong tide in the run. When we reached the shelter of Earl Island, Daddy dropped anchor. We were happily jigging for cod when suddenly a whale came up right beside us. Sally and I screamed. I watched in awe as its sleek black body rolled through the surface of the sea.

"Tis a small one," Daddy said.

"Don't look very small ta me," I piped up.

"Tis only a grumpus. He won't hurt ya."

We watched as it kept surfacing and blowing spray into the air. Eventually, Daddy decided to find another spot to jig, so he started up the engine. Sally was standing in the boat, still marvelling over the whale.

"Ya better sit down, Sally," Daddy said before putting the engine into gear.

"Nah. I be awright."

Daddy put the engine into gear, and Sally went flying backward into the boat, falling over the tot (seat) and landing in the bottom among the fish and the gore. I laughed so hard I couldn't jig, but Sally didn't think it was funny at first. Then, before we knew it, we were all laughing.

I wasn't paying attention to what I was doing, and when I threw the jigger back over the side of the boat, the hook pierced my leg, going deep into the flesh past the barb. In seconds I was crying instead of laughing. The jigger wouldn't come out, so the choice was either to rip it out or let Daddy cut it out. I screamed when he opened his pocket knife and put the blade against my leg, though I knew there was no other way. One quick cut placed skillfully along the steel hook and the jigger fell from my leg. But there was blood everywhere. I have the scar to this day. That ended our fishing excursion. When we got back to our house, Mommy bandaged the wound and it healed in a less than a week. We laughed so hard that we cried at the events of the day, with Sal's sore rump and my aching leg.

Being only 12 but going on 20, I was beginning to enjoy part of my life. I found some teen magazines, and all of a sudden felt grown up. I wasn't peeing in my bed anymore, so I was feeling a little better about myself. I tried to ignore Mommy's constant badgering about my being stuck up, conceited, and lazy.

In late summer, before school started, I began to go out at night as late as I dared. Mommy cursed and swore at me because she was worried that I'd get into trouble. I wanted to show off my new clothes and wear makeup, but my mother wouldn't allow makeup, so I had to wait until I got away from home to put it on. My new friends and I had a wonderful time pretending to be grown-ups. After all, I was working and making my own money.

Back in school in September 1955, I sat in my seat on the first day and gazed at the front of the room to inspect the new teacher.

"My name is Mr. Cooper [not his real name], and I'm from Newfoundland," he said.

I couldn't help but laugh at his accent, which was different from ours. Newfoundland was still alien to me despite my trip to the hospital in St. Anthony. In our history and geography books we'd read about the pulp and paper mills and the log drives in Corner Brook and on the Exploits River, but I didn't really know much about the place.

Shortly after school started, my class was asked to stay behind one day. Puzzled, we looked at one another. A new minister, the Reverend Tibbo, came to Cartwright in 1955. His wife, whom I'd worked for periodically during the summer, came into our classroom and asked if we wanted to form a Girl Guides group.

"Whass Girl Guides?" I asked a girl sitting behind me, but got no reply.

Mrs. Tibbo tried to explain the history of Girl Guides in Canada and Cartwright specifically. She told us that the first Girl Guides in this part of Canada was started in Cartwright in 1924 and was the very first in Newfoundland or Labrador. For a number of years, Guiding had faded but then was brought back in 1938 under the leadership of Betty Sparshot and Cora Fequet. However, it became inactive again after their departure. Mrs. Tibbo thought it might be a good idea to start Girl Guides here again.

The reverend's wife went on to tell us about, patrols, uniforms, the Guide Law, and the Guide Promise. It sounded complicated. *Would I ever be able to do all that?* I asked myself. But Mrs. Tibbo explained that it would be fun, that we would learn valuable life lessons, and that we would earn badges.

"Badges, miss?" I asked.

"Yes, you'll get the opportunity to earn badges if you're willing to strive for them."

"Strive?"

"Work, Josephine. If you work for them."

So Guiding in Cartwright got underway once more, and I was a member of the Daffodil Patrol. It all happened so quickly. Uniforms were ordered, and sashes, ropes, badges, and all the other paraphernalia arrived in various packages. Every week we met in the little church.

We learned the Guide Motto, which was "Be prepared," and the Guide Promise — "I promise on my honour to do my best. To do my duty to God and the Queen. To help other people at all times and to obey the Guide Law." We also learned the Guide Law and the Guide Creed.

There were 15 of us, ranging in ages from 12 to 16. Of course, I was one of the smaller girls. I loved every moment of Guiding — learning how to tie knots, about bugs, and about leaves and trees. And I loved the long hikes we took.

Eventually, Clarice Hopkins took over as captain from Mrs. Tibbo, and Mrs. Keddie from Lockwood came and taught us sewing. I wanted to earn all the badges, and worked hard at my homemaker's, cook's, and rope-tying badges. I've carried the lessons I learned in Girl Guides with me throughout my life.

On our Girl Guide hikes we travelled to Goose Cove, Black Head Hill, or the pond at Lark's Harbour. Those trips were heavenly. As we hiked, we sang songs like "She'll Be Coming 'Round the Mountain" and "Row, Row, Row Your Boat."

My baby brother, Phillip, was a year old and starting to toddle about. He was also able to babble a few words. I loved the way Mommy talked to her babies. She was expecting yet another one and was as big as a puncheon tub. I didn't ask any questions but paid attention to some of the rumours I'd heard about babies. When I heard other girls talk about "their periods," I wondered what that was. However, I was too scared to ask and no one offered to tell me. Then Marcie got her period.

"Yer a woman now, Marcie," Mommy said to my sister without elaborating.

I saw shame in Marcie's eyes and felt shame for her, but had no idea why we were ashamed. Marcie was a smart, good-looking young girl with the voice of an angel. She was in her early teens and was dating a few boys at that time. I loved her so and wanted to be just like her.

My mother gave birth to her thirteenth child in September 1955 around the time I became a Girl Guide. It was turning cold, and we were preparing the house for the winter. Hunting season for waterfowl was exciting for us because, for the most part, we'd been eating fish all summer. Things had changed rapidly at home. We'd arrived in Cartwright three years ago with Sam, Marcie, me, Sal, Rhoda, Eddie, and Winnie. Now we had Dora, Phillip, and Tony, making our little home very crowded.

Then, when Tony was four months old, he got quite sick. Of course, my mother had no way of knowing how ill he was. A few days later, early in the morning, she climbed the ladder to our loft, something she never did.

"Whass wrong, Mommy?" I asked.

"Baby Tony died last night," she said sadly.

28

Coping with Tragedy

When wee Tony died at only four months old, I was either too busy or too wrapped up in my own misery to know how sick he'd been. At age 13 I was ignorant about many aspects of life, including death. Nothing was explained, so I had to figure everything out on my own. I knew he went to heaven. But where was that? Mommy told us he wasn't ever coming back to us, so I experienced sadness as I'd never felt before.

This was the fourth time my parents had endured the grief of losing a child. His tiny body lay at the wake in a box draped in white linen in the bedroom. I'd never seen a dead body before and was afraid to look closely at him. Seeing the sadness in the eyes of my siblings was painful. Their faces were full of questions and puzzlement. Most of them were too young to understand what had happened to their little brother.

"Whass wrong wit Tony, Mommy?" three-year-old Dora asked.

"Little Tony's gone to heaven, Doey," my mother answered quietly.

My tears mingled with the boiling cornmeal as I stirred the dogs' food on the dark porch. The only light source was the firelight filtering through the cracks in the stove. As the eerie illumination danced around the room, I thought of poor little Tony and wept. I wondered if I could have done anything to help.

Girl Guides were my only escape from the sadness and the seemingly endless rules and responsibilities at home. Guiding also offered me a few hours to forget the pain of the abuse I always carried with me.

I excelled at sewing and became one of the top Girl Guides in needlework. I think I'd inherited some of my mother's talents. She had taught me how to do different stitches and how to embroider, and I'd discovered that sewing gave me a great sense of accomplishment. After all, Mommy's sewing was now reaching the far corners of the globe by way of the tourists who travelled on the *Kyle* each summer.

Life kept improving financially for my parents. When Daddy got his paycheque, he harnessed the dogs and went to the store to stock up on food and supplies. Although our budget was limited, when our earnings were combined with fresh game, we ate better than ever before. Sometimes we even had eggs, apples, oranges, cookies, and a whole waxed bologna, which my mother hung on a nail on the porch.

"Awright!" Mommy cried one day. "Which one of ya little blood-of-a-ones was digging at this bologna dis time?" She took the bologna from its nail and slapped it on the kitchen table.

"Twasn't me!" several of us said in unison.

"Me, neither," piped up another child.

Mommy didn't have the energy to beat all of us, so she said, "If I ever catch yas in the act, ya'll git the lacin of yer life."

Somewhere along the journey of my short life, I'd become a thief. I'd stolen from the children at Lockwood. I stole from my classmates at St. Peter's. I stole from the Company Store a few times. And when Mommy went out on cleaning jobs, I filched chunks of bologna and pinched cookies and other goodies she'd hidden in our porch loft.

One day, after Daddy brought home some food, I watched as Mommy piled tins of Vienna sausages into the crude cupboard on the inside porch. I got my chance after school a few days later when nobody was home and I went snooping for the sausages. When I found the tins, I grabbed one, went outside, stood at the end of the house in a snowbank, and began eating. They were delicious. However, I didn't know that Sally was visiting Alma next door. Chewing happily on a sausage, I glanced up suddenly. There was Sally staring at me! I didn't know what to say.

"Do ya want one, Sal?" I finally asked, pushing the can toward her.

"No, I don't. And I'm gonna tell Mommy, too." She walked away quickly.

I was done for and knew it. I'd been caught red-handed. True to her word, Sally blabbed to our mother.

"Ya little blood-of-a-one!" Mommy yelled. "What did ya go an do a ting like that fer?" She grabbed a belt. *Whack! Whack!* Again and again. I started to cry because it hurt so much. She gave me one of the worst beatings of my life that day, one I'll never forget.

Marcie was growing up fast, and I felt as if I were losing my best friend. She was dating Austin Pardy, one of our neighbours. His parents, Austin and Betty, were prominent members of our community. Austin was a respected war veteran, and Betty was from Great Britain. They had three children: Austin Junior, my friend Cynthia, and David, the youngest. David was cute, and I had a crush on him. Marcie was 15 years old. She and Austin Junior fell madly in love, and Marcie got pregnant. It was understood that they would get married and that was exactly what happened. I wasn't allowed to attend the wedding because I had to stay home and look after the youngsters. Mommy and Daddy were heartbroken, and so was I. My sister, my guardian and mentor all of my life, was suddenly gone.

At first I liked Austin. He was an extremely funny little man and made us laugh. He even won over Mommy for a time. However, he couldn't hold a job and drank a lot. My mother was against the drink.

In the spring of 1956, after the snow started melting, Austin, Marcie, Sammy, several neighbours, and I built a little house for the newlyweds on the hill off the fork leading to High Road. Although Marcie was only 15, she seemed much older and went about setting up her house and getting ready for the arrival of their baby. My sister was heartbroken when she lost the baby. Her first-born son died of complications at birth. She got pregnant again, and Terry was born, healthy and strong. Although I spent as much time as I could at her house, I didn't pay much attention to Marcie's life. I was too wrapped up in my own little world of growing up.

In March 1956, Sammy turned 19. He was a man now — tall, muscular, strong, and healthy, a son to be proud of. Sammy was a real tease when he was home, always needling somebody, especially Rhoda. Once he made her so angry, she threw a pair of scissors at him and they stuck in his leg. Mommy gave Rhoda the beating of her life. He nicknamed Sally Ol' Ding-Derry. I have no idea where that nickname came from. When Sammy wasn't busy pampering his dog team and training them for the Easter races, he was hunting small game, hauling wood and water for Mommy, or playing his guitar and mandolin. He was playing well by now and had learned a lot of new songs. Since he couldn't read, we wrote the songs out for him and read them to him until he memorized them.

Sammy searched the radio stations for songs by Hank Williams, Hank Snow, Conway Twitty, Kitty Wells, and even Elvis Presley. Elvis wasn't his favourite singer. He liked songs such as "I'm So Lonesome I Could Cry," "Honky Tonk Man," and "Old Shep." Mommy and Daddy were so proud of him when he won the dog team race one year. Sammy didn't seem surprised at all and took it all in stride. He was very pleased with his team, though.

Sammy continued to work for the Hudson's Bay Company on the salmon-collecting boat. Even though the collector was a fairly big vessel, about 40 or 50 feet long, there were only two workers — skipper Robert Coombs and my brother.

In the summer of 1956 I was once more working for Mrs. Massie, and since Marcie was now married, I had to work for Mrs. Moores, as well. With those two jobs and babysitting for what seemed like half of Cartwright, I was short-tempered and detested having to do anything at home or look after all my younger siblings.

Early one morning I shuffled up the road, heading for Mrs. Massie's house, feeling sorry for myself. Being a little bit early for work, I meandered onto the Hudson's Bay wharf and gazed into the sea. Flatfish and sculpins scurried among the rocks, and seaweed swayed with the tide. It was so peaceful there all alone. What was I going to do? What would become of me? I didn't like my life now. I thought about Marcie. I cried for her and her dead baby. I cried for Tony, my dead baby brother. Then I felt ashamed of hating my life and thought of Mommy. She was expecting yet another baby. Where were we going to put that one?

Then I thought about Sammy and how my mother pampered him and catered to his every whim. She treated him as if he was special. Every day when he got home from the salmon collector she washed his back. Why couldn't she treat me like that? Life was miserable, I thought, and I didn't want to go to work. But I had to go. So I picked myself up and dragged my feet up the path to Mrs. Massie's back door.

Mrs. Massie's children were playing outside already. They were getting bigger. Little Rickie was finally potty-trained. My schoolmates, Don and Lloyd, seemed to stay out of my way. I envied them. I started picking up the dishes, making the beds, and getting on with my day. *At least I'll have the night off,* I thought as I yanked the blankets off one of the beds.

Every day around four o'clock my mother watched for the salmon collector to come around the point as she prepared supper. On this day it was sunny and hot, with not a ripple on the water. We had all returned from work and were waiting for Sammy to arrive so we could have supper.

When I glanced out the window, I spied Uncle Bucky coming across the marsh toward our house, swaying and staggering as though he were drunk. He came in the door and banged the wall with his fist, yelling incoherently, muttering something about a damn boat and about Sammy falling overboard. Uncle Bucky seemed crazy. Everyone hurried over to him. Daddy settled Uncle Bucky into a chair and tried to calm him so we could make sense of what he was babbling.

"Sammy's in de ... de water!" Uncle Bucky spluttered. "Men tryin ta fetch him out, but they couldn't reach him in time. De men is still lookin."

"What?" my father demanded.

"Sammy drowned! They couldn't get ta him in time an he's gone! The men is still lookin fer him."

Mommy went into labour with the shock. People started coming in and hugging my mother, and then she was whisked away to the hospital across the harbour. I was left alone with my younger siblings. *What do I do now?* I kept wondering. *Do I go ahead and feed the kids? What should I do?* I kept gazing out the window as the boats searched for my brother's body.

It didn't take them long to find him. When they did, they discovered that he had kicked off one of his hip rubbers. He was an excellent swimmer, but once his hip rubbers filled with water, he didn't have a chance. They dragged him under. I remember thinking that no one could drown on such a beautiful day. Maybe in a violent storm someone might get washed overboard, but not on a day like this one.

In the days that followed we heard the whole story. When the salmon collector cruised into Cartwright's harbour that day, there were a number of small motorboats lined up along the Company wharf. They'd come to shop for supplies. This caused a jam-up at the wharf, and there wasn't enough room for the collector to dock. Sammy stood on the bow of the collector, his hip rubbers pulled up, waiting to throw the rope to somebody on the wharf. Robert, the skipper, decided to circle and wait for the other vessels to leave the wharf. As he turned the wheel to veer away from the dock, he threw Sammy off the bow.

The nurse across the harbour had a dilemma — what to do with our extremely distraught mother? In the little Cartwright hospital, and in a super-altered state, my mother gave birth to Linda that day. After giving birth to 14 babies, my mother was sent to St. Anthony Hospital in Newfoundland for a hysterectomy, leaving me to care for the little ones.

I don't remember Sammy's funeral. As a matter of fact, I didn't even know where he was buried until many years later. I couldn't bring myself to go there. I shut down emotionally at that point. For me it was better not to feel anything.

Although it was very difficult, I did the best I could to take care of my siblings. Dad had to go to work, of course, and I had to keep the household going. One day he wanted me to cook ducks for supper.

"Ducks, Daddy? I dunno how ta cook them."

"I know, Jimmy. I'll show ya."

The ducks were sitting in the heat and would spoil if they weren't cooked, so I had to try. Daddy stuffed the ducks for me before he went to work. He also instructed me on what to do. Even though I'd watched Mom cook ducks many times, I hadn't paid much attention.

"Get the big pot, Jimmy, an render out some salt pork. Then put the birds in it. Pour water on 'em an let 'em cook."

"How do I make duff, Daddy?"

"Ya don hafta make duff, Jimmy. I'll finish that when I come home."

Just after dinner, I stoked the fire, put the ducks in the pot, filled it with water, and let them cook. However, I'd put too much water in the pot and had forgotten to add salt. When Daddy came home and lifted the lid, he saw that everything was a mess. All the stuffing was soaked out of the birds and was floating around in the pot.

"What have ya got done, Jimmy?" he asked, bewildered.

"Dunno, Daddy," I said, half laughing, half crying.

We looked at each other, laughed, and then cried.

29

Early Teens

The dynamics of our family changed drastically after Sammy's death. With Linda, our new baby sister, clutched tightly in her arms, Mommy returned from the hospital beaten and grief-stricken. She was recovering from a hysterectomy and having a baby, but no suffering could compare with the devastation of losing Sammy, her pride and joy. And she had the overwhelming job of finding food, caring for a newborn, and attending to her family.

I was still working and babysitting for several people in the community and was now mature enough to realize I needed to help my mother. So I did whatever I could. Alma, my mother's best friend, was wonderful. She was there for Mommy every day, and the people in Cartwright gave freely of their food, time, compassion, and support. Aunt Dulcie and Uncle Bucky helped out a great deal, too.

My body was changing rapidly now, and I didn't understand what was happening to me. Hair was growing in certain places, my bust was filling out, and there was absolutely no one I could talk to about everything. I was becoming more interested in my appearance, and being an oversensitive person, any negative comment from my mother hurt me deeply.

One day two of my closest friends and I were playing in the woods. We talked about life as we knew it and eventually started chatting about menstruation. All three of us had older sisters who menstruated, and we were curious about what that involved.

"How do they do that?" one of the girls asked.

"Dunno, maid, but I sees blood on their clothes," the other girl said.

"Yeh, but where do it come from — their bums or from that other place?"

Our curiosity was so intense that we took down our pants and shoved sticks up our vaginas to make them bleed. They did bleed, but not because of any period. We had no idea we could have hurt ourselves badly. We were curious little girls trying to find answers to some fundamental questions. No one would speak of such things to their children. It was just too shameful.

I was beginning to notice a few boys at school. When I saw up-the-harbour girls flirting with boys, I wanted to compete with them, so I ordered more new clothes from the Eaton's catalogue. I was proud that I could pay for them myself.

My greatest challenge was to get a little more freedom from my mother and family obligations. I was determined to find ways to go out more often. The simplest method was to work hard and earn permission but that didn't seem to do the trick. So I started not to care about my mother's approval. I was aware of the consequences of disobeying her. I knew that when I stayed out too late I'd get a beating. For the most part I was on my own. With Marcie married and Sammy in heaven, I had no one to keep me in check.

Books and magazines were passed around town, and eventually I got my hands on them. The pictures were breathtaking. I drooled over full-page spreads of Ricky Nelson, Bobby Darin, and Elvis Presley. How could they look so perfect? I was in love with all of them. Although I didn't often get the opportunity, I listened to songs on the radio about lost love such as "It Don't Hurt Anymore," "I Can't Help It If I'm Still in Love with You," and "Dear John."

Gradually, the citizens of Cartwright got used to the American military invasion. The GIs roaming the streets wore nice clothes and looked sexy in peaked caps and skintight T-shirts. From a distance I studied their tall, lean bodies, their mannerisms, the way they walked. Some of the GIs seemed very young, not to mention handsome. I went to the Company Store and Fequet's Store frequently, hoping to see a certain fellow and get his attention.

I was a lonely little girl trying too hard to be a grown-up. I had big dreams of getting away from Cartwright. Although I didn't know where in the world I wanted to go, or even what the world was really like, I dreamed of being a singer like Bobby Darin or Johnny Cash, or an actress like Elizabeth Taylor. She was so beautiful!

All my friends were getting taller, so I fretted about my height. Was I going to stay this small forever? Feelings stirred within my body that I didn't understand and didn't know how to react to. My need to be liked, the craving to be cared for and cared about, was overwhelming, and the desire to be loved raged through me like wildfire. I would get a crush on someone in an instant, but found it difficult to speak. Always I felt inferior and out of place.

My mother worried about the GIs. "Stay way from them ol fellers if ya knows what's good fer ya." She feared the arrival of the ships that brought materials for the military base. "An I don't even wanna hear bout you bein up round dat dock when those boats comes in."

"I won't go down dere, Mommy," I assured her. "Don't worry."

"Don't go near them ol fellers. God only knows what they'll do ta ya."

For the most part I did stay away from those men, but I wanted to go because I knew other girls had visited the dock and had no problems.

When school started up again in September 1956, I got interested in a few of the boys in my class. Being a two-room school with all grades, some of the boys were older than I was. Dave Pardy, Cynthia's brother, was cute. My heart thumped every time I went to visit her and saw him. Finally, he asked me out. I was thrilled to be going on a date. We walked along High Road hand in hand. For a long time we kissed, and the feelings that had been stirring in my tiny body grew even more frightening and disturbing.

In January 1957 I turned 14. I began dating GIs and believed them when they told me they loved me. I believed them when they said I was attractive, smart, and beautiful. I believed every promise. I gave them my mind, soul, spirit, and body. I gave them sex freely, as though it was the most natural thing in the world to do. And maybe it was, but at 14? It felt wonderful to be held, kissed, caressed, and told that I was special. But during intercourse I felt absolutely nothing. Now I ask myself why I kept doing it. The answer is simple: I craved attention, longed for affection and the moment of feeling loved.

I didn't know what being "easy" meant and had never heard of promiscuity. I had no idea I could be an object to be passed around like candy, the source of a cruel bet or another notch on the trunk of a spruce. In search of love I had an evening ritual. I washed the dishes, helped my mother get the little ones to bed, put them to sleep, walked the floor with them, sang them a lullaby, and then I could get ready to go out.

I had ordered a hairbrush and a makeup set from the Eaton's catalogue. Now I stood in front of the only mirror in our house, brushed my hair, and applied my lipstick.

"Don put too much a dat ol stuff on, Jos, an don be so conceited," my mother growled.

"I'm not conceited," I insisted.

I wanted to smack her and tell her to shut up and leave me alone, but I gritted my teeth and continued to put on my lipstick, trying to ignore her cutting comments. I thought it better not to argue with her or I might not get out at all.

That was the way that winter went for me. I tried to listen to my mother some of the time, but life got more and more unbearable. I didn't care how much pain Mommy was in. I couldn't see beyond my own self-centred issues to care about her or anyone else. I was getting some of my needs met, and that was all that mattered to me.

I started dating a GI named Jerry during the winter of 1957. I told him I was 16, and he seemed to believe me, even though I looked 12. After getting away from the house in the evening, I went to the fork in the road where the trucks stopped to let the GIs off. That was where we met. We walked across High Road to the power plant. Jerry had a key. When we entered the power plant, we found it dark, noisy, and smelling of fuel. We weren't supposed to be in there, so Jerry didn't turn on the lights. He used a cigarette lighter to find a decent spot to spread his jacket for us to lie on. A few other couples were lying on the concrete floor. As I stretched beside Jerry, I felt shame and guilt, but I didn't have the courage to say no to him. I needed the affection he was giving me so desperately and talked myself into thinking it was all right. The sexual act didn't give me any pleasure, and I could hear the other couples doing the same thing.

"Do you love me?" I asked Jerry.

"Of course, I love you, Josie. You're beautiful." He fumbled with my clothing. "Are you a virgin?" he whispered in my ear.

"Whass a virgin?"

"Have you ever done this before?"

"Dunno," I muttered.

My mind flashed back to the terrible experience I'd had as a little girl in the woodshed at Lockwood. I didn't know what to say. My body became rigid. All the warm feelings that had been aroused as a result of Jerry's caresses suddenly vanished. Why couldn't I stop this craziness? But I knew I couldn't. I just couldn't …

Jerry and I dated for most of that winter. And aside from the sex, which I managed to block out, it was fun. We often walked hand in hand along High Road beneath a pitch-black sky shimmering with northern lights, our boots crunching across the hard-packed snow on a crisp, cold night. When Jerry told me about his country and the way he lived there, I was entranced.

There was a dance at the military base every Saturday night and locals were allowed to go. Although I was only 14, I felt grown up and beautiful in my new pink dress, all puffed out with a new crinoline. I was in heaven as my boyfriend waltzed me across the floor to "Lonely Boy" and "Puppy Love." This was a different kind of dancing than the stomping we did at our house.

I missed Sammy terribly, as did we all. There were no more opportunities to teach him words to a song, no more having him tease poor Rhoda out of her wits, no more calling my sister, Sally, Ol' Ding-Derry, no more borrowing his dog team to go randying, and no more would Mommy scrub him down each day when he got back from work. No music was played in our house for the rest of that year. Daddy didn't play his accordion at night, and the radio wasn't tuned into Wheeling, West Virginia's sad country songs.

But even my sorrow didn't stop me from fantasizing. I constantly daydreamed of escaping. Maybe I would marry a GI and move to the United States. I wanted a tall, dark, and handsome man because that was what I'd read about in magazines. I wanted roast beef dinners, running water, electric lights, a swimming pool, and smiling, happy children with store-bought clothing. That was what I hope for. However, the outside world and age 16 seemed far away. Even Spotted Island seemed too distant. I cried late into the night and was finally rescued by blessed sleep.

Even though sadness hung heavily in our home, the rest of us had to carry on. With our mother incapacitated with grief, the bigger ones took care of the little ones and we managed to survive. When winter approached, water from the high tides came all the way up the bank to our porch. The path to school that skirted the Pettens' fence was underwater. We had to cling to the fence posts so we didn't get wet. Making our way through the driving rain, we struggled up the path to the little schoolhouse on the hill. A fresh coat of paint and the newly swept floor didn't mask the building's mustiness.

I had to repeat grade seven, so I wasn't happy at school. Besides, the Massie boys were there, and I knew that after classes I had to work for their family. I felt shame for being poor, for having to go to school with the children of the people I worked for, for the things I was doing at night with boys. I felt powerless to change anything, so I retreated into daydreams. I longed to get away. I was certainly not going to do what Marcie did. My life was going to be better.

Since I was the oldest living at home, Mommy allowed me to move into Sammy's old bedroom downstairs. That was bittersweet for me, though I was happy to have my own room finally.

I still wanted to fit in with my family but didn't spend much time at home because my mother was always cursing me. She called me a bloody fool, a blood-of-a-one, a blood-of-a-bitch, and a little Christer. According to her, I was proud, conceited, lazy, and a good-for-nothing.

That was an atmosphere I didn't want to live in. I hated the wailing of the youngsters. Cleaning clothes on our washboard skinned my knuckles. Scrubbing the linoleum floor that Daddy had brought from the dump tore up my hands because of the nails, since we didn't have glue to paste it down. Filling the lamps with kerosene and cleaning their chimneys was a hated chore. Lugging water from across the marsh was back-breaking, even though we now used a wooden hoop to balance the buckets. The ever-present stench of the slop pail was nauseating; emptying it was disgusting. Sitting on the sawhorse so Daddy could cut wood was bone-chillingly cold in the winter. Lugging wood into the house was exhausting. I was never allowed to sit for any length of time. I felt sorry for myself and found that the more Mommy wanted me to do the less I wanted to do anything.

Maybe if I hadn't spent two years at Lockwood, or if I hadn't been in nicer homes when I worked for people, I wouldn't have had anything to compare my life to. But I was observant and paid attention to stories I'd read in books and magazines. I could see that life was different elsewhere. When I was little, I couldn't comprehend the meaning of poor and rich, clean and dirty, good and bad, nor did I have any idea what healthy living should be. Now, at 14, I knew that a lot of people had lifestyles quite different than the one I had. I didn't blame anyone for that. We certainly had more material things than ever before. We had more access to food and medical treatment and certainly had more money coming in. The Curls were better off than they had been when there was nothing but stark wilderness and total isolation.

The population at the bottom, as we called the area adjacent to the marsh, was growing. There were now five houses stretching to Big Brook. The Hamel family had built a new home across the brook. Johnny Hamel, his wife, Minnie, and several children were the first Pentecostal people to move to Cartwright from Goose Cove. Soon they were holding Sunday night services in their house.

One Sunday my friend Dora Learning and I attended a service. We entered the house and took seats at the back. Everyone waited for the minister to start. People were dressed in their Sunday best, with bandanas tied under their chins. Then the singing began, and as it gained momentum, people waved their arms and moaned as if they were dying. The scene reminded me of the time Sammy had taken me to Goose Cove.

Uncle Johnny Holwell came to live in Cartwright. He was from up the shore and was a good friend of my parents. He moved into a house up the harbour with Levinia, his daughter, who was older than I was.

I loved Uncle Johnny, and his presence was a blessing to our family. He made us a little wall cabinet to go over our washbasin, which meant we were finally able to get rid of the Rinso box we were using. And he made another cabinet for my room, which thrilled me. The cabinets were similar to bathroom medicine ones with mirrors in their doors. I could keep all my treasures and makeup in it.

Uncle Johnny played the violin and showed me how to play a song in 10 minutes. He was patient and understanding and one of the kindest people I'd ever met. I learned how to play the fiddle thanks to him. Unfortunately, though, when I moved, I no longer had opportunities to practise and forgot everything Uncle Johnny had taught me.

In our community, Sunday was a time for cruising (visiting people). If you stayed at home, any number of people might drop in. No one knocked on doors; they simply walked in. And not all of them were real aunts and uncles. The children just called them that.

Linda Mullins, who became one of my favourite people, had recently moved to Cartwright from Happy Valley–Goose Bay. Even though she was almost old enough to be my mother, we became friends. I liked the way she talked. She told me about Goose Bay, about the world, and about sex. Linda was the one who explained pubic hair and what to expect when I started my menstrual cycle. She drew diagrams and tried to make me understand what would take place in my body each month, what would happen when I got pregnant, and that babies weren't found in stumps or under rocks. Through her I learned about bodily hygiene, deodorants, powders, and makeup. She talked to me about feelings, and because of that I grew to love her dearly.

In the late spring of 1957, I met a young construction worker who I'll call George. He had come to work at the military base, and I really liked him. George taught me how to drive his stake truck, which gave me a sense of excitement and freedom as we raced along High Road at 50 miles per hour, dust feathering behind us.

It wasn't long before I discovered that George was married and had a wife and family in Newfoundland. I was so angry. He was no better than the GIs I'd been dating. I immediately broke up with him, but wasn't strong enough to tell him that he'd taken advantage of me and that I felt cheap and cheated.

Then I met a young man who arrived on the *Kyle* from Happy Valley–Goose Bay. He lived there with his adopted parents and had come to visit Joyce Pardy, his birth mother in Cartwright. Joyce was the lady we'd lived with while Daddy was building our house. The young man's name was Murray Pardy. I was intrigued by him. After all, he was from somewhere else, so he had to be interesting. I didn't know how old he was, but I thought he was quite cute. One evening while we were hanging around the Company Store he asked me to go out with him, and I was elated. We went for a walk on Flag Staff Hill. Starry-eyed, we gazed across the North Atlantic, awed by the beauty all around us. A full moon cast light straight at us. It was the beginning of a very special relationship. Murray was wonderful to me. He was kind, gentle, funny, and a fantastic kisser.

Part of Murray's charm was that he was extremely handsome. He dressed like the teen idols I'd seen in magazines — Ricky Nelson, Bobby Darin, Fabian. I was in love at last! I knew what I felt this time wasn't the same as what I'd experienced with the GIs and local boys I'd dated. Murray sparked emotions deep within me, ones I'd never encountered before. And that frightened me.

We were having so much fun that I began to neglect my work and got into trouble with my mother. She didn't like Murray, but I didn't care what she said. I was going to do what I wanted.

Then, suddenly, Murray was gone. He had to return to Happy Valley–Goose Bay but promised me he'd write and would be back next summer. We exchanged love letters during the winter, but whenever a cute boy asked me out I couldn't refuse. I felt guilty cheating on Murray but couldn't resist.

In January 1958 I turned 15. I rebelled against my mother at every turn. My attitude toward her was terrible. I didn't care what she thought. I was going to date any boy I wanted to and stay out as long as I felt like. Despite what she said, I didn't go to church on Sunday anymore and refused to stay home and babysit for her. To me, that winter, the weeks and months seemed to drag on forever. I wanted Murray, my boyfriend. I wanted to feel his arms around me, wanted him to make me feel special. I loved him so.

30

Growing Up

In the spring of 1958, at age 15, though I was belligerent with my mother, I was a mature and responsible teenager in other ways. I was different than a 15-year-old is today. I'd been working since age 11. I knew how to run a household, care for children, and cook a meal.

One of our popular winter pastimes was card playing. On a Sunday night in early spring it was cold and wet outside. I didn't want to make the long trek to church, so I went to a friend's house to play One Twenties, a popular card game then.

"Whass yer bid, Jos?"

"I bid 20."

"Twenty-five."

"Go on, den," I dared her.

"Hearts."

I glanced at my partner across the table, then eyed my hostess. "Hearts! I hope *yer* partner can help ya." I was holding the highest trump!

We had so much fun together. However, somebody told my mother. Skipping church was reason enough for a beating, but playing cards on Sunday when I was supposed to be in church was a deadly sin.

Mommy was waiting for me when I stepped in the door. *Whack!* The first blow was a backhand across my face, which almost knocked me off my feet. As I tried to fight my mother off, she grabbed a piece of bank line, the closest thing to her. Bank line is a hard, tightly woven rope, and I felt every twist and fibre as it sliced into my body.

"Mommy, Mommy, stop, stop!" I cried, groping for the rope, tears blinding me. Finally, I yanked it from her, paused for a moment, then stared her straight in the eye. "Dis is the las time ya'll ever lay a hand on me!"

She didn't say anything.

I threw the rope into the corner of the locker and raced outside. Excruciating pain shot through my body thanks to the impact of the bank line, but that wasn't remotely anything like the agony I felt inside as I scrambled up the road. I hated her! I hated her so much!

In the late 1950s there were a lot of big changes in Cartwright. Walking to the store on High Road made me feel proud. Stately new homes graced the main street, with a church on one side and the striking RCMP residence on the other. Our church's steeple pierced the cobalt-blue Labrador sky, and its bell could be heard throughout the community. However, there had been problems.

During the early construction of the church, on an extremely windy day while I was walking to school, something awful happened. I was holding my coat tightly around my neck and fighting a blizzard with every breath. Glancing up to make sure I was following the road, I noticed that the roof had blown right off the church. I felt so sad for the men who had worked so hard. But these were Cartwright men — strong, hardy fishermen who took everything in stride. It wasn't long before the roof was rebuilt and Mommy had one more place to add to her list of places to clean.

The first time I stepped inside the doors of the new church I was impressed with the shiny lacquered seats and exquisite pulpit. I enjoyed a few sermons, but for the most part I didn't want to be there. A favourite memory from that church was Marcie's voice ringing out above everyone else's, crystal clear and perfectly in tune as she sang, "Nearer God to thee, nearer to thee."

I missed Marcie. We'd been close during our years at Lockwood, but with both of us working so hard and her early marriage to Austin, we had little time to be together. Consequently, we'd grown apart.

By this time Cartwright had a policeman. Mr. Cheeseman, our Royal Canadian Mounted Police officer, had been living in a little bungalow on Low Road. When I turned 15, the new RCMP residence was completed and Mommy got the job cleaning it. The Cheesemans were from Ontario. My mother was very impressed with the fancy way Mr. Cheeseman talked.

The old RCMP residence became a snack bar for a short time. Whenever my friends and I walked up to the counter for a snack, I'd feel a sense of well-being and happiness. At last I had money in my pocket!

"Can I have a Coke an a Tootsie Roll, please?" I'd ask.

"That'll be 25 cents."

I was still surprised that I could afford such luxuries.

Marcie had a new baby, little Terry, and it wasn't long before she was expecting another. I wondered if she was going to be like our mother and have more than a dozen youngsters. I wanted a child of my own some day, but only when I was older and after I married a rich man and was living in a fine-looking house with all the lovely things I'd read about in *True Story*.

I hadn't grown since I was 12 and seemed stuck at five feet and 100 pounds. I looked younger than I was, but inside I felt much older. I was losing my tomboy ways and becoming more ladylike. I wanted to be a grand lady with manners, poise, and social class. I wanted to be a dancer or an actress and wished fervently that I could get out of Cartwright and live the good life.

Mommy had stopped having babies. My siblings were growing. Linda was now two years old. Tony, had he lived, would have been three. Phillip was four and spoiled rotten, since he was a boy. Dora was five, her golden locks and blue eyes standing out from the rest of us. Winnie, now six, was dark-skinned and quite pretty. Eddy was eight years old and becoming a little man. Rhoda was 12 and growing tall and thin. She had grown out of the horrible nosebleeds that had almost killed her. Sally was 14 and beautiful, with clean features and black hair. She was also taller than I was and really intelligent. She kept us in stitches with laughter and had a special relationship with our parents, which I envied. After all, she'd spent more time at home with them than I had. She was learning to dress nicely and had started dating boys.

I got a shock in 1958. At age fifteen I had my first period.

"Yer a woman now, Josie," my mother said. "So act like one." That was the extent of her advice.

It was a good thing I had started late. Otherwise I might have gotten pregnant when I was 13.

There was still a week of school to get through, and I wasn't feeling good about my final exams. Besides, the *Kyle* was due any day now, and I knew Murray would be on it. All I cared about was spending time with him. I needed someone to stop the hurt I felt inside. In my fragile, insecure, and needy state I felt deserted, rejected, and used. I didn't know if I loved Murray or not. I knew he loved me, because he'd told me so in the letters I'd received all winter. I was looking forward to seeing him, but Mommy hated him, though to this day I don't know why. She never bothered to tell me.

Finally, around the end of June, I heard welcome news on the radio. "The *Kyle* left Battle Harbour four o'clock this morning," the announcer said.

"Murray's gonna be onboard for sure," I whispered to Sally.

"The *Kyle* left Black Tickle at midnight last night" was the news from the Marconi station.

"She's gettin closer, Sal!" I said.

I hitched a ride with a friend to the harbour when the *Kyle* docked. As I approached the ship, I noticed people dressed in strange clothes standing along the top railing. I was soon informed that they were tourists. Some of our neighbours had been told that tourists didn't know what to make of my people, especially those of us with dark skin and piercing blue eyes. We were a peculiar lot, they thought. Tourists had also told neighbours that we appeared to be tough, hardy, and happy.

We didn't know what to make of the tourists, either. They looked very odd and very rich. Today, though, I didn't give them much thought as I scurried up the gangplank and onto the ship in search of Murray.

As I was making my way to the galley to scrounge an apple as I usually did, there he was! He looked so handsome. His Brylcreemed hair was slicked back with a single curl that hung down his forehead just like the one Ricky Nelson had. And he was dressed in tight blue jeans and a fancy windbreaker. We embraced and began looking for a way to get off the *Kyle*. We wanted to be alone. As I raced down the gangplank hand in hand with my sweetheart, I was overjoyed that he'd come back to me.

We hurried up Flag Staff Hill, frolicked in the blackberry bushes, and kissed. His lips were soft and gentle, and his crooning words telling me how much he'd missed me made me feel very special. We made love in the blackberry bushes, with a gentle breeze blowing in from the sea, then rolled over and watched the clouds as they floated effortlessly across the sky. I wanted that moment to last forever.

During the summer of 1958, Mommy and Alma were asked to clean Lockwood School. While she was there my mother talked to the new house mother about a job for me. She didn't, of course, bother to consult me.

"I got ya a job fer the summer, Josie," Mommy said as she dropped her pail onto the locker one day after work. "They want ya ta go as a cook at Lockwood."

"Cook!" I wailed. "I dunno how ta cook! Ya never taught me how ta cook."

"Ya'll learn quick nough. An they want ya ta start tomarra."

"Tomarra! Why so soon?" I was shocked, angry, and terrified. I'd been looking forward to a few weeks of freedom with Murray.

I lay in bed that night and thought about my years at Lockwood. The terrible things that had happened to me swarmed in my mind, especially the rapes and the mental and physical abuse. Until now they'd been pushed back into my subconscious. I started to worry about tomorrow. I'd developed an arrogant attitude and didn't like anyone giving me orders. Somehow, though, I made up my mind do my best, the way I'd been drilled to do since I was 11 and even earlier when I was a student at Lockwood. It helped that I was going to be paid $30 a month. Up until I started working for Mrs. Massie I'd never seen a dollar bill in my life — maybe a nickel or a copper, but nothing larger than that.

The next morning I woke up early and lit the fire for my parents as I'd done so many times before. It was still chilly as I gathered my clothes to go across the harbour.

"Marnin, Jimmy," Daddy said as he limped out of the bedroom. "Gettin ready ta go, is ya?"

"Yeh, Daddy. I don't have much ta take, anyway."

"We're gonna miss ya, Jimmy," he whispered, not wanting to wake anybody.

"I'm gonna miss ya, too, Daddy. I'll be back often. I'm only going across the harbour."

I rubbed my father's shoulders gently and thought how much I didn't really know him. Would I ever get to know my parents? I loved Daddy so much, but I couldn't tell him. My tongue was stuck. Then I heard my mother get up up and wondered what she was going to say. She was always so unpredictable.

"Marnin," she said as she lifted the damper off the stove. The glow from the fire illuminated her face. As always, she moved the wood to the side where it got the best draft, picked up several junks, laid them carefully in the stove, and replaced the damper. Then she took her long, waist-length hair, pulled a comb through its fine, silky length, and rolled it into the familiar bun she always wore. While doing so, she glanced out the window, bending a little because our windows were so low. "Looks like it might rain today, Tom," she said in the special voice she used only for Daddy. "Is ya goin jiggin?"

"Yeh. I'll drop Jimmy off at de mission, jig a few fish, and go feed de dogs."

"Awright. Need yer grub bag packed?"

Their conversations were instinctive, routine, and cordial. Daddy always touched her tenderly as she passed him.

"I got my stuff ready, Mommy," I said.

"That's good, Josie. Now, ya be a good girl an listen ta the house mothers."

She had called me *Josie*. That meant she was feeling sympathetic toward me, perhaps a little sad watching me get ready to go. I looked at all my little brothers and sisters who had crawled out of their various sleeping bunks, all those little ones who over the years I'd complained so much about. Tears welled in my eyes as I hugged each one and then walked out the door. Some of my siblings followed Daddy and me to the wharf, stood on the bank, and waved as my father pushed our little boat into the water.

With blinding tears I gazed back at the home Daddy had built five years earlier and thought of everything that had happened to us there. That house was crammed to the rafters with bodies, but it was always warm and cozy to walk into on a cold day. The smell of my mother's freshly baked bread always made my mouth water and my spirits soar.

That day our boat's little Johnson engine purred as we chugged across the harbour. I thought of all the wonderful times my father and I had experienced together in the five years since I'd come home from Lockwood. I thought of how lovingly he had cut the cod jigger out of my leg. I knew I would miss him so.

We soon arrived at the long mission wharf that I'd climbed so many times before. Daddy handed me the pillowcase I'd stuffed with my clothing, and our eyes locked. I saw the love there. We both knew this was a major turning point in my life. Blinded by tears, yet not wanting to make a fuss, I clambered up the ladder and started toward the dormitory. Daddy and I never hugged. We never said what was in our hearts.

When I got to the school, I poked my head in to say hello to the Bird family. The kids were all grown now. As usual Aunt Susie had bread in the oven, and the familiar smell was wonderful.

I strode past the mission store where Mommy's sewing was on display in the window along with the work of many other talented residents from our community. I walked up the hill past the machine shop. The doors were still open, and Mickey was inside fixing something. As I strolled past the school and playground, I recalled times of great joy and unforgettable sorrow.

It was quiet now with the children away at home for the summer. The early planting of the garden was showing great promise, and the grounds, except the play area and pathways, were covered with lush green grass. The classrooms gleamed with new paint. Repairs were being done on the fences and playground equipment. I looked beyond the school to the hospital and remembered having to lie for weeks with my legs under a wooden structure because of tuberculosis. And I recalled the joy of knowing Emma Tulak, who had also been ravaged with consumption. Other, much more painful memories crowded my mind, but I pushed them away. This time things at Lockwood were going to be very different.

Climbing the steps leading to the entrance of the school, I knocked. It felt strange to rap on this door. I didn't feel worthy of using it. After all, only invited guests and important people usually had the privilege. But I reminded myself that I was here as a worker now and was entitled to use the front door. I knocked again and waited. Finally, I heard footsteps.

The door opened, and a large, nicely dressed lady with short, dark hair took my hand. "Hello. You must be Josie Curl. Welcome to our team. My name is Miss Lowe. Come on in and I'll introduce you to Miss Bethel."

"Awright, miss" was all I could mumble. I was terrified and didn't know why.

"We're so glad you decided to take this job even though you're awfully young. We've heard wonderful things about your work."

"Yeh, miss?"

"*Yes*, we have, Josie." She emphasized my mispronunciation of the word *yes* with a meaningful look. "I'm sure you won't let us down. We'll see how you do during the summer. If you do well we'll have you back when you get out of school."

"Okay, miss." I was pleased about the comment on my work, but angry at her for correcting my grammar. I was impressed with their American accents. Fancy talk, I called it.

We walked through the kitchen where I'd be working and on into her suite. I hadn't seen the suite since Mrs. Forsyth was house mother when I was only eight. It looked different. I was aware of pleasant music playing on a radio somewhere. When I sat in a plush chair, I was nervous and shaky. After introducing me to Miss Bethel, Miss Lowe said, "Your day will start at six o'clock and finish around seven in the evening, but you can have a couple of hours off in the afternoon. Does that sound reasonable?"

"Oh, yes, miss. Sounds good."

"You're not to bring boys into the dorm," Miss Bethel added firmly. "There will be no loud music. And you have to be in by 10:30 at night. Your bedroom is at the top of the staff stairway."

"Awright, miss."

I walked back through the dining room to get my bag from the hallway and then went upstairs. I stopped at the little girls' dormitory and stared at what used to be my bed. The beds were stripped bare now except for the cold rubber sheets, which were still on the two beds closest to the door. I wondered how Florence was doing. Memories flooded me with pain, and tears welled inside as I thought of the cruelty I'd endured.

As soon as I opened the door to my new bedroom, I felt as if I were an intruder. All of this couldn't be for me. A lovely chenille bedspread covered the bed, and there was a bureau and a closet for my clothes and curtains on the window.

Throwing myself onto the bed, I placed my hands behind my head. It was thrilling to finally be on my own. I got up and put my few pathetic belongings away. I had so very little. But that would soon change. I was going to order new clothes from the Eaton's catalogue as soon as possible. Being away from home and free from conflict with my mother was a new lease on life.

Even in the Lockwood kitchen I could hear the music of Pat Boone, Doris Day, Judy Garland, and Nat King Cole coming from Miss Lowe and Miss

Bethel's radio in their airy suite. House plants placed on the big dining-room tables and in some of the windows added beauty and fragrance to the dormitory and made the establishment far more cheerful, pleasant, and welcoming than I remembered from my student days.

The kitchen was well equipped and several steps up from the pieces of broken glass and scraps of lace on an orange crate in my parents' home. This was the real thing! There were two enormous stoves and a gigantic pantry and sink. A long counter spanned one wall, with big windows facing onto the harbour. The colossal cooking pots were almost as big as I was, and there were utensils in spacious drawers to work with. The floor was covered with brown linoleum. Food was safely locked in storage rooms in the basement. The teachers and house mothers had their own well-stocked pantry filled with special foods I'd never seen before.

We had a staff dining room to the right of the kitchen. The first thing I noticed when I entered that room was a record player sitting on a table against the wall. We were actually allowed to play our own music! I was ecstatic to see "Jailhouse Rock" by Elvis Presley and other .45s by Jerry Lee Lewis, Conway Twitty, and Fats Domino.

"Do you have a boyfriend, Josie?" Bessie, one of the other workers, asked me at dinner.

"Yeh. He jus come on de *Kyle* from Happy Valley."

"A boyfriend from Happy Valley? Well, well, well. What's his name?"

"Murray Pardy."

I felt intimidated by Bessie, though I had no idea why. Maybe it was because she was much older and more experienced than I was. Also she was from up the shore and not a local girl.

I learned my job quickly and took it very seriously. Fresh apples had arrived on the *Kyle*, so one of my first tasks was to bake apple pies. Miss Bethel watched me, which made me extremely nervous. I realized she was probably assessing my abilities. A delectable aroma filled the kitchen as the pies baked. They turned out beautifully.

"Josie, you're a natural," Miss Bethel said.

"Oh, thank you, miss." I smiled, not accustomed to being praised for my work.

My last big job that first day was to make bread. I only had to make two loaves because there were no children at the school yet. Even so, it was a challenge to master the size of that bread pan and to manipulate the dough into the right consistency. The bread at Lockwood was always whole wheat, of course, which brought back memories of my days at school here and how much I detested that kind of bread.

As I was to learn, my first duty every morning was to bake the bread for the day. When the children returned, I baked six loaves every morning. Each day, as soon as the bread was in the oven, I put a big pot on the stove to make porridge. Except for the occasional time when we switched to cream of wheat, we had porridge almost every morning.

I felt strange as I set the staff table for dinner, and couldn't help looking at the record player. I didn't know who owned it and was afraid to ask. Finally, after supper during a little break, I asked Elsie, one of the other staff members, if I could play a record.

"Go ahead," she told me. "It's there for all of us to use."

I was overjoyed. Oh, how I loved music! Someday soon I, too, would own a record player.

As I settled into my new life, I felt as if I'd become truly unshackled. Even though my days were long and I did a split shift, I loved the work. I could do anything I wanted and go anywhere I desired as long as I did my job and met the curfew. Therefore, I could go out with my boyfriend.

With only a skeleton crew for the summer, I didn't have to work hard initially. I enjoyed my downtime immensely, and during the afternoon break on rainy days, I started reading again. I was coming into my own, becoming my own person.

As the first week of school approached, I knew I didn't want to go home. I wondered if I could keep the summer job permanently and decided to ask the house mothers if that was possible. One day I mustered up the courage and knocked on the staff door. "Miss, I was wonderin if I could keep my job fer de winter."

"Oh, yes, Josie," Miss Lowe said. "You've become a great little cook and we'd love to have you stay. But what about your parents?"

"Dunno, miss. I'll talk ta them tomarra. I know my mother's gonna be mad, but I wasn't doin well in school, anyway."

"Well, then, talk to them and let us know as soon as possible, all right?"

"Yeh, miss, and thank you."

The next day I was off duty, so I took the mission boat *Loon* across the harbour to speak to my mother. As I was striding down the road, a knot grew in my stomach. I was still very much afraid of my mother. I opened the door of our house onto a familiar scene. It was Monday, and Mommy was heating water in large pots on the stove to fill the galvanized washtub. The entire floor was covered with dirty laundry. I wouldn't have my knuckles skinned today, though, I thought. For a moment I faltered, trying to find the courage to tell her. Finally, I just blurted it out. "Mommy, I'm not goin back ta school. They want me ta stay on at Lockwood."

"Ya bloody little fool, Jos. Ya knows yer not gonna quit school yet." She paused for a moment, then added in a tone that made me shudder. "We'll jus see bout dat, won't we?"

She asked if I could watch the youngsters so she could go to the store that afternoon, and I said yes. A little later in the day I saw Mommy coming across the marsh with the minister! I knew it was about me and that they were going to try to get me to return to school. I was very surprised. I had no idea that education was so important to my mother.

"Josie, do you think it's a good idea to be quitting school so young?" the minister asked.

"No, sir, I don't. But I like my job an I'm good at it. An besides I can help Mommy feed de youngsters."

"Your parents are very concerned about you."

"Yeh?" was all I could say.

I hadn't expected this. In our community the minister was next to God.

"What do you expect to do for the rest of your life, Josie?" he asked.

"Dunno. All I know is, I'm *not* goin back ta school. And dat's all der is to it! Ya can't make me go back, either."

Mommy thought I'd listen to the minister, but I didn't. Finally, he glanced at my mother and shrugged. "That's all we can do, Flossie. Her mind's made up."

Poor Mommy. She didn't know what to say or do. She wasn't used to dealing with situations she couldn't control. I took great pleasure at seeing defeat on her face. Before she could say anything more, however, I walked out the door.

Back at Lockwood, I told my bosses what had happened and that my mother had asked the minister to try to talk me into going back to school.

"Your parents have a right to be concerned, Josie," Miss Lowe said. "However, we're glad you're going to stay on."

The return of the children in September brought back many memories for me. My heart went out to the little ones who came for the first time. Things hadn't changed much from when I first arrived five years ago. I helped out wherever I could and tried to reassure the kids that they would be all right. I told them they would learn wonderful things, make new friends, and eat good food. I knew that, like me, some of them came from poor families with very little food. As I walked by the dormitory that first night of school and heard the children crying themselves to sleep, my heart ached for them.

My workload jumped as I changed from feeding a skeleton crew of 10 people to providing food for 50 children. Each morning I woke up at five, placed six loaves of bread in baking pans and stuffed them into the oven, put the coffee pots on, cooked the porridge, made KLIM or cocoa, and then prepared toast. After all that, I dished everything out to the starving children.

When breakfast was done, I got dinner ready, following the menu posted on the wall. After that, during my few hours of free time, I sometimes rested or stole a few minutes with Murray. As a rule, I saw him in the evenings. I had to start supper at three o'clock, swo it didn't leave me much time in the afternoons.

Supper was usually cod, trout, salmon, or artic char, which was stewed, fried, boiled, broiled, or baked. After hunting season opened, we might be lucky enough to acquire rabbits or partridges. As soon as supper was cleared away, I had to make bread for the next day. Then I was done. After a short breather, Murray showed up and we took a boat across the harbour to visit my family or hiked to the dam, battling flies the whole time.

Sometimes the bigger girls were given assignments to help me. Another big girl was employed as a maid to serve the house mothers during meals. The girls had to listen and respond immediately to the dinner bell. Sometimes the bigger girls were delegated to make bread for me, which was a huge help.

I thoroughly enjoyed playing music on the record player and getting to know the other staff members as they arrived to take their positions for the winter. Another cook, the teachers, the laundry women, the sewing lady, and the aides arrived one after the other. We all got along well. I discovered that I was able to carry on a conversation with people and functioned satisfactorily in the workplace despite my youth.

Murray stayed in Cartwright for several weeks during the summer of 1958. I pretended not to hear my mother's complaints about him every time I visited my family. She would never stop me from seeing him, especially now that I'd moved away from her badgering. It didn't matter to me what she thought. I loved Murray, and the summer flew by with him. Before I knew it, August had arrived and he had to return to Happy Valley–Goose Bay. My sweetheart was leaving me once again, and my dream returned.

I was falling, falling, falling … never reaching the ground.

31

Love and Conflict

W ith the arrival of June 1959 I had worked at Lockwood for a full year. The halls were now filled with whispers and giggles as the children got more and more excited about returning home.

"I didn't get ta go home after my first year," I told a little girl named Cathy as I helped her find her own clothing.

"Oh, miss! That musta been sad fer ya."

"Yeh, it was." It still seemed odd that the kids were calling *me* miss now.

Now that it was summer again my heart was glad. Murray was coming for a few weeks once more, and I could hardly wait to see him. We'd written to each other all winter and spring. I hadn't told him about the occasional American GI I'd dated.

For the staff, work didn't stop when the children left. The mission went into maintenance mode, and several locals were hired along with Mickey Bird to get the place in perfect shape for the next group of children in the fall. I didn't qualify for holidays that summer, so I filled in for the other girls in their jobs. I learned how to do the laundry and enjoyed hanging out the wash on the many clotheslines strung around the grounds.

In the mornings we were still awakened by the crowing of a rooster at the crack of dawn. It didn't bother me. As an early riser, I was already up and working when he crowed. Mickey was busy preparing the garden for the summer season, and new lettuce was already breaking the surface. It reminded me of the time Mrs. Forsyth sent me to the garden to pick fresh lettuce and I almost drowned myself when I cut through the water hose. In midsummer, chickens and piglets arrived on the *Kyle*. As I watched the pigs being unloaded, I recalled as a wee girl jumping onto their backs and falling off into the muck. I remembered Mrs. Forsyth sending me to collect eggs from the hens' pen. I'd liked watching them cackle and fight.

Our winter's supply of dry goods arrived on the *Kyle*, and as I unpacked box after box and placed their contents on the storage shelves, I recalled how I had once snuck into the storeroom to steal dried apricots and apples and nuts. When I put away the Christmas decorations, I thought of my childhood Christmas at Lockwood when I sneaked into the attic and saw the toys we were to receive. The attic was a mysterious place to me when I was small.

As my second summer waned and as September approached, we got ready for the returning children. Nothing had changed from the year before. I helped out with the children and enjoyed telling them about my earlier time at Lockwood. The first thing we had to do every fall was rid the children's little heads of lice. Then each child was stripped of personal belongings and issued mission clothing, a toothbrush, rubber boots, et cetera. Rules were laid out for the kids to interpret in their own way or suffer the consequences if they were disobedient. Oh, how I remembered the many times I endured those consequences. My heart went out to the little ones attending school for the first time. Watching them rekindled old memories of the fear and loneliness I'd experienced during my first few nights.

I wasn't a bad person. I wasn't a lazy good-for-nothing or a bloody fool, as my mother so often told me. I didn't want to think of the years when I lived in that tiny, overstuffed shack she was so proud of. I didn't want to remember the cruel way she treated me. I didn't understand why my mother hated me so much. My childhood had taught me how to take care of myself and how to fend off malicious remarks from other children. Despite it all, I felt I'd survived with some measure of pride.

Before Lockwood I had happy memories, too — living in Roaches Brook in the wintertime and randying down the hillside on the tiny komatik my father had made. And there were memories of Spotted Island, as well — roaming rocky hillsides, picking berries, playing tag or Alley Over. How well I remembered that springtime of my childhood when I claimed a tiny puppy for a little while until it got too big to drag around by its feet, head dragging on the ground. And there were cherished memories of playing house, my sealskin moccasins tied neatly around my ankles.

By the fall of 1959, at age 16, I'd been working at Lockwood for 14 months and had settled in comfortably with my job, co-workers, and bosses. Murray had returned to Happy Valley–Goose Bay, and even though I missed him terribly, I was resilient and bounced back quickly when he was gone.

Lockwood started bringing in a group of U.S. soldiers on Saturday afternoons to entertain the children. I became interested in the lead singer and guitar player named Richard Falkner (not his last name). He wasn't the tall, dark, and handsome man of my dreams. Actually, he was the opposite — short and stubby with a freckled face and a receding hairline. His hair reminded me of red ochre, and he had the softest blue eyes I'd ever seen. Even though I knew my mother would never approve of him, I started a relationship. He was kind to me and extremely considerate. We both enjoyed hiking through the woods, skating, skiing, and frolicking in the snow. I knew he was older than I was, but when he told me he was twice my age, I had second thoughts about him. I certainly didn't want Mommy to find out how old he was. So I dated him secretly for a while, but that didn't sit well with my conscience.

"Ya gotta meet Mom an Dad soon, Dick," I said softly one night.

"All right, sweetheart. We'll do that soon."

As the day of the meeting approached, my anxiety increased. I was ashamed of my home and all the little snot-nosed youngsters running around. We couldn't warn my parents that we were coming because they didn't have a telephone. I fretted that the house would be in a mess.

When we reached the house, I glanced at Dick with all the love I felt inside. Mommy couldn't possibly be mean to him. He was a gentleman, well-mannered, and polite. I pulled the rope that lifted the latch from its cradle on the opposite side of the door. It was hot inside because my mother was baking. Immediately, I could see she didn't approve, and Dick's friendly comment about the wonderful aroma of freshly baked bread went unanswered.

"Hello, Mom and Dad. This is Dick … um … Richard Falkner. Dick, this is Flossie an Tom Curl."

"Good day, sir," Daddy said, reaching out to take Dick's outstretched hand.

"I'm pleased to meet you, Mr. Curl."

Mommy was speechless. Unable to look Dick in the eye, she finally managed to mumble, "Good day ta ya, too, sir."

"You have a beautiful daughter, Mr. and Mrs. Curl. And even though she's young, I'd like your permission to marry her."

This was a shock to me! My parents seemed stunned. I wrapped my arms around Dick and gave him a big kiss right in front of my parents. I'd brought GIs home before, and even though Mommy never approved of me dating them, she never got nasty with them. It wasn't what she said to Dick, but how she said it that told the story.

Her face was grim. "We'll jus see bout dat."

Suddenly, the room filled with tension. Dick and I thought the best thing to do was to get out of there.

"Oh, Richard," I murmured as soon as we were outside, "do ya really wanna marry me?"

"Yes, Josie. You've told me many times how you want to get away from here."

"Yeh, but … what can she do?" I asked as we strapped on our skis. "Can she stop me?"

"I don't know, Josie. All I know is that I love you. I want to marry you and show you a life you never imagined possible. And don't worry. It'll work out. Besides, how can she stop you?"

"Dunno, Dick," I mumbled, feeling breathless.

My mind was in turmoil. Daddy hadn't said anything. It was as though he didn't exist. I wondered what he thought of Dick, of our getting married. I so wanted his approval.

I had to meet my 10:30 p.m. curfew at Lockwood, so we headed back across the harbour. The swish of our skis on the snow helped ease my anxious mind. The northern lights undulating across the sky, along with the full moon, made it as light as day and filled me with awe. *I'm getting married!* I thought. *Dick wants to take me away to the United States, away from this godforsaken place to a completely new life. He's promised to love me and take care of me forever.*

Dick was wonderful to me. I'd never been treated with so much respect and kindness before. We kept to ourselves for the most part. There really wasn't much we could do other than go for a walk in the woods and find somewhere out of the way to share our love. Dick told me I was beautiful, that I was mature for my age, and that I would make a wonderful wife. He explained what it would be like to live in the United States and told me about the thousands of cars, the theatres, the fancy restaurants, and the gorgeous homes. He spoke of his house in Decatur, Illinois, and how I could make it ours. It seemed so far away to me. My eyes were like saucers as I tried to visualize everything, but I couldn't really comprehend it all. I loved Dick so much and was looking forward to spending the rest of my life with him.

About a month later Dick came across the harbour and told me he had to go back to the United States to tie up some loose ends and take care of a few things. He promised he'd be back. I clung to him and sobbed, "Please, Dick! Don't leave me!" But there was nothing he could do. He had to go.

When he was gone, I missed him terribly and my heart ached.

Then one day, shortly afterward, Miss Bethel approached me. "Josie, I've been asked to tell you that your parents want to see you."

"Wha fer?" I asked. I wasn't up to talking to my mother just then.

"I don't know, Josie, but Martha will cover your shift and you'd better go this afternoon."

"Okay, miss."

The ice was too thin to walk on, so I had to go around the harbour. It was a long, lonely trek. Not looking where I was going, I stepped on a huge, rusty nail that went deep into my foot. I sat on the ground and cried, not only from the pain in my foot but also from fear and anguish. Bleeding, I hobbled the rest of the way to my house and limped inside. The minister was there! I glared at my mother and sat on the edge of the locker, rubbing my foot. What was going on?

"My goodness!" the minister cried. "What happened to your foot?"

"Stepped on a nail," I said, shaking. "Whass goin on, Mommy? Why's de minister here?"

"He'll tell ya now," she said, averting her eyes.

The minister shifted his weight and took a deep breath. Beads of sweat rolled onto his white collar. "Josie, I'm afraid I have some bad news about Mr. Falkner."

"W-what is it?" I stammered.

"Shortly after he returned to the States, he was hit by a car and killed."

"No, no, no! Thass not true! Can't be true. I was talkin ta him las night!"

"It happened last night, Josie, around eleven o'clock. That's all we know so far."

"Yer lyin! Tis not true!" My heart pounded so hard I couldn't breathe. "No, no, no! He's gonna come an get me an take me away. He promised!" I sobbed as I ran out of the house.

I couldn't believe what was happening and wandered the road for hours. My tender, loving, caring Dick couldn't be dead.

But it seemed he was dead and that all my hopes for the future were shattered, that my dreams of living in a beautiful house with a bathroom, running water, and electric lights would never happen now. I had even imagined driving my own car.

I can't remember much about the rest of that summer other than deep sadness and regret. I grieved for months.

I was 54 years old before I found out the truth of what had happened that summer of 1959. My mother told me the story on her deathbed as she was dying of liver cancer. I had long since forgiven her for my rough childhood and had grown to love her deeply. We talked and talked, and one day I mentioned Richard Falkner.

"I got rid of him," she said.

"What?"

"I had the minister talk to the base commander, and they shipped him out," she rasped, struggling with the ravages of her terrible disease. "I wasn't gonna have dat ol feller marryin ya an takin ya away ta some strange place, an dat was dat."

I was stunned that she would do such a thing, but I didn't get upset. As a mother of four grown children myself, I knew how she felt and what she must have gone through. She had dealt with the situation the only way she'd known how.

"You did that for me, Mom?" I asked, stroking her thin face.

She closed her eyes and settled back against her pillow. "God only knows what mighta happened ta ya."

I had always thought my mother didn't love me. But her actions concerning Dick told me a great deal more about my mother. Even though she didn't have the capacity to show her love, even though she'd never held me that I could remember, she still cared about me.

I had hated her all those years. What a waste of precious time that could have been spent loving her instead. In the end, I actually thought her actions had been right. She knew I would get over Dick eventually and that someday I'd find someone else. After all, I was only 16 and he was 32.

But at the time I was heartbroken. I was grateful that my job kept me busy, and I threw myself into helping with the children whenever I could. I tried not to think of Richard. I was still receiving the occasional letter from Murray. He knew about Richard, but he refused to give up on me. So once he heard what had happened, he came back to Cartwright that summer to reclaim my love. It was wonderful to see him. Even though I couldn't be my carefree, high-spirited self, I appreciated his love and support and clung to him like a lost puppy when he had to return to Happy Valley–Goose Bay at summer's end.

Still, I was tired of Murray's comings and goings, tired of the on-off relationship, tired of writing letters, and tired of lying about any new GI I was dating. Most of all, I was weary of having to ward off any man who got within breathing distance of my body.

Lockwood's year passed in its predictable rhythm: trips to the dam, long hikes in the woods, and walks across the harbour to the Company Store. My mind returned to happier times such as the Easter fair when people came from near and far to compete in dog team races, shooting matches, tug-of-war competitions, and many other events. Memories of Sammy and his all-white dog team filled me with pain and pride. How I missed him!

That Easter I wanted to make a basket and speculated what I'd put in it and what I'd serve for dinner in our staff dining room. I wanted candles and music, and hoped my basket winner would be a certain fellow I liked from up the shore. However, I never made that basket. Being poor had left its scar. I was too scared and felt too inferior. I didn't have the courage to make an Easter basket.

I loved to ski, so during my two hours off in the afternoon in March, when the weather warmed up enough to travel, I strapped skis on and skied across the harbour to visit my family. I'd been away from home almost two years now, and the youngsters were getting bigger. My relationship with my mother hadn't changed much, though I felt she respected me for my good reputation at work. Sometimes I thought she was even a little proud of me, but she lacked the capacity to express that. I found it very difficult to forgive her back then. Too much damage had been done.

"I'll be glad when yer all grown up an gone," she said so many times when I was little. Such harsh comments were hard to forget.

During the spring months at Lockwood, the children enjoyed the warmer weather and went flying down the hillsides on pieces of cardboard or whatever they could find. The bigger ones braved the hills on skis made of barrel staves, as I had done not so long ago. The snow melted quickly, though, and as soon as patches of ground appeared, little girls scratched hopscotch squares into the muddy ground. Skipping ropes carefully tucked away since Christmas were now being used to hop and skip joyfully around the grounds. I longed to join them as they built playhouses on the hillside behind the dormitory. I wondered if they were as possessive of their pieces of dishes and scraps of lace as I had been.

The year rolled by, and soon it was time for the children to return to their homes once again. In a few short days they wouldn't have to line up to go to the bathroom, take cod liver oil, or get their hands, ears, and teeth checked. Soon they would be able to roam the hills of their fishing villages, catch flatfish, sculpins, and thornbacks in the landwash, and play tag or Alley Over. Soon they would be free.

As I look back, I realize that not much had changed at Lockwood. The policies and procedures and the way the children were treated were much the same. All the rules and regulations governing the school were carefully prescribed. Even though some of the house mothers tried to be compassionate, it was hard for them to break through Dr. Grenfell's rigid vision of how children were to be treated. What we referred to as "old English rule" persisted until Lockwood closed its doors forever in the mid-1960s.

32

Leaving Childhood Behind

In 1960 I turned 17, and even though I felt mature, at only five feet tall I still looked like a little girl. My naturally curly brown hair, which had been growing for years because my mother wouldn't let me cut it, hung in a wavy mass just past my shoulders. I clipped it to the side with a barrette. My pale hazel eyes stood out in contrast to my olive complexion. Being part Inuit, people could never figure out what nationality I was. "You're a peculiar-looking person," a stranger once told me.

I had become an independent, self-sufficient person. Boys told me I had a lot of sex appeal, whatever that meant. I wanted to be sexy because I liked the attention. The whistles and compliments made me feel good. Gradually, I got over the heartbreak of losing Richard and was doing my best to carry on.

After working at Lockwood for two years, I decided I wanted to take a vacation so I could go to Spotted Island for a short visit. I had longed to return there every year since my family and I had left when I was seven.

That summer I received a letter from Murray on the first trip of the *Kyle*. He said he'd found employment for me in Happy Valley–Goose Bay as a nanny for the postmistress. The job was mine if I wanted it. I was ecstatic! Murray had figured out an escape for me. He and I had been writing each other since we'd begun dating two years earlier. However, I wasn't the type of girl to sit around and wait. Being promiscuous from an early age, I did what I had to do to get my needs met.

There were no telephones in that part of the world then or any other form of communication, just letters. Riddled with guilt, I sat down and wrote Murray that I would take the job but wanted to go to Spotted Island first. The rugged beauty of that place amid the icebergs was pulling me back to its rocky shores.

When the day came for me to leave on my holiday, I scanned the water anxiously and was delighted to spot the *Kyle* cruising into Cartwright's harbour. The silence of the morning was shattered as the vessel's huge horn bellowed, calling those who were buying, selling, and travelling to come to the ship. As the *Kyle* anchored in the harbour, little boats of all sizes paddled and chugged their way to its side.

I grabbed the suitcase I'd packed several days before and hitched a ride on the mission truck down to the wharf where I climbed aboard the *Loon* to cross the harbour. When I finally reached the *Kyle*, I clambered up its gangplank, made my way past the galley, and arrived at the purser's office to purchase my ticket. It was only a half-day cruise, so I didn't need a cabin.

I noticed a few of the stewards eyeing me as cat whistles escaped their brazen lips. This was going to be exciting! I loved the attention and lapped it up.

After finding a spot to put down my bag, and with my ticket in hand, I went to the galley to scrounge an apple as I'd done many times before. The boat was full of tourists wearing fancy raincoats and rubber boots in fashions I'd never seen before. Tourists scared me, so I kept my distance from them. As far as I was concerned, they could have been from another planet. We weren't allowed up on *their* deck, as if they were too good to mingle with us. My inferiority complex was always fuelled when tourists were around.

As the *Kyle* weighed anchor, I went up on deck to look around the harbour. Facing our house at the bottom, Lockwood was on my right and the community of Cartwright on my left. I thought about my life at home and at Lockwood and the way events in both places seemed to intermingle. Images of extreme cruelty flashed through my mind, but harshness wasn't the only thing I remembered. Blissful recollections also came to mind: my store-bought boots and clothes, my brand-new skates, Richard Falkner's unconditional love ...

I spent the first few hours on deck savouring the sight of dazzling white icebergs drifting in the icy water like enormous stately ships. My mother feared these icebergs, but to me they were magnificent. They either floated freely among the many small islands scattered along the coast or got stuck in shallows or secluded coves. Sometimes a high tide set them free again to continue their southward journeys. As we cruised past the icebergs, I noticed their different shapes. Some had been worn smooth and were scooped out by the constant lashing of the sea so that they resembled giant slides that refracted colours like a prism.

The jagged coastal cliffs wore bonnets of various berry bushes, while the hills appeared soft and rounded from a distance clad in their greys, blues, and purples. As always, the salty sea air and craggy beauty of Labrador filled me with joy.

My thoughts were interrupted by music coming from inside the boat. Being an ardent music lover, I made my way to the music room where a tourist was playing the piano. I was thrilled and ventured closer. Other people were playing cards and entertaining themselves, as well. Shortly afterward, someone started playing the accordion, which was more to my taste. The familiar tune had everyone tapping their toes and clapping their hands.

> I's the b'y that builds the boat
> And I's the b'y that sails her.
> I's the b'y that catches the fish
> And brings them home to Lizer.

When the dinner bell rang, people made their way into the dining room. I can't remember *what* we ate, but I certainly recall *how* we ate. We were served in a manner I had only read about in magazines. Seated at tables covered in white linen tablecloths with sparkling linen napkins, we used gleaming cutlery and fancy dinnerware. I felt so grand!

After dinner I returned to the music room to listen to the music and eavesdrop on a few tall tales. The smoking room on the *Kyle* was famous for the men who told tall tales about their Labrador hunting trips — yarns where someone got shot or was drowned, dog teams plunged through the ice, limbs were severed, teeth were knocked out, and eyes were blinded. Each storyteller tried to outdo the other.

Then someone hollered, "We're getting close to Spotted Island!"

"That's my home," I said as much to myself as anyone else.

As we rounded the point, Spotted Island, my favourite place in the whole world, came into full view. I was ecstatic. Tears trickled down my cheeks as the little houses perched on stilts and stages became visible. My mind raced from one delightful memory to another. Once again I'd witness the making of the fish!

The community was bustling with activity. The fishermen were back from the traps, and cod were being pronged onto the stages from gore-filled boats. It was wonderful to see the drying bawns and flakes. Soon they would be covered with salt cod. The ocean breezes dried the cod completely in just a few days in the hot afternoon sunlight. As a little girl, always wanting to help, I'd enjoyed the process of drying fish. We always had to watch for clouds, and I recalled the hustle and bustle of having to rebundle and cover the cod before the rain came.

As the *Kyle* anchored in the harbour, little boats turned toward us while fisherman in oilskins and jumpers came to take us ashore. Instantly, all the activity shifted and everyone was busy unloading and loading goods. Men, women, and children took part in this regular, but always exciting, event. Boatloads of salt and other goods were hoisted out of the *Kyle*'s hold and precariously lowered into motorboats bobbing on the waves.

I retrieved my bag from its shelf and clambered aboard a slimy little boat. As it putt-putted to shore, I was overwhelmed with emotion. Hastily wiping tears away with my sleeve, I climbed onto the stagehead and was greeted by Violet Dyson, who had gathered with her neighbours to see the *Kyle*. Since much of Labrador still didn't have modern communications, I wasn't able to telephone her, and she'd had no idea I was coming.

We walked up the path past the little brook and into Violet's house. My family's house had been abandoned during the years we'd been away. I peered inside and saw the familiar wooden floors and remembered how Mommy had put sand in a burlap bag and used it along with her homemade lye soap to scrub them. She'd scrubbed so hard that the softer wood was literally worn away, leaving the knots sticking up.

I didn't know what people did on a holiday, since I'd never been on one before. I felt a little lost and strange with nothing to do.

A few American GIs roamed the village. I wondered what they were looking for. They were like scavengers. Perhaps, I thought, they were looking for young girls to take advantage of. Even if that was true, I was still interested in them. Searching for a little excitement, I wandered out onto the point behind the oil tank. Several young men were rambling over the rocks and taking pictures.

"Whass that?" I asked one shyly.

"It's a Polaroid camera. My name's Dan. What's yours?"

"Josie Curl," I mumbled, unable to look up and speak properly.

"Can I take your picture, Josie?"

"Awright." Then I was curious. "How does it work? How come ya got de snap awready?" We always called photographs snaps.

"Because it's a Polaroid. See?" He explained how it worked. "Would you like to go for a ride in my truck?"

"Yeh," I murmured.

I was scared and excited as I climbed aboard his truck. Off we rumbled up the hill on a rocky road. I couldn't help but marvel at the rugged beauty of Spotted Island. I hadn't realized the place was so big. Three Island was away in the distance, named for the three tiny islands in the middle. Ponds trapped in pockets of solid rock reflected the sky like mirrors. Finally, we reached the highest point on the island and had a panoramic view of the North Atlantic.

As we made our way back to the village, I asked Dan to stop the truck so I could study this isolated, windswept place I loved so much. Several houses were empty because the families had moved away to find work, just as our father had done. When we lived here, there were only 25 families whose houses perched precariously on logs and solid rock foundations. It was amazing that they hadn't blown off the rocks years ago.

Dan and I went behind the oil tank and kissed for a while. "What's a beautiful gal like you doin' in a place like this?" he finally asked me.

"Tis my home. Where's yer home?"

"Texas."

"Where's Texas?"

There were people all around, so I was afraid to get into heavy smooching for fear of being seen. However, as the sun dipped behind the horizon and darkness fell, I couldn't resist the loving attention, the words of praise, and the feelings stirring within me. I felt special and loved, and that was what I was after.

Violet Dyson was a soft-spoken, generous soul. Although I wasn't sure why, she was known as Sister or Sis to my family but was actually my first cousin. Compared to her husband, Esau, she was tiny with fair skin and blue eyes. Although a kind and gentle soul, Esau was a big man with a large face and head that gave him great presence, and he carried himself in a way that demanded respect. The Dysons had six children.

The big bell that rang without fail to call the fishermen up at mug-up time and mealtime was located at Esau's house. And one of my most vivid early memories was the loud ringing of that bell and all the huskies howling in unison. But now when the bell rang, Daddy wouldn't come up from the stagehead for his supper, nor would he limp across Mommy's freshly scrubbed floor and plop onto his settle. Those days were gone forever. My father was now a dynamite blaster making a regular income and was home every evening after supper to play his accordion, cut wood shavings for the fire, and tell the little ones a story or two.

The *Kyle* had delivered supplies to stock the little store across the brook in the big house. Sis had also replenished her pantry with foods I'd never seen before.

"Whass dis?" I asked as I reached for what looked like bread. The slices were so white and perfectly shaped they looked as if they'd been popped out of a mould. I never saw anything like them before. I'd only seen mom's homemade bread and Lockwood's whole wheat.

"Dass baker's bread," one of the children piped up smugly.

"Whass baker's bread? An where'd it come from?"

"It come on de steamer," another child added, going to the pantry. In a moment he brought out a jar of Miracle Whip. I'd never seen that before, either.

"Whass dis den?" I asked, eyeing the bottle.

"Tis Miracle Whip."

"Yeh, I can read. But what is it?"

"Tis mayonnaise fer makin sanwiches."

"Sure. I knows how ta make dat stuff. I makes it at Lockwood."

"Not like dis ya don't," the boy said. "Try it."

I spread some mayonnaise on the baker's bread and took a bite. It was delicious. Just as I was finishing the dishes, Dan knocked on the door and asked if I wanted to go for a ride in his truck. I never turned down a ride, so I grabbed my sweater from the chair and ran out the door.

"Jus be careful," Sis said.

I didn't answer. I was free to do as I pleased. As soon as I got into the truck, Dan put it into gear and we took a spin around the island. Taking a deep breath, I gazed across the island. It was breathtakingly gorgeous in the late-evening sunset. Dan stopped the truck at the exact point where the pink sky reflected off the distant ponds. He took out his Polaroid camera and snapped some pictures of the view. The Polaroid process fascinated me. I watched as each picture became clearer before my eyes.

"You're so beautiful tonight, Josie. Can I take your picture?"

"Yeh."

"I mean ..." He paused meaningfully. "Can I take a picture of your ... you know ..."

"My what?"

"Just lift your skirt a bit."

It suddenly dawned on me what he wanted to do, and I felt a stab of fear. This wasn't fun anymore. I didn't want to lift my skirt. As always, though, I didn't have it in me to say no. So I slowly raised my skirt. He kept prodding me by telling me how beautiful I was, then coaxed me to remove my panties.

"This is a Polaroid. No one will ever see it. I'll tear it up afterward. I promise."

I felt contempt for him, but I pretended I was enjoying it. I simply didn't have the willpower to resist his demands. He came to me, and we kissed passionately. That was what I needed, and the lovemaking was well worth it. I simply concentrated on the feelings. The only thing that mattered was that he loved me. When he was done, I fixed my rumpled clothing, and then we drove back to the village. We clambered around the rocks for a while, with Dan taking more pictures. I kept thinking he really was a handsome guy, but now I look back on that episode with sorrow.

My holidays were coming to an end and I would have to return to Cartwright on the *Kyle*'s next trip northward from St. John's. I didn't want to go back. I kept thinking of the letter from Murray asking me to go to Happy Valley–Goose Bay to work. He was in Cartwright now and would travel with me. It was my way out, and it was an excellent opportunity for another job. The pay would be $60 a month, he'd said. That was double what I was getting at Lockwood. Suddenly, there was no doubt in mind that I would go with Murray.

One night at the Dysons' house as we were all sleeping, the *Kyle*'s whistle blew through the village, waking everyone up. No one knew exactly when the *Kyle* would arrive, so the whistle was a heads-up for everyone who wanted to travel or send goods. People jumped into their clothes and ran down to the harbour from all directions. I grabbed my suitcase and followed Violet's family to the stagehead. It was a stormy night, but the *Kyle* waited for no one.

As we motored out to the steamer, I strained to see. Behind us the lights of my childhood home grew dimmer. I thought of Dan and knew I'd never see him again. Despite the Polaroid incident, he'd been kind to me. Tears trickled down my cheek as I thought of the happy times I'd spent on Spotted Island as a little girl. My heart was filled with love for Sammy. If only he hadn't died so young. If only Marcie hadn't gotten married so young. And if only I hadn't had to work from such a young age, I might have had a fighting chance to know my family better. I loved Sally, but I was jealous of her relationship with our mother. They seemed close, and I longed for that kind of intimacy, because despite everything she'd done to me, I loved my mother.

The sea surged wildly, tossing our little boat like a wood chip as we pulled alongside the *Kyle*. Boarding was almost impossible. Our boat and the other launches were heaved around like rag dolls.

"Okay, Josie, get ready ta grab de ropes!" Esau's son, Charlie, hollered over the roaring wind.

I did as I was told. It was so rough that I was certain I was going to end up in the freezing water. I managed to grip the rope railing and climbed aboard. Soon the old ship blew its horn, and we lurched out into open water.

As the *Kyle* rounded the point, Spotted Island's lights disappeared in the darkness. I hung on to the rails and cried. Why was I crying? For a lost love? A vanished childhood? I didn't know my own heart then. I didn't know why I cried or what I wanted. I was running away from all the things that had hurt me.

Because my family had moved from Spotted Island while I was away at Lockwood, I'd always felt disconnected and misplaced. It nourished my spirit to see the island once more and made me feel free to move on. I was happy to have experienced the old ways again. I'd seen the fishing boats leave in the pre-dawn and return at midday loaded with fish. I'd seen the women clean their hand-hooked mats in the landwash and talk about the flies, or the weather, or the condition of the fish, or the state of their bodies and minds, or the health of their youngsters. There were so many things to chat about in the landwash. This vacation had been a soul-searching experience that had given me a sort of closure.

My heart beat rapidly as I thought of what was going to happen tomorrow. I was going to tell my mother that I wasn't coming home, that I was going on to Happy Valley–Goose Bay with Murray. As I sat next to one of the ship's velvet-draped windows, I thought about Murray's letter. Throughout the voyage I was preoccupied with what my mother was going to do to me. But what could she do? I was 17, after all, a grown woman and old enough to make my own decisions.

The *Kyle*'s whistle blew as we entered the channel leading into Cartwright's harbour. The wind had died down, and the air was so still that sounds could be heard from one side of the harbour to the other. The release of the anchor shook the ship and the noise echoed throughout the surrounding hills. Little boats of all sizes and descriptions left the wharf to greet us.

I watched intently as the *Kyle* lowered its gangplank. The old ship was so much a part of our lives on the Labrador coast. It was our lifeline to the world and brought fishermen to fish for cod each summer. The *Kyle* delivered new clothing and wares to our stores, brought us our mail, and supplied us with fresh fruit and candies. It also connected loved ones and even brought the minister to marry them.

I ran to the purser's office to find out how long we were going to be in Cartwright's harbour. I was informed that we would be about an hour. I hitched a ride on the first boat ashore, which unloaded at the Hudson's Bay Company wharf near the centre of town, then ran as fast as I could to my parents' house. I was on a mission and needed to get this confrontation behind me.

Mommy was at the window when I entered the house. She turned and stared at me. I could see that she sensed something was up. Briefly, I hugged her and felt her body stiffen.

"Mommy, I'm goin on ta Goose Bay," I blurted.

"Jos, ya bloody little fool! Ya can't do dat! What about yer job?"

"I gotta job in Happy Valley. Murray got me one."

"Murray got ya one? That bastard! I'll kill him!"

"Mommy, I'm goin and ya can't stop me!" I knew how she felt about Murray, but I didn't care. "I gotta go. De steamer's leavin soon an I don wanna miss it."

That was it. No hug. Nothing. I just raced out the door. I didn't even hug my little brothers and sisters as I sprinted toward Low Road, tears streaming down my face. My mother didn't approve of my leaving, but it shouldn't have been that way.

I hitched a ride on the first boat going back to the *Kyle* for another load of freight. My eyes were glued to the outline of my parents' house. I wondered what my mother was thinking.

When we came alongside the *Kyle*, I climbed the ladder once again. As soon as I was aboard, I went to the purser's office, blinded by tears, and paid for my passage to Happy Valley–Goose Bay. Thank goodness Murray was there. He held me as I sobbed uncontrollably, then told me that he'd paid my fare already.

"It's gonna be all right, Josie," he whispered.

"I know, but why couldn't she wish me luck, or tell me ta be good, or smack me or sometin?"

"Cuz she was surprised. She didn't know what ta say or do."

Our emotions were raw as we strolled around the *Kyle*'s decks. Finally, I regained my composure and stopped to chat with several girls waiting at the galley for a treat.

"I'm goin ta Happy Valley," I told them.

"Yer leavin fer good, Josie?" one of the girls asked.

"Yeh. Fer good. I gotta job in Happy Valley."

"Yer some lucky, maid," another girl said enviously.

But I didn't really want to speak to anybody. After about a half-hour, which seemed like two hours, the anchor clanged back up, shaking the whole ship. We were moving and I was leaving!

As the *Kyle* turned around, my eyes found the little house at the bottom of the harbour. Mommy had been so proud when we moved there seven years earlier, and I'd been happy that we weren't living with strangers anymore. Although it was now packed to the rafters with youngsters, it was a reasonably cheerful place. I wondered then what was wrong with me.

My parents' house stood in a cluster now. Other homes had been built nearby, and we had grown into a little community. Most of the houses were only tarpaper shacks in various stages of construction. With tears still streaming down my face, I clung to the railing until I lost sight of our home.

Lockwood School, the dormitory, and the mission hospital were now in focus as we passed. The first time I had been to the mission hospital I was four and badly torn up by husky dogs. So many memories … I thought of the rapes and abuse I'd endured. Were there any fond memories of Lockwood? Yes, there were some. Holidays were special. I saw my first movie there, discovered how to fight for myself, and learned, sadly, how to hate.

My mind travelled back to the beginning of it all when Claire Forsyth, the Lockwood house mother and nurse who had loved me and wanted to adopt me, actually took another girl and abandoned me. Why couldn't I have been the one she wanted? What would I have been like if I'd gone to the United States and become Mrs. Forsyth's daughter?

I thought of the cruelty I'd endured for being a bedwetter. Where had those barbaric ideas come from, anyway? I was angry and glad that I was leaving this place. I never wanted to see Lockwood again. As I watched Cartwright vanish, my thoughts turned to my family. Would they miss me?

The *Kyle* sliced through the waves and glided past soaring cliffs as I recalled the cod-jigging trips with Daddy and Sammy at this very spot. Tears welled again as I thought about my brother and the terrible day he drowned. I leaned over the railing and watched seawater swirl back from the bow, creating heaps of white foam. Raising my head, I gazed out to sea. It was a healing tonic just to see the North Atlantic whitecaps roll endlessly into one another. We passed the little island where Sammy and I had gone birding. We'd picked eggs from the nests there. The memory of that day was so sweet.

I thought of Miss Bethel and Miss Lowe, my bosses at Lockwood, and wondered if they were upset with me. They had no cook now but had a few weeks to find another one before the students returned in September. I shifted my thoughts to my new and exciting adventure. I was leaving Cartwright. I was leaving the rules and orders of my mother and Lockwood School. I was free.

The trip to Happy Valley–Goose Bay took 14 hours, and all the time I was snuggled in the arms of my boyfriend. We were inseparable. He didn't need to know about all the others I'd been with, and anyway, he didn't seem to care. I was with him now, and we loved each other. I was grateful to him for finding me the job and getting me out of Cartwright. All I knew about my future position was that my boss's name was Mrs. Crawford and that she was the postmistress, and I wondered if I would be able to handle the work. Shrugging away my worries, I burrowed deeper into Murray's willing arms.

As the *Kyle* steamed closer to our destination, I clung to my boyfriend as if he were a life raft. He explained to me what it was like where we were going. Of course, I didn't comprehend half of what he was saying, but I got more and more excited. He told me about the movie theatre, the restaurant, the cars, and his motorcycle.

I was on my way to a whole new life.

Glossary

Babbish: Sealskin strips.

Bank line: Hard, tightly woven rope.

Bawn: A stretch of pebbly rocks on which salted cod are dried.

Beachy bird: A type of sandpiper.

Belly crater: Ice mound on a rock.

Boil-up: A hot drink (usually tea) and a snack when away from home.
    See **Mug-up**.

Brewis: Stew made of hardtack soaked in water and boiled.

Bridge: Verandah.

Civil: Calm.

Cruise: Visit people.

Cuff: Mitten.

Dicky: Parka.

Doughboy: Boiled dumpling.

Duff: Dumpling.

Duffle: A coarse, heavy woollen material like thick felt.

Flake: A rack for drying fish.

Horn junk: Wooden cradles.

In the hole: In debt.

Jannie: Mummer.

Jig, Jigger: A piece of lead often shaped like a fish with two hooks in the mouth used for catching fish. The jig is jerked up and down in the water to attract a fish.

Jigging: To fish with a jig or jigger.

Junk: Log.

Kingwak: Bits of roasted bread dough.

Komatik: Wooden sleigh.

Marconi operator: Radio operator.

Mug-up: A break for a hot drink, especially tea, and snacks during a journey. See **Boil-up**.

Ninny bag: Small pack for a trip.

Pan: To jump between ice floes.

Pick: To pluck.

Pinny: Pinafore.

Puncheon: Tub.

Quintal: A measure of cod equivalent to 112 pounds.

Randy: To go sledding.

Reeve: To stick.

Rip: To cut.

Scitter: To slide (on ice).

Settle: Settee.

Sish over: To form a thin layer of ice.

Slob: Ice chip.

Smitch: Smoke.

Sound bone: Backbone.

Split: Dry wood cut into kindling.

Steady: A still spot in a brook or stream.

Tickle: A tiny inlet.

To be found: To be born.

Toe: Cotton wool.

Tot: A seat.

Trap: A four-sided box to catch fish.

Turr: A murre, a large seabird.

Ulu: Rounded knife for cleaning animal pelts.

More Great
Non-Fiction from Dundurn

Little White Squaw
A White Woman's Story of Abuse, Addiction, and Reconciliation
by Eve Mills Nash and Kenneth J. Harvey
978-0-88878-427-8
$22.95

Eve Mills Nash, with the help of co-author Kenneth J. Harvey, tells a hard-hitting tale of a life of violence at the hands of the men in her life, starting with her early marriage to Stan, an Ontario Mohawk. From early childhood, Nash was surrounded by the alcohol-fuelled groping of male fingers during her parents' parties and found respite in their discarded wine. Harrowing yet life-affirming, this blistering account of life on the cusp of New Brunswick's Native community sees the Little White Squaw and her children balance precariously between two seemingly irreconcilable cultures and colours.

Go to School, You're a Little Black Boy
The Honourable Lincoln M. Alexander: A Memoir
by Lincoln M. Alexander with Herb Shoveller
978-1-55488-733-0
$26.99

Born in Toronto in 1922, Lincoln Alexander embarked on an exemplary life path that has involved military service for his country, a successful political career, a thriving law career, and vocal advocacy on subjects ranging from antiracism to the importance of education. This biography traces a remarkable series of events from Alexander's early life to the present that helped shape the charismatic and influential leader whose impact continues to be felt today. Alexander's is the ultimate, uplifting Canadian success story, the embodiment of what defines Canada.

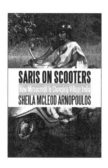

Saris on Scooters
How Microcredit Is Changing Village India
by Sheila McLeod Arnopoulos
978-1-55488-722-4
$29.99

Renowned author and journalist Sheila McLeod Arnopoulos uses her talent for investigative reporting to take us deep into the poorest villages in India. Yet, far from being passive victims of their circumstances, the women who live there have joined forces and are making astute use of microcredit to break the cycle of poverty. After witnessing these women's inspiring success stories first-hand, Arnopoulos has come to believe that such villages have a potential strength equal to that of modern, high-tech cities in India.

Available at your favourite bookseller.

DUNDURN PRESS
w w w . d u n d u r n . c o m

What did you think of this book?
Visit www.dundurn.com for reviews, videos, updates, and more!